FREAKS NO MORE!

Don't call them "freaks." It's an ugly word. Yet there is an uglier one—used by the medical profession for years: monsters. But they weren't—and aren't—monsters. Or freaks. They are Very Special People—burdened by their strangeness, but gifted with a rare dignity and courage.

Different as they are from us, they can inspire us with the undefeated spirit they share in the face of overwhelming odds. The true story of their accomplishments is not only astonishing, but heartwarming. You'll never feel the same once you meet these

VERY SPECIAL PEOPLE
The Struggles, Loves and Triumphs of Human Oddities
by Frederick Drimmer

VERY SPECIAL PEOPLE

The Struggles, Loves and Triumphs of Human Oddities

Frederick Drimmer

BANTAM BOOKS · TORONTO · NEW YORK · LONDON

RLI: $\dfrac{\text{VLM 7 (VLR 6–9)}}{\text{IL 7–adult}}$

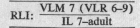

VERY SPECIAL PEOPLE

*A Bantam Book / published by arrangement with
Amjon Publishers, Inc.*

PRINTING HISTORY
*Amjon edition published November 1973
2nd printing .. February 1974   3rd printing .... May 1974
4th printing ... September 1974
Bantam edition / April 1976*

Contents

Prologue   ix

Part 1   Chained for Life

1   Chang and Eng: The Original Siamese Twins   3
2   More Than One . . . Yet Not Two   28
3   Millie-Christine: The Two-Headed Girl   38
4   The Tocci Brothers: The Two-Headed Boy   46
5   Violet and Daisy Hilton: Sold into Slavery   53
6   The Biddenden Maids, Radica-Doodica, and
    Other Remarkable Siamese Twins   63

Part 2   Armless and Legless Wonders

7   Carl Unthan: The Armless Fiddler   73
8   Tripp and Bowen: On a Bicycle Built for Two   87
9   Kingston, Kobelkoff, and Other Wonders   94

Part 3   The Hairy People

10   Mme. Clofullia   107
11   Annie Jones: The Bearded Girl   120
12   France's Most Celebrated Bearded Lady   127
13   Some Modern Bearded Ladies   132
14   The Hairy, Hairy People   141
15   The Long-Haired Ones   148

Part 4   The Little People

16   The Amazing Career of General Tom Thumb   155
17   Tom Thumb and Lavinia Warren   172
18   Why—and What—Is a Midget?   183
19   Famous Little People of Past and Present   190

Part 5   There Were Giants in the Earth

20   What—and Why—Is a Giant?   215
21   Byrne and Cotter: The Two Irish Giants   222
22   Swan and Bates: Two Giants in Love   231
23   Jack Earle: The Lonely Giant   242
24   Robert Wadlow: The Alton Giant   247
25   Giants Yesterday and Today   254

Part 6   Fat and Skinny

26   They Don't Come Any Heavier   265
27   Celesta Geyer and William J. Cobb: from
       Heavyweight to Lightweight   274
28   Living Skeletons   282

Part 7   An Odd Lot

29   Zip and Other Pinheads   291
30   Half-Man, Half-Woman   298
31   Unzie the Albino and Other Oddities   304

Part 8   Very, Very Special People

32   The Strange Fate of Julia Pastrana   311
33   Grace McDaniels: The Mule-Faced Woman   320
34   The Elephant Man by Sir Frederick Treves   322

Epilog   347
In Appreciation   349
Bibliography   353

Prologue

When the idea of writing a book about Very Special People was first suggested to me, it raised many questions in my mind. To find the answers, I sent my daughter, Jean, out to Baraboo, Wisconsin.

Baraboo, little known to the public, occupies a large place in the history of the American circus. It was the home of the Ringling Brothers when they were getting their start in the 1880s. Later it was the winter quarters of their circus. The memory of the brothers is still green in Baraboo, and today you can see a circus there all summer long and visit the Circus World Museum. It was to the library and archives building of the museum that I sent my daughter.

Jean spent hours and hours poring over old photographs, newspaper clippings, circus programs, books, and letters written by and about human oddities. My questions were more than answered by the briefcase full of Xeroxes and notes that she brought home.

But Jean brought back something more. It was a nightmare she'd had—a deeply disturbing dream inspired by the unusual people into whose lives and feelings the Baraboo archives had given her a glimpse. Here's how she related it to me.

"In my dream I was all alone. I was walking down a strange street in a strange town.

"Out of nowhere, a crowd of men, women, and children appeared. They swirled around me. . . .

"Suddenly I noticed the children were pointing their fingers at me. The men began to laugh. The women turned away or covered their eyes. Horror was written on their faces.

"I examined myself all over. I didn't have far to look.

"My arms had disappeared.

"In their place, growing directly out of my shoulders, were two very small, slender hands.

"But otherwise I was the same person I had always been.

" 'Stop looking at me like that!' I cried to the people surrounding me. 'What if I am physically different from you? I am still a human being like you. Treat me like one. I have the same feelings—exactly the same feelings as you.

" 'I am you!' "

The plea my daughter uttered in her dream has been the plea of human oddities through the ages. They have always wanted to be treated as equals by their fellows. But their wishes have seldom been satisfied.

Odd Man Out

The rest of mankind has always belittled the "odd man out." Essentially, because he's different—and it's human nature to look down on someone who is different from you, unless he has something you envy, like wealth or talent.

Yet, although people have disowned or depreciated the human oddity, they've usually flocked to see him. They may shudder with horror and cover their eyes with their fingers, but they always peek between them. They are morbidly fascinated by the human being who is formed differently from them.

Gawking at human oddities has been a popular pastime ever since they were first exhibited at fairs during the Middle Ages, and earlier. The living skeleton, the giant, the dwarf, the bearded lady have always drawn crowds who wanted to look, wonder, and, like Doubting Thomas, touch. During the Renaissance and later, the barons and princes of Europe, who owned everything else, also had their own hunchback dwarf jesters and giant porters and soldiers.

The Comprachicos

Human oddities were so highly prized that sometimes, it seems, they were even made to order. In *The Man Who Laughs,* Victor Hugo told of the *comprachicos*. The word, in Spanish, means "buyers of children." These people, according to Hugo, purchased young children and deformed them. "They took a man and made a muzzle; they stunted growth; they distorted the features." Then they sold their creations to traveling carnivals and collectors of human oddities.

Hugo also told of Chinese dealers who took a small child and put him in a grotesquely shaped porcelain vase without a top or a bottom. At night they laid the vase on its side, so the child could sleep; in the morning they set it upright again. They kept the child in it for years, while his flesh and bones grew according to its shape. Then they smashed the vase.

"The child comes out—and, behold, there is a man in the shape of a mug!"

Motives for Wonder

People look at human oddities for a variety of reasons.

Some find it an astonishing experience—and it is—to see a woman like Bella Carter, with an authentic tail growing between her shoulders. Or a pair of twins like the Tocci brothers, who were separate boys down to the sixth rib—but below that were a single person.

Some look at human oddities with a curiosity that is fundamentally scientific. They speculate about the hormonal imbalance that makes Tom Thumb a midget only twenty-five inches high and Robert Earl Hughes a mountain of flesh weighing over one thousand pounds. They are interested in the whys and wherefores.

Others—perhaps almost all of us—may look at human oddities for a reason that we seldom perceive. "It is merely one more additional attempt on the part of the individual," said George Brinton Beal, "to demonstrate a proof that he is better than some other individual, more perfect, more beautiful, less repulsive."

According to Dexter Fellows, publicity man for the Ringling Brothers and Barnum & Bailey Circus, "There is an equally large number of persons who attend the sideshow to pity rather than to gloat."

Clyde Ingalls, boss of the sideshow for Ringling Brothers, gave an interesting personal reason. "When I look at freaks, it makes me content by comparison to be less than perfect," he said.

Ugly Words

"Freaks" is an ugly word. There are uglier ones. One used by the medical profession is "monsters." A monster, scientifically speaking, is a person (or a plant or an animal) that deviates from the usual, normal type. The word comes from a Latin root (the same one as in the word "monitor") meaning "to warn." In ancient times or in backward places, when a human oddity was born, people took it to be a warning from heaven that they had sinned and were going to be punished. Their first act of repentance, naturally, was to kill the "monster." This was almost the fate of a number of the people you will come to know in this book, including Chang and Eng, the original Siamese twins.

People may be different from everyone else but they don't enjoy being called monsters. If they work in circus sideshows they may jokingly refer to each other as "freaks," but they don't relish it when anyone else applies that epithet to them. They prefer to be described as performers.

"Prodigies"

They've often spoken out on the subject. One memorable occasion was on January 6, 1898, when the Barnum and Bailey Circus was in England. The members of the sideshow—including two you'll get to know better in these pages, a lovable bearded lady named Annie Jones and a handsome Indian named Laloo, who had another body growing out of his own—held a meeting in which they formally protested against being called freaks. (As usual, a publicity man—Tody Hamilton—was in back of the action, but he was only capitalizing on authentic sentiment.)

The press paid considerable attention to what it called the "Uprising of the Freaks" and many people wrote to the papers proposing alternate terms. "Prodigies," a word suggested by Canon Wilberforce of Westminster Abbey, was chosen by the performers as the most satisfactory substitute. They took their decision to James A. Bailey, who accepted it. From then on, "prodigies" replaced "freaks" on the banners of the Greatest Show on Earth.

By 1903 the old word was back again. But the performers were never happy with it. Eventually the circus gave in, and the sideshow was called "the Congress of Strange People."

But they weren't—and aren't—strange. They are very special. They carry a special burden—and they carry it with dignity and courage. That is why, in this book, you'll rarely find them called freaks unless it's in a quotation from another source. I call them "Very Special People." And that, as you will soon see, is what they are.

Why Human Oddities Occur

"We call that against nature which goes against custom," said Michel de Montaigne, a French sage.

"There is nothing, whatsoever it may be, that is not according to nature."

The human oddity is natural, but nature has played a bitter prank on him. Often that prank is irremediable. The person's condition may be the result of some sudden, unexplainable genetic change or the emergence of some buried trait, dictated by the laws of heredity. The thyroid, the adrenal, the pituitary, or some other gland may misfire or go on a rampage. Or, while the individual is still an embryo rapidly taking form in his mother's womb, she may contract a disease or suffer an injury that does permanent damage to him. Or she may take a seemingly harmless medicine, like thalidomide, that hasn't been adequately tested (governments and drug companies have much to answer for on this score) and give birth to a deformed infant.

Sometimes the fertilized egg in the mother's womb starts to divide to form identical twins. But then, in the middle of the job—who can say why?—it stops. The twins are born, and they may be very beautiful, but they're joined by a thong of flesh, or they're connected at the head, the shoulder, the base of the spine, or in other strange ways.

Sometimes the culprit isn't nature but nurture. A person may just have learned bad eating habits. When you've practiced them long enough, they're almost impossible to break. This is often the story of the fat ladies and gentlemen of the sideshow—and possibly some of the thin ones.

Nowadays, doctors can do something to help many of these people. In earlier times—and that means up until a few decades ago—almost nothing could be done. Medical science hadn't advanced enough. The knowledge or the technique simply wasn't there. What you were born—armless, legless, a giant, a bearded lady, a dwarf, a Siamese twin—that you remained.

Unwanted and Unloved

If you're born a human oddity, your fate is not an enviable one. Every day of your life, starting in infancy, you are made aware that you are not as others are. And—especially if you're young—unconsciously you may interpret that to mean you're not as good.

As a Very Special Person, you probably will have a bitterly unhappy childhood. Even if you're loved by your mother and father (many parents try to get rid of unnormal children), you may not be accepted by your brothers and sisters, and your peers will certainly make mock of you. You may spend most or all of your days in an institution. Or you may hide from the world, to avoid the punishment it inflicts on those who differ from the rest in mind or body.

Life is not full of ego-building experiences for the Very Special Person. Nikolai Kobelkoff was born without arms or legs in Russia in the last century. When his mother finally got up her nerve and took him out of doors, her neighbors looked at him and crossed themselves. When little Carl Unthan, an armless child, sat by the coffin of his younger brother, he heard his kindly neighbors and relatives whispering—somehow, loud enough for him to hear—that God had taken the wrong child. As a boy, Jack Earle, the Texas giant, had to race home down alleyways to avoid the gibes of other children.

When you grow up, things, instead of getting better, may get worse. You may find it hard or impossible to get a job. If you're a very fat girl you won't fit into the ordinary office chair. If you're a midget you'll fit into it, but you'll have a problem getting up there. And when you want to marry? It may not be so easy to find a mate. (Think of the problems faced by Siamese twins.)

Romance and the Very Special People

Surprisingly enough, many of the Very Special People manage to marry and stay married. Often, they mate with normal people. The normal may find the unnormal exotic or endowed with some special quality they value. You might be surprised at how many bearded ladies have been adored by their bearded or beardless mates and how many midgets have been married to people of average stature.

According to Dick Best, who managed some of the most successful Very Special People in show business, 90 percent of human oddities marry normal people. My research tends to support this observation to a good degree. "I have never heard of a marriage between a freak and a normal person ending in divorce," Best said. You'll find a few divorces, however, among the people in this book.

Many of the Very Special People mate with their own kind. Tom Thumb found a miniature helpmate whom he adored. (Abraham Lincoln and Ulysses S. Grant adored her, too.) Emmett, "the Alligator Boy"—his body was covered with scales—and Priscilla, whose skin was so hairy that she was called "the Monkey Girl," had a marriage so happy that some who were physically normal envied them, and they had a normal child. Jean Tomaini, the legless acrobat, and her handsome giant husband, Al, were a loving pair.

Very Special Careers

The Very Special People not only find love—they frequently find Very Special careers for themselves. It's often been observed that nature seems to compensate them for what it has denied them, by giving them an unusual talent or a drive that brings them achievement far beyond the norm.

Tommy Jacobsen, born without arms, wasn't satisfied just to learn how to feed and dress himself with his feet. He went on to learn how to play the piano with his toes and became an outstanding performer. Eli Bowen, legless, was a superb acrobat. Ducornet, armless, has a permanent place in the history of French painting.

As you will discover again and again in these pages, the lives of many Very Special People show that the human spirit may be confined to an unnormal body but it isn't necessarily limited by it.

Sometimes it may be strengthened.

The Sideshow and Human Oddities

Human oddities often used to earn their liveli-
hoods by working in the carnival and circus sideshow.
Some still do, but every year fewer and fewer are seen.
Ringling Brothers hasn't had a bearded lady or a pair
of Siamese twins in the basement at Madison Square
Garden for a long time.

Taste has changed. The wave of interest in human
oddities that P. T. Barnum rode to fame and fortune in
the nineteenth century has disappeared with the unso-
phisticated age that engendered it. Today, many feel it's
wrong to display unnormally formed human beings for
profit, and numerous cities and states have laws prohib-
iting it. So does at least one country, the Soviet Union.
As Dominic Vivona of Amusements of America, a top
carnival, says, "Years ago there was no other way for a
freak of nature to make a living except by joining a
show. Now they get jobs."

But not all do or can. Many still appear with carnivals, and they feel they have a right to. In December,
1971, a group of human oddities had a round-table
discussion on Channel Thirteen in New York City.
Among them were the giant Eddie Carmel, a 712-
pounder named Big Jim, an albino named Sandra Reed,
and Dolly Regan, described as half-woman, half-child.
They agreed that the Russians were right to forbid
exhibitions of human oddities, but pointed out that the
Soviet Government gives them special training and hires
them for jobs. "Not like here," the discussants emphasized. In America's "free" society, they said, there is no
alternative to the sideshow. "If it was not for carnivals,
we wouldn't have a chance. You get more respect in a
sideshow; in the street you'd have to be a beggar." Or,
as Dick Best put it, "An alligator girl can't be a waitress
or a receptionist, a nurse, or a baby sitter . . . And
who's going to support these people if they can't support themselves?" Agreeing with this opinion, in 1972
the Florida Supreme Court struck down a 1921 law

against "freak shows," ruling that the state has no business telling anyone he cannot earn an honest living.

What Is Normal?

In the circus and carnival, the human oddity is taken for granted. People in show business won't stare at him, and he can associate with others of his own kind. There you can find, seated around the same table playing cards together, a woman who weighs six hundred pounds, a girl with a body shaped like a frog's, and a man with three legs. The person shuffling and dealing has no hands—he does it all with his toes. "Nobody sits around feeling sorry for himself or anybody else," Dick Best observed. "You could be accepted there if you had nine arms and ten heads."

Human oddities and others in show business tend to flock together. Since they traditionally work with carnivals and circuses in the warm months and are idle in the winter, they've tended to settle in the South, where the cold months are more comfortable. After John Ringling moved the winter quarters of his circus to Sarasota in the 1920s, many of his employees made their homes there, or in Tampa. Gibsonton, nine miles south of Tampa, is known as the carnival capital of America. It is full of circus folk and perhaps has more Very Special People than any other community in the country. The other residents don't look on them as oddities, but as neighbors and fellow members of the Elks or the PTA. They lead a normal life, raising their families like other Americans and taking part in local affairs.

In such a town, normalcy counts for little. Sometimes you can even get the fleeting impression that the normal human being is the exception—and the oddity is normal.

When you come right down to it, what is normal? Except for their appearance, the Very Special People are the same as ordinary human beings. As my daughter Jean's dream expressed it so basically, they have the same feelings as the rest of us. Only their bodies are different.

Perhaps we can leave the last word on the subject to one of the Very Special People.

"If the truth were known," said a wise old trouper named Lady Olga, stroking her long gray beard, "we're all freaks together."

Very Special People

PART 1

CHAINED FOR LIFE

1

Chang and Eng:
The Original Siamese Twins

The Siamese people are fond of saying that they have given three things to the world. One is white elephants. Another is Siamese cats. And the third is Siamese twins.

Twins who are joined together physically have been known since the beginning of time. But Chang and Eng (see photo insert), born in Siam in 1811, were the most famous pair in history. They toured Europe and the United states repeatedly, exhibiting themselves to millions of people. They were examined and elaborately described by the most distinguished physicians of two continents. So celebrated did the two become that all twins whose bodies are physically connected have been called Siamese twins ever since.

Oddly enough, the original Siamese twins weren't Siamese, but Chinese. Their father was a Chinese fisherman; their mother was half-Chinese, half-Malay. The couple had settled in Siam in the hope that they could make a better living there. In their native village and

3

throughout Siam the two boys were always known as the Chinese twins.

The twins were born on May 11, 1811, in Meklong, a tiny fishing village sixty miles from Bangkok, capital of Siam (Thailand). The family already had four children, all normal. Their mother, thirty-five years old, was a well-proportioned, attractive woman. The birth was an easy one: the twins were quite tiny. They came into the world simultaneously, the head of one tucked neatly between the legs of the other.

The babies were handsome and both were boys, which should have furnished occasion for rejoicing. But in one respect they were very different from any other children that had ever been seen in the little village. They were bound to each other at the breastbone by a stout thong of flesh. In the middle of it was a common umbilicus or belly button.

Why Are Siamese Twins Born?

Siamese twins, or conjoined twins, basically are identical twins. Identical twins develop from a single egg fertilized by a single sperm. The egg then divides completely in two, and the twins have the same sex and the same physical characteristics. In the case of Siamese twins, however, the egg fails to divide perfectly.

At the point where division is incomplete, the twins stay attached to each other. Some are joined at the back, the abdomen, the chest, or even the top of the head. Some are connected by a band of tissue. They may have organs or limbs in common. Most are born dead or die shortly after birth.

Miraculously, the twins born that day in Meklong lived. And they were to continue to live for a long time, despite the ligament that connected them.

That ligament was to be their destiny. Because of it they were never to spend a moment apart or have a secret from each other. They were to eat together, sleep together, work together, marry together, sit by the fire together, grow old together. Finally they were to die together.

An Evil Omen

The parents named the twins Chang and Eng. In pictures of the brothers Eng is the one on the left, Chang the one on the right, when they are facing you.

In a backward country like Siam, any event out of the commonplace—and particularly a birth like this one—was likely to be taken as a sign from the gods. The people of the countryside believed the conjoined twins were an omen that the end of the world was at hand. News of the birth was carried up the river to Bangkok, where it reached the ears of the king. For a while, it is said, he considered having the extraordinary infants put to death. But he thought better of it and the baby boys were left in peace.

The twins brought celebrity to Meklong. People came by land and water to have a look at the strange little beings. Siamese doctors suggested to the parents that the infants should be cut apart or burned apart so that they might lead separate lives. But their mother decided it was better to have two babies who were connected but alive than two who were separated but dead, and she refused the physicians' suggestions.

Lengthening the Ligament

The twins' family lived in a floating house built upon a raft moored in a river. The house was made of bamboo and thatched with leaves. Here, when they were old enough, Chang and Eng crawled on the floor and finally learned to walk.

At the start, the twins found every movement a tremendous problem. Not only were the children bound together—they were bound face to face. If they were to move at all they had to move simultaneously. Each had to time his actions to those of the other. Otherwise they came tumbling down in a writhing heap of arms and legs.

The babies, their mother saw, would have greater freedom of action if the band of flesh could be lengthened. She kept pulling them apart and exercising them so as to exert pressure on the ligament. Always she urged them to face away from each other as much as possible.

It was a moment of triumph for the mother when she found that her sons, by constant effort and practice, had stretched the ligament so much that they were able to stand side by side. Not quite like other boys. But almost.

Two Distinct Personalities

In appearance Chang and Eng resembled each other closely, but they had distinct personalities which emerged more and more clearly as the years went by. Although they had to coordinate their movements, it was necessary for one to be the leader, the other the follower. The first role naturally fell to Chang; he was more aggressive and decisive than his brother. He also had the quicker temper. If there was an argument between the two, Eng was usually the one who would give in. Some people felt that Chang was brighter than Eng, but a dominant personality often creates such an impression.

The boys disagreed occasionally. Once in a while they had a severe fight. But most of the time they showed complete sympathy and affection for each other.

Like Two Dancers

In their movements Chang and Eng reminded people of a couple who have been dancing together for years. Long experience had bred a sixth sense in them. Each could anticipate the other's next move and follow it up smoothly and faultlessly. To many it seemed as though each boy could read the other's mind.

The ligament that bound the twins was an object of great curiosity to everyone. If someone touched it in the exact middle, both boys responded. On the other hand, if it was touched more toward one of them, only that one felt the touch.

The band eventually could stretch to a length of 4½ inches. It was as thick as a forearm and had great strength. If one of the twins was picked up and the other hung suspended by the ligament, neither complained of any pain. When one of the boys fell the other could pull him upright by the band. They enjoyed tumbling head over heels in bed, and did so with great freedom. Often, in their sleep, they changed positions. To do this, one would roll completely over the other—without either of them awakening.

Earning a Living

Living on the river, young Chang and Eng spent endless hours in and around the water. They learned to handle a small boat, to dive and swim, and catch fish. In spite of their handicap, they attempted everything the other children did and played with them as equals.

By 1819 the twins' family had grown to include ten children. That year misfortune struck. The twins, then eight years old, lost their father. All the youngsters who were able to had to help support the family. Chang and Eng first tried making coconut oil. Then they became peddlers in the floating market of boats on the river. They had a quick smile and a native charm. People found it hard to resist the salesmanship of these small human oddities, who would pour out a torrent of words simultaneously and finish each other's sentences. Later they turned to breeding ducks, preserved the eggs, and sold them.

At the Royal Court

For Chang and Eng, 1824 was a gala year. A new king had come to the throne and he asked that the famous twins be brought to his palace in Bangkok so he could see them. It was an extraordinary honor, and the boys were carefully tutored in all the niceties of court etiquette.

At the royal palace Chang and Eng were led into a

vast hall decorated in gold, lavender, and crimson. High above them, on a lofty throne, sat the king, Rama III, under a canopy of nine gilded umbrellas. The youngsters prostrated themselves and touched their foreheads to the floor in unison as they had been taught. Rama asked them questions about themselves, their family, and how they earned their livelihood.

All at once Chang and Eng heard a loud crash of gongs, and curtains swept in front of the king. The boys drew back in terror, but they had no reason to. It was simply the end of their audience with King Rama.

Next the twins were taken on a tour of the palace. They were received by the king's wives—he had seven hundred of them—who were greatly interested in the two unusual youngsters and gave them presents.

The boys were coming to be recognized as one of the national assets of Siam. A few years afterward a special embassy was sent to the neighboring country of Indo-China, and Chang and Eng were chosen to go along. At the state banquet all eyes were fastened on them. Their moment of glory was short-lived, but it left the boys with a hunger for a better life and a desire to see other lands and other people.

Hunter Discovers the Twins

In 1824 a Scottish merchant named Robert Hunter glimpsed a curious sight. He was crossing the river and in the distance he saw swimming in the water a creature that looked like a monster out of a Siamese legend. It seemed to have two heads and an unusual number of limbs and it moved with a strange and sinuous grace. When the creature climbed out of the water the merchant saw with astonishment that it was really two young boys who were bound to each other by an unbelievable band of flesh.

Hunter approached the two boys. He found them friendly and eager to talk. The merchant learned where they lived and something of their history. He was impressed by the skill with which they had adapted to their handicap and the cheerfulness with which they bore it.

It was only the first of many meetings between Hunter and Chang and Eng. The merchant visited the boys at home and met their mother. He became deeply interested in the youngsters. As events were to show, his involvement was not entirely disinterested. Hunter was a shrewd businessman, with a keen eye for good merchandise, and he realized with a sudden quickening of the pulses that the world had not seen anything like Chang and Eng in his lifetime. He began to tell the twins about the wonderful countries that lay on the other side of the globe. At the same time he approached the government of Siam and asked for permission to take the boys to Europe.

The government declined Hunter's request. But the hard-headed merchant was far from discouraged. The boys were young and he had time.

Goodbye to Siam

In 1829 Hunter's patience was rewarded. Captain Abel Coffin, master of the American trading vessel *Sachem*, arrived in Bangkok. Coffin was a business associate of Hunter's, and the Scot proposed that they form a partnership and take the twins to the West and exhibit them. The two men approached the twins' mother. Offering her a cash payment for her permission to let the boys go, they promised to take good care of them and bring them back in a few years. They didn't have to persuade Chang and Eng.

The permission of the government still needed to be obtained. It had been refused before, but Hunter now had an argument he felt would be persuasive. Siam was eager to increase its contact with the West, and he told the king that the twins would be an excellent advertisement for the country. And so, in April, 1829, the *Sachem* headed out to sea with Hunter and Coffin and two seventeen-year-old boys whose hearts were bursting with excitement.

The Siamese Twins in the United States

The *Sachem*'s destination was Boston. The trip took four months. In that time, associating with Coffin, Hunter, and the American crew, Chang and Eng learned to speak English.

The ship docked in August, 1829. Renting a huge tent—it was large enough to hold several thousand people—the partners began to publicize the two youngsters. The promoters' expectations were great, and they weren't disappointed. Billed as "the Siamese Double Boys," Chang and Eng appeared before densely packed audiences at every performance. People paid a premium price, from two to six dollars apiece, to see this eighth wonder of the world. The sensation they caused was probably not to be matched until fifteen years later, when P. T. Barnum exhibited General Tom Thumb, the celebrated midget.

Not only laymen were intrigued by the unusual spectacle. The leaders of the medical profession were eager to see and study the twins. At Harvard University, Professor J. C. Warren of the medical college examined them and wrote a report on his findings. He concluded that the ligament connecting Chang and Eng contained nerves, arteries, and veins. If one of the twins were to die, he warned, the ligament should be severed at once or the surviving twin would die soon afterward.

From Boston Chang and Eng were taken to Providence, Philadelphia and other cities. Whether they were prompted by their managers or found it dull standing quietly on the stage while the public listened to a lecture about them, they soon developed an act. They performed, often in unison, a complex series of movements, which included bending their bodies in all directions and turning somersaults. They also would carry a portly member of the audience as much as one hundred feet without showing signs of strain.

In mid-October, after a highly successful exhibition in New York, the twins and their managers embarked for England.

Success in England

In London, Hunt and Coffin rented a room at the Egyptian Hall, one of the city's major showplaces, where Tom Thumb was later to score a great success. Already, in America, the partners had periodically encountered complaints that the Siamese twins were a fake, and they decided to forestall similar charges in England. They extended invitations to a group of prominent British literary and scientific men, among them members of the Royal College of Surgeons, to come to a private meeting with the twins at the hall.

The guests found themselves both impressed with the anatomical peculiarity of the boys (most physicians had seen Siamese twins only in jars) and pleased with their personalities. The president of the Royal College of Surgeons, Leigh Thomas, and over thirty of his colleagues signed a certificate testifying to their approbation of the exhibition. Joshua Brookes, a noted anatomist, provided a document declaring that the twins "constitute a most extraordinary *Lusus Naturae* [sport of nature], the first instance I have ever seen of a double living child; they being totally devoid of deception, afford a very interesting spectacle, and they are highly deserving of public patronage."

Chang and Eng were featured in articles in the English press. Members of the royal family came to see them. The English public was fascinated by them. The gentleness and sweetness of their dispositions, and their physical attractiveness struck the public all the more forcefully because of their unfortunate deformity. People commented that the twins, standing with their arms draped around each other—one of their favorite poses—looked like a group of statuary.

An artist's representation at this period shows the boys in Siamese costumes. They have handsome, soulful oriental faces, with long braids fastened on top of their heads. (Later they cut off the braids.) Each holds a racket in his hand while the other arm embraces his brother. At their feet lies a shuttlecock. Chang and Eng had become masters of the game of battledore and shuttlecock, ancestor of our modern badminton, and often included a match in their act.

Foreigners frequently suffer in the damp, foggy London climate and the visitors from sunny Siam were no exception. That winter, for the first time in their lives the twins saw snow. They also came down with severe colds, sore throats, and chest pains. Hunter and Coffin, seeing their golden goose suddenly endangered, summoned Dr. G. B. Bolton, a prominent surgeon whom they had engaged to be the twins' personal physician. Following his advice, Chang and Eng were outfitted with leather waistcoats, and a leather blanket was obtained for their bed. They were soon on their feet again.

Medical Tests Galore

Doctors continued to take advantage of the rare opportunity to study and test the Siamese twins. Politely, Chang and Eng put up with their questions, thumpings, and experiments. Each of the youths was fed different foods for twenty-four hours and their body wastes were examined. The conclusion was that their digestive tracts were completely independent of each other.

X rays were still seventy years in the future. Although the twins' connecting band was measured and studied endlessly, no one could be sure what vital organs were contained in it. Almost without exception, physicians warned that it would be extremely dangerous to sever it in order to separate the brothers.

Dr. Bolton, the twins' physician, was among those who published studies on them. He noted that they were about five feet two inches tall (Chang was actually an inch shorter) and weighed one hundred and eighty pounds together. "Their bodies and limbs," he observed, "are well-formed but the spine of Chang, who habitually holds his arm over the shoulder of Eng, is considerably curved laterally, apparently the result of this long-continued habit... They are cleanly and delicate in their habits and mutually assist each other. They are exceedingly affectionate and docile and grateful for every kindness shown them." He found them remarkably quick in intellect and was struck by their fondness for music.

After a long stay in London, the twins' managers took them on an extensive tour of the British Isles. "The Wonderful and Extraordinary Siamese Boys, eighteen years of age and joined together by Nature!" advertisements proclaimed. "Since their arrival in England they have been visited by Queen Adelaide, and several of the Royal Family, Prince Esterhazy, Charles 10th, Duchesses de Berri and Angouleme, and many thousand Ladies and Gentlemen of distinction, who universally have expressed their satisfaction of the exhibition."

Banned in France

After traveling twenty-five hundred miles in Britain, the showmen made plans to tour the Continent. To their surprise the French Government refused to permit the twins to enter. The French subscribed to the doctrine of "maternal impressions"—which held that if a pregnant woman saw an unpleasant sight or was frightened in some way, it might leave its mark on her unborn child. People told the story, for example, of a woman who saw her husband killed by a lion—and then bore a son who had a lion's mane and a face covered with long hair. (This tale was circulated about Lionel the Lion-Faced Man, later widely exhibited in Europe and the United States.) The effect of maternal impressions was widely believed in at the time; medical science rejects the belief completely today.

Although France was closed to them, the rest of Europe welcomed the Siamese twins. They traveled from one major city to another, playing to packed houses and stirring wonder everywhere they went.

Hunter had taken a long leave of absence from his business affairs in Siam. He now had to return. Having realized a substantial profit on his investment in Chang and Eng, he sold out his interest to Captain Coffin.

In 1831–32 the twins were back in the United States, touring the country. They were well on their way to becoming a household word on two continents.

Attack on a Doctor

Although Dr. Bolton described the twins as "docile," they weren't always so. Once, when they were appearing in Alabama, a doctor wanted to examine the band that connected them. The twins did not relish the idea of baring their bodies on a platform in front of an audience and they refused. Indignant, the doctor declared they were fakes.

Boiling with rage, the twins flung themselves at the physician and knocked him down. Fights broke out throughout the room and it was only with difficulty that Chang and Eng extricated themselves from the melee. They did not escape the law, however. They were arrested and had to deposit $350 with their pledge to keep the peace.

The Angry Twins

At another time, in Philadelphia, the twins almost ran afoul of the law again. Shaking hands with the youths, a man squeezed Chang's hand very hard. Chang took a swing at him. The injured party went before a magistrate and said he wanted Chang arrested for assault and battery. But the magistrate pointed out that the twins presented a peculiar legal problem: it would be impossible to arrest Chang without also taking his brother into custody. If the innocent Eng was jailed, he could bring a charge of false arrest against the plaintiff. Astonished, the man dropped the charge.

Chang and Eng were very sensitive to being stared at when they were off the stage. Sometimes, if there were guests for dinner, the youths might suddenly discover that someone was watching how they cut their food or put it in their mouths. To discourage the inquisitive person, they would catch his eye, pointedly put down their knives and forks, and remain immobile.

When the guest saw what had happened he would quickly look away.

The Twins' Compassion

The twins felt a deep compassion for people who were physically handicapped. During one performance they noticed a man without arms and legs who was seated in the audience. Declaring that fate had dealt more kindly with them than it had with him, they gave him a present.

On another occasion Chang and Eng saw a one-eyed man among the spectators. Calling the theater manager, they asked him to refund half of the man's admission fee—since he could see only half of what others did!

A Lively Sense of Humor

Chang and Eng were also noted for their lively sense of humor. One story that went the rounds for years concerned a trip that they made on a train. Before the brothers climbed on board, only Chang bought a ticket. Taking a seat on the train, the twins covered themselves with a cloak that concealed the telltale ligament.

When the conductor came through, Chang handed in his ticket. Eng, however, shook his head.

"Your ticket, sir," said the conductor.

"I have no ticket."

"Pay or leave the car."

"I won't pay. But I will get out if my brother does."

The brother disagreed. "I have paid," said Chang, "and I don't mean to get out."

The conductor called the brakeman, a stout Dutchman. As he came up to the twins—and before he could open his mouth—Chang and Eng dropped the cloak. In their troublesome passengers the trainmen suddenly recognized the world-famous Siamese twins, and everyone burst into laughter. The brothers, of course, had no intention of bringing the issue to a legal test, and Eng paid for his ticket.

On Their Own

Exactly what financial arrangement Captain Coffin had with the twins up to this time isn't clear. Unquestionably, he was pocketing the lion's share of the money they earned. In their contacts with American show business, Chang and Eng became aware that they had a right to more money than they were receiving.

In May, 1832, Chang and Eng reached the age of twenty-one. Legally they were adults. They at once notified Coffin that they considered their contract with him at an end; henceforth they intended to manage their own affairs.

Something of the bad feeling between the youths and their manager emerges from a letter they wrote to their old friend Robert Hunter, with whom they continued to correspond.

"He told us," they wrote, referring to Coffin, "that the arrangement with the Government [of Siam] was for *seven* years, and that 2½ years was mentioned to our mother in order to quiet her fears and prevent any obstacle from being in the way of our leaving home with him. However, this kind of double dealing was but badly calculated to induce us to remain with him any longer. . . We have nearly completed the tour of the United States, being now in the 19th state of the 24 which compose the Union."

In their letter, Chang and Eng mentioned their wish to return to Siam. This desire cropped up again and again in their letters and conversations. The twins became acquainted with an American lady, Mrs. Roper-Feudge, who often traveled in the Orient. When she was about to leave for Siam she told them she would like to visit their mother and family and bring them a message.

"Tell them we are coming home sometime," Chang said. "When we have made money enough," added Eng.

But Siam was a long way off. As the years went by, the twins put down deep roots in America. They were never to see their mother again.

The Twins and P. T. Barnum

Just as all roads proverbially once led to Rome, the roads traveled by the Very Special People in America in the nineteenth century led to P. T. Barnum. On his stage appeared such famous oddities as Jo-Jo the Dog-Faced Boy; Anna Swan, the Nova Scotia giantess; Annie Jones and Mme. Clofullia, the bearded ladies, and many others whose stories are told in these pages. Inevitably, in their turn, the Siamese twins came to Barnum, too.

The premier impresario of his time, Barnum has been called "the Shakespeare of advertising." Many of the human curiosities he promoted were discovered by him (with the help of his agents). The Siamese twins hardly needed to be introduced to the public when they signed up with him. But many people still believed they were fraudulent, and in this he saw the possibility of a major exploitation. His first step was to obtain a medical certificate so he could prove they were authentic conjoined twins. Then he launched his advertising campaign and put them on display in the mid-1830s. Crowds poured in to see the brothers, and both they and Barnum profited handsomely.

Curiously, the showman makes only passing reference to Chang and Eng in his autobiography, although he devotes whole chapters to his other successes, like Tom Thumb and Jenny Lind. Apparently he was not overfond of Chang and Eng. For their part, they appear to have felt the same way about him. After their dealings with Captain Coffin, they were already somewhat jaundiced about promoters and their promises.

A Horse Named Bob

The twins' stay with Barnum was only an interim affair. For years they toured under their own management. Methodical businessmen, the brothers kept a careful record of their outlays. Their ledger book, written in the elegant hand of the day, is still in the possession of their descendants. The twins must have been considerable smokers, for their expenditures in June, 1832, included an item of nine dollars for five hundred cigars. Also recorded were items of $72.50 for a horse named Bob, $2.75 for a bridle, and $4.50 for "horsekeeping ('Bob')." The ledger shows an expenditure of $86.02 for whisky and beer in a single week. It lists outlays for printed handbills and boys to distribute them, as well as newspaper advertising expenses.

Bouncing along behind Bob in their buggy, the twins traveled from one corner of the country to another, giving exhibitions. Agents were sent on ahead with handbills and posters, advertising the coming of "the United Brothers, Chang-Eng." The fee for admittance was usually fifty cents. They also sold "a very superior likeness, executed in lithograph, and suitable for framing." The sale of pamphlets containing an account of their life and adventures, with a report on the medical findings of distinguished doctors who had examined them, was another source of income.

In 1836 the brothers were back in Europe again. They traveled from city to city, renting a room and giving performances. It was a profitable way of life—but an exhausting one.

Backwoods Settlers

In 1839 Chang and Eng were twenty-eight years of age. They had been appearing in public for about ten years and had amassed some sixty thousand dollars. They were tired of the hard, roving life of itinerant curiosities and were eager to settle down somewhere.

In June, they decided Wilkesboro, a small town in the Blue Ridge foothills of North Carolina, was that somewhere. It was backwoods country. The inhabitants lived in log cabins and earned their living by farming, and the brothers liked their life style.

Now the entries in the twins' ledger suddenly

change. There are expenditures for bolts of cloth, brandy, buckets, spoons, tablecloths, fishing hooks, and shot, among other items. We suppose that Chang and Eng began their retirement from show business by opening a country store in Wilkesboro. We also suppose the town didn't need the store, for not long afterward the twins were busy as farmers. By the end of the year they had bought 110 acres in Trap Hill, not far away, paying for it with a bag of silver. They also built a house.

A letter that Chang and Eng wrote in 1842 to Robert Hunter gives a picture of their new way of life. "We . . . raise our own corn and hogs—we enjoy ourselves pretty well, but have not as yet got married. But we are making love pretty fast, and if we get a couple of nice wives we will be sure to let you know about it. We weigh 200 lbs. (together) and are pretty stout fellows at that!!!! . . . We have wood and water in great abundance and our neighbors are all on an equality, and none are very rich—people live comfortably, but each man tills his own soil."

Chang and Eng Bunker

Siam had faded into the past. Chang and Eng had a permanent home in North Carolina and they were American in language and outlook. Why not, they thought, become Americans in fact?

In October, 1839, soon after they settled in Wilkesboro, the twins filed a declaration of intent to become American citizens in Wilkes Superior Court. Raising their right hands, they took their oath of allegiance to their new homeland. They had no last name. They were listed simply as "Chang and Eng, Siamese Twins."

By 1844 the brothers decided that, like their neighbors, they should have a family name. In the fall term of Wilkes Superior Court they presented a petition to adopt the name Bunker. Their request was granted. Where did they find the name? We can't be sure. Correspondence in the possession of the North Carolina Divi-

sion of Archives and History suggests that the twins
had an old friend named Bunker.

Love and the Siamese Twins

Not far from the Chang-Eng property lived David
Yates, a farmer and part-time clergyman, and his
family, which included nine daughters. They were
Quakers, of Irish and Dutch ancestry. Chang and Eng
met two of the Yates girls, Adelaide and Sarah Ann,
and began to go out with them. The twins were in their
early thirties, the girls about nineteen and twenty.

According to Kay Hunter, who has told the story
in her interesting book, *Duet for a Lifetime*, when the
twins appeared in public with the girls the townsfolk
were appalled. They liked Chang and Eng well
enough—but not enough to see them keeping company
with girls who were not only white, but normal as well.

Yates first learned that his daughters were dating
Chang and Eng when people began to smash his windows. He also received threats that his crops would be
burned unless he pulled in the reins on his two girls.
The twins were told that they should keep away from
Wilkesboro womenfolk—if they knew what was good
for them.

In spite of the warnings, Chang and Eng continued
to court Adelaide and Sarah Ann. The twins had lived
without love a long time—too long to give it up when
they had finally found it. But only too mindful of the
difficulties that lay ahead, they went to Philadelphia
and quickly arranged for a surgical separation. It was a
dangerous step to take, and they knew it. In the nick of
time their sweethearts found out what they were con-
templating. The operation was never performed.

In April, 1843, in a double wedding, Eng was
married to Sarah Ann and Chang to Adelaide. The two
couples moved into the twins' house and settled down
to life together. It was a novel kind of married life and
it required novel adjustments. But, different as it was
from any other, in its fundamentals it was the same.
Both marriages were happy, fruitful, and lasting.

Soon Chang and Eng were making a new kind of entry in their ledger book. Instead of expenditures, now they listed the children that were being born to them and their wives. They wrote down no more than each child's name and date of birth. They felt no need to indicate to whom each child belonged.

When the last name was finally entered many years later, Eng had fathered seven boys and five girls and Chang seven girls and three boys. All twenty-two children were normal except for a son and daughter of Chang's who were deaf mutes. In the 1850s the twins reappeared on the stage. They needed additional funds, they said, to provide their children with a liberal education.

With the years the families grew too big to remain comfortably beneath the some roof. The twins bought land in nearby White Plains and built two houses, one for each family, about a mile apart. Chang and Eng spent three days in one house and the next three days in the other. They followed this schedule year in and year out, in winter and summer, in sickness and health. In Eng's house, Eng was the master and his brother had to bow to his wishes; in Chang's house, Chang called the tune.

A New Way of Life

For the Very Special People, life is often a story of meeting new challenges and overcoming them. In the North Carolina backwoods Chang and Eng found themselves in a situation different from any they had known before. As usual, they adapted, quickly and efficiently. They learned to plough and they became crack shots. Wielding an axe became second nature to them. They enjoyed felling trees and helping their neighbors raise new houses. Reportedly, they cut the logs used to build the White Plains Baptist Church, to which they belonged, and they shingled their own barn. The two are credited with developing a special method of chopping wood dictated by their need to stand in the same place when working. Chang would strike the tree with his axe angled in one direction and then Eng would swing with his blade angled in the opposite direction.

The twins were fond of society. Long afterward, old-timers told Archie Robertson, a newsman, "They'd entertain you royally so long as they didn't think you'd just come to see them out of curiosity." Eng enjoyed playing cards with his friends or checkers with the children. Chang didn't—but if he was in Eng's house he had to go along with his brother's wishes, so, while Eng played, Chang was likely to be reading a book or dozing. However, there were many activities both enjoyed. Reading poetry or history aloud to each other was one of them.

The Civil War

Mark Twain was a contemporary of the Siamese twins, and like other Americans he was greatly interested in them. He wrote an elaborate spoof on the brothers in which he pretended he knew them intimately. Among other things, he declared that one of them was born two years after the other. During the Civil War, said Twain, "they were strong partisans, and both fought gallantly all through the great struggle— Eng on the Union side and Chang on the Confederate. They took each other prisoners at Seven Oaks . . ."

Of course, the twins didn't serve in the war. They were southerners, however—well-to-do ones at that— and the conflict brought financial ruin to them. Before the war they had sold the bulk of their real estate, taking notes, which were secured by mortgages. The notes were repaid with Confederate money, which proved to be worthless. The brothers owned slaves, but the war set them free. Moreover, the economy was at a standstill, so there was no market for the crops the twins grew on their farms. With their fortunes gone and large families to support, somewhat reluctantly Chang and Eng returned again to P. T. Barnum.

Back in Show Business

The years had taken their toll of the brothers. When Chang and Eng reappeared in New York City they were not the overwhelming success they had once been. But they still had a worldwide reputation. Barnum determined to exploit it.

"I sent them to Great Britain," he wrote, "where, in all the principal places, and for about a year, their levees [shows] were always crowded. In all probability the great success attending this enterprise was much enhanced, if not actually caused, by extensive announcements in advance that the main purpose of Chang-Eng's visit to Europe was to consult the most eminent medical and surgical talent with regard to the safety of separating the twins."

Although Barnum, in an effort to draw the crowds, ballyhooed the brothers' interest in being separated, his statements were not far from the truth. The need for a surgical separation had come to weigh increasingly on the twins' minds. They viewed with dread the day—which was inevitably drawing closer—when one of them would die and the other find himself bound to a corpse.

In London, Chang and Eng called on Sir William Ferguson of the Royal College of Surgeons and asked his opinion on a surgical separation. Sir William examined them. He found Chang's arteries were showing marked degenerative changes, foreshadowing that he might be the first to go. In view of the age of the twins—they were now in their upper fifties—Sir William advised against the operation.

In Edinburgh the twins consulted Sir James Simpson, professor of medicine and midwifery (as obstetrics was then known), who made history when he introduced chloroform to ease the pangs of delivery. Sir James told them he considered separation would be "perilous" and counseled against it. In a lecture he gave on Chang and Eng he said they had lived longer than any other conjoined twins he knew of.

Troubled Times

After several years in Europe, during which the twins sometimes included their wives and some of their children in their performances, they returned home. On shipboard, Chang suffered a stroke. Henceforth he was to be partially paralyzed on his right side. His condition imposed a heavy burden not just on himself but on his brother as well. He also became increasingly deaf.

With these afflictions it's hardly surprising that Chang was frequently depressed and turned more and more to alcohol for relief. He had always been the more irritable of the two. Now it became almost impossible for Eng to live with him. He had little choice, however.

Mark Twain, in his humorous sketch on the twins, makes Chang an ardent prohibitionist and Eng a heavy drinker. Because of the physical link between the two, according to Twain, whenever Eng got drunk it would inevitably cause his brother to become intoxicated. In real life, of course, Chang was the drinker and Eng the teetotaler. Strangely enough, Chang's drinking never affected Eng. Possibly Chang was simply more sensitive to alcohol than his nondrinking twin. However, Eng hardly found it reassuring to have to watch Chang ruining his health with alcohol.

When Chang was in Eng's house, Eng had the right to tell him when to stop drinking, and he had to obey. In his own house, however, Chang was free to drink himself into insensibility. Once, when Chang was in his cups, the twins had such a violent argument that they broke furniture and burned it. A peace officer was called in and the twins were placed under a bond. After that they found it was easier to stay out of trouble if they did not speak to each other when they were upset.

"Look at Your Uncle—Quickly!"

In January, 1874, when the twins were staying at Chang's house he came down with a severe case of bronchitis. Their physician, Dr. Hollingsworth, was called. Chang soon showed some improvement. When the day came for the regular move to Eng's, Chang insisted on making it, although his brother argued against it. It was a damp, wintry day, and they traveled in an open carriage as usual.

On the following night, Friday, the twins went to bed. After a while Chang woke his brother.

"I'm having trouble breathing," he gasped. "I must get up."

The two got out of bed. To keep off the chill they made a fire. For a few hours they sat in front of it in their big double chair. Then Eng got sleepy, and succeeded in persuading his brother to go back to bed.

In the middle of the night Eng awoke in a cold sweat. He had a frightening presentiment that something had happened to his brother. He listened for Chang's hoarse breathing but he heard nothing. He shook him. Chang did not stir.

Eng was confused and terrified. "Help!" he called. "Help!"

In a few minutes one of his sons padded into the room. "What is it, Father?" he asked tensely.

"Look at your uncle—quickly!"

The boy examined the quiet form next to his father.

Finally he said, "Uncle Chang is dead."

"Then I am going also," Eng said. Uncontrollable spasms wracked his frame. "My last hour is come!"

The family was awake by now. One of the boys was sent to call Dr. Hollingsworth at Mount Airy. If there ever was to be a right time to risk separating the twins, that time was now.

But Mount Airy was three long miles away. It took a while for the boy to reach the doctor's house—and a while for the doctor to gather up his instruments.

In the meantime Eng was contorted with severe cramps. His family massaged him. They assured him Dr. Hollingsworth was coming and all would be well.

"Move Chang closer," Eng whispered. "I am very bad off."

Eng was weakening, but he seemed less frightened.

Now he said, "May God have mercy on my soul!" He became very still. After a while his wife noticed that he had stopped breathing. The date was January 17, 1874.

The Autopsy

Two weeks later the bodies of the brothers were removed to Jefferson Medical College in Philadelphia. Doctors were eager to perform an autopsy on the most famous Siamese twins in history. They wanted to determine not only the cause of both deaths but how closely the twins had been linked in life.

In making the autopsy, the surgeons were hampered by restrictions laid down by the twins' families, who did not want the bodies mutilated. The examination suggested that Chang had died of a cerebral clot. The cause of Eng's death, however, was more difficult to establish. "Eng," declared one of the examining physicians finally, "probably died of fright, as the distended bladder seemed to point to a profound emotional disturbance."

The surgeons probed the ligament joining the twins. They discovered that an artery linked the two circulatory systems, and Eng's veins were almost devoid of blood. The blood had flowed out through the artery and into the body of Chang, possibly causing Eng's cramps and death. Whether an operation to separate the twins could have been successfully performed was impossible to say.

If Chang and Eng were born today, their story could be a very different one. With the aid of modern diagnostic procedures, surgeons can tell exactly how Siamese twins are joined, what organs they share in common, and whether they can be separated successfully. Surgical separation of conjoined twins is a frequent occurrence. In some cases, however, it is possible to save only one of the twins.

Chang and Eng were buried in the graveyard of the Baptist Church at White Plains, which they helped to build. In time their wives were laid to rest beside them: Sarah Ann, who passed away in 1892, and Adelaide in 1917.

Many of the twins' descendants still live in the same community and attend the same church. All told, over one thousand people—among them a railroad president and an Air Force general—trace their descent from the original Siamese twins.

There have been some twins among them, but none were linked together like their two renowned ancestors.

2

More Than One...
Yet Not Two

"More than one ... yet not two." These strange words describe the fantastic human beings you're going to read about in this chapter. Among them are some of the greatest anatomical and physiological curiosities that have ever lived.

The names of some of these extraordinary people were well known to sideshow fans of a generation ago. You may have heard of them: Frank Lentini, "the Three-Legged Wonder"; Myrtle Corbin, "the Four-Legged Girl from Texas"; Betty Lou Williams, "the Girl with Four Legs and Three Arms," and others equally famous. Their drawing power was fabulous. Thirty or forty years ago they were earning up to a thousand dollars a week. And they were worth every penny of it to the circuses and sideshows that employed them, for they packed in the crowds of bug-eyed curiosity seekers show after show.

What were these Very Special People? What made them so Very Special?

These human oddities had a great deal in common

with Siamese twins. A booklet about one of them, Jean Libbera, who was sometimes billed as "the Man with Two Bodies," described him this way: "Not one child and not two children, but more than one, yet not two." Like Siamese twins, Jean Libbera and his counterparts developed from a single fertilized egg that failed to divide completely. For some unknown reason, however, the egg's growth was extremely erratic. Instead of splitting into two fairly equal and symmetrical bodies, as is the case with most conjoined twins, it formed two bodies that were . . . very different.

Siamese twins—with a difference. One body was normal in size and appearance. The other body was stunted. It was just a miniature, the size of a small child or a big doll. Or it was only part of a human being. *And it grew out of the body of the normal twin.*

The little twin might be almost complete. It might be a whole small body from the neck down. Or a whole small body from the waist down. It might be the upper part of a body, with a large, deformed head. The twin might be just one or two legs. It might be just a head—fused to the head of its completely normal twin. Sometimes a portion of the partial twin might be enclosed within the body of the larger twin. Doctors call the larger twin an "autosite," the smaller one a "parasite."

Most oddities of this kind, like most conjoined twins, are stillborn. Nature chooses this way to rectify her gravest mistakes. In addition, some that are born alive are perhaps not given the slap on the buttocks that traditionally starts an infant breathing. But others have a special strength. Against great odds, they fight for life and survive in a cold and hostile world.

This chapter is the story of a number of these extraordinary beings.

Colloredo: the Cavalier with Two Bodies

One of the most celebrated human oddities of the past was Lazarus-Joannes Baptista Colloredo. Born in 1617 in Geneva, Switzerland, Colloredo was exhibited all over Europe and studied by noted scientists. He had a little brother growing out of his breast. Both were baptized; the larger brother was named Lazarus, the smaller Joannes Baptista. (Since there were two heads, the church held that both could be baptized.)

The anatomist Bartholinus's description of the strange twins provides an interesting picture:

"The little brother had but one, and that the left leg and foot, which hung down; he had two arms, but no more than three fingers on each hand. If pressure was made against his breast, he moved his hands, ears and lips. He received no food or nourishment but through the medium of the body of his greater brother Lazarus.

"As he slept, sweated and stirred, when his greater brother was awake and not in motion and without perspiration, their vital and animal parts seem to be distinct from each other. . . . The head of the little brother was well formed and covered with hair but his eyes were closed, and his respiration but weak, for when I held a feather to his mouth and nostrils, they gave but little motion. His mouth was ever open and gaping, but I discovered no want of teeth, though no part of him seemed to increase in size [with the years] except his head, which was much larger than that of his greater brother Lazarus, deformed and with long dangling hair."

Both of the twins possessed beards. Lazarus took good care of his own, but the twin's was neglected. Joannes Baptista had genitals but they were not perfect.

Except for his twin, Lazarus was a completely normal person. He was described as a comely man, of average stature, with the manners and accomplishments of a courtier. He married and became the father of several children. Whenever he went out, he covered his little brother with his cloak.

"He was commonly in good spirits," Bartholinus wrote, "though now and then a little dejected when thinking of his future fate, and, as he presaged, the death of his brother."

Born with Two Heads

A memorable case of an individual with a "super-numerary" or extra head was reported in the Transactions of the Royal Philosophical Society for 1791. This was a Bengalese child born in 1783. The extra head grew on top of the normal one, crown to crown, and was turned sideways, facing to the right. Sir Everard Home reported on the child to the noted anatomist John Hunter.

"The body of the child was naturally formed," wrote Home, "but the head appeared double, there being besides the proper head another of the same size and to appearance almost equally perfect, attached to its upper part ...

"When the child was six months old, both of the heads were covered with black hair in nearly the same quantity ... The natural head had nothing uncommon in appearance, the eyes were attentive to objects, but the body was emaciated. The parents, who were poor, carried it about the streets in Calcutta as a curiosity to be seen for money ...

"When the child was roused, the eyes of both heads moved at the same time. Tears flowed from the eyes of the superior [upper] head but never from the eyes of the other. When it smiled, the features of the superior head sympathized in this action. It seemed to feel little or no pain when the superior head was pinched.

"When it was a little over the age of two years, the mother went out to fetch some water and upon her return found the child dead from the bite of a cobra. . . ."

An examination revealed that the upper head had a brain and nervous system of its own. The double skulls later passed into the possession of the Royal College of Surgeons in London.

Louise L.: "La Dame à Quatre Jambes"

A notable human oddity that lived to adulthood was Louise L., known as *"La dame à quatre jambes"* ("the lady with four legs"). Born in France in 1869, Louise had attached to her pelvis a second rudimentary pelvis from which grew two deformed or atrophied legs. Looking at her, it almost appeared as if the two legs were emerging from her sexual organs. Her vulva seemed to be virtually obliterated.

At the point where the two legs joined Louise's body there were two rudimentary breasts, one smaller than the other. The fragmentary twin had no primary sex organs. The limbs weighed about seventeen and one-half pounds and were not capable of movement. However, Louise could usually tell when they had been touched, and where.

In spite of this almost unbelievable handicap Louise not only married—she became the mother of two healthy, well-formed children!

Laloo and His Little "Sister"

Around the turn of the century a man named Laloo (see photo insert) was a familiar sight in American and European sideshows, including Barnum's. He was a dark, slender person, a Mohammedan, born in Oudh, India, in 1874. Attached to the lower part of his breastbone was a small twin. Laloo was the second of four children. All the others were normal. He married in 1894 in Philadelphia, and his wife traveled with him.

Laloo's twin lacked a head; its upper part grew directly out of his body. It had two arms and legs, but the forearms were defective. It showed no signs of a pulse, but the limbs were sensitive and when they were touched Laloo could tell where. The blood streams of the two were connected; if Laloo's temperature rose and he perspired, the twin reacted in the same way.

Laloo's miniature twin possessed a well-developed penis and pubic hair, but testicles were lacking. It was reported that erections of the penis occurred. The twin had a urinary system of its own and urine was discharged independently of Laloo's control.

Identical twins—whether normal, Siamese, or parasitic—are always of the same sex. This was of course the case with Laloo and his twin. However, the managers of the dime museums where he was employed pretended otherwise. To attract the gullible masses, they advertised that Laloo's twin was a sister, and they dressed the little body in female clothes.

Betty Lou Williams: "The Girl with Four Legs and Three Arms"

Betty Lou Williams was an extremely handsome and shapely black girl who enjoyed great popularity with circus audiences. Yet while they admired her beauty they couldn't fail to be moved to sympathy by her strange deformity. For growing out of Betty's left side was part of a little sister in miniature. Her twin consisted of a body from the waist downward, with two legs and a single misplaced arm.

It was a curious sight to see Betty, smiling prettily and looking as natural as could be in her two-piece bathing suit, with one hand on her hip—and the other holding up the weird little twin attached to her side.

Betty was so popular she was widely imitated by fraudulent sideshow operators. It wasn't uncommon for an attractive girl to appear before the public with a tiny deformed body of rubber strapped to her shapely torso. But Betty, like the other human oddities in this chapter, was real. Among other things, she had to pack away very substantial meals—since she was eating for two!

Betty reportedly died in 1955 of an asthma attack. She was one of the best liked and most generous of sideshow people. In her prime she earned close to a thousand dollars a week. With it she bought a large farm for her father and put her brothers and sisters through college.

Jean Libbera: "Jean and Jacques"

Like Betty Lou Williams, Jean Libbera was one of the highest paid of the Very Special People. Like her, he had a miniature twin growing out of his body. It was so well formed that he (or his manager) even gave it a name, "Jacques." Libbera was often billed as "Jean and Jacques" or "the Man with Two Bodies." He traveled with Barnum and Bailey and other shows.

Jean Libbera was born in Rome, Italy, in 1884, the fourth of thirteen children. By a strange coincidence the third child was formed the same as Jean, but it died immediately after birth.

The body of "Jacques"—what there was of it— was strikingly perfect. It had hips, thighs, arms, and legs, and was complete down to the nails on the fingers and toes. It drew its circulation from its big brother's body and it had a strong bone structure. The nervous systems were connected, too, and Jean could tell whenever "Jacques" was touched.

In Germany, a Professor Berdenheimer is said to have made a thorough study of Jean, using X rays. His report declared that imbedded in Jean's body was a structure resembling a rudimentary head.

Except for his strange twin, Jean was the same as other people. He was married and the father of four children, all completely normal.

When Jean went out at night, he often wore a white tie and tails. Like Colloredo, hundreds of years earlier, he also wore a cape, which covered the body of his twin. People looking at him seldom noticed the bulge it produced—and never imagined that the man in front of them was one of the most special of Very Special People.

Frank Lentini: "The Three-Legged Wonder"

People are occasionally born with extra toes or fingers. Frank Lentini was born with a whole extra leg projecting from his back.

Frank always insisted that the extra limb didn't bother him in the least. However, he couldn't walk on it because it was too high up. "But he could use it as a stool," said Harry Lewiston, who worked with him in the circus. "He was the only man I ever knew of who could sit down any time, any place, without bothering to drag up a chair. The leg was functional to such a degree, Frank could even kick a ball with it, which provided a good tag for his part of the show."

Frank Lentini was born Francesco Lentini in Rosolini, a town in Sicily, in 1889. He was one of twelve children, but the only one who came into the world with more than the regulation number of legs. The extra limb was actually part of another body—a partial twin. The leg was attached to Frank's skeleton by a rudimentary pelvis, and with it he also had a rudimentary set of genital organs. Of course the circuses with which he appeared couldn't forgo the opportunity to proclaim that he possessed "two complete sets of male organs."

Frank was never able to use his extra leg for walking. When he reached his sixth year the rest of his body started to outgrow the third leg, so that in time it was some inches shorter than his other legs. His own two legs were of different lengths—thirty-nine inches and thirty-eight inches, respectively. The extra leg was thirty-six inches long. A left leg, it was almost normal, except that it had a club foot and, growing from the knee, another small foot that you can discern in our photograph.

The Lentini family immigrated to the United States when Frank was a child. For years he traveled with Buffalo Bill's Wild West Show, Ringling Brothers and Barnum & Bailey, and many others. Pictures of him show us an attractive, friendly-looking man, normal in every respect but the extra limb.

Although the leg provided him with a good livelihood, Lentini said he would gladly have traded it for a chance to lead a quiet, inconspicuous life. But, reportedly, surgeons who examined him advised against an operation. The leg was connected to his spine, and amputation, they said, would be exceedingly dangerous. If it didn't result in death, it could cause complete paralysis.

To Lentini, as a youngster, the leg was a source of constant and excruciating embarrassment. Almost every day he noticed someone staring at him and heard the remark, "Isn't that a pity!" When he reached the age at which boys enjoy taking part in vigorous outdoor games, his handicap kept him on the sidelines. The realization of his peculiarity plunged him into a deep depression. He hated himself and he withdrew from people. His folks did everything they could to help him adjust to his situation—but they couldn't convince him that life was worth living.

One day the boy was taken to visit an institution for the handicapped. It was full of children with severe problems. He saw boys and girls who were doomed to spend their lives groping in darkness, or who were deaf, mute, gruesomely deformed, or crippled. All, he noticed, had come to grips with their handicaps. They weren't complaining about their fate; instead they were striving to make the best of things as they were. Whereas he, by contrast—he who could see, hear, speak, and walk—spent his days feeling sorry for himself.

"The visit to that institution," he said later, "unpleasant though it was because of the misery I saw there, was the best thing that could have happened to me. From that time to this I've never complained. I think life is beautiful and I enjoy living it."

So Frank Lentini learned to accept his leg. He learned to do things with it. "I can get about just as well and with the same ease as any normal person," he said. "I can walk, run, jump, ride a bicycle or a horse, ice-skate or roller-skate, and drive my own car. I can swim. I even have an advantage over the other fellow in swimming—I use the extra limb as a rudder!"

Sometimes he was asked how he bought a shoe for his extra foot. "Well, here's how. I buy two pairs and give the extra left shoe to a one-legged friend of mine who had the misfortune to lose his right leg. So, you see, every time I buy a pair of shoes I really do a good deed along with it."

Another question he was often asked was: Does the extra limb bother you in sleeping? It didn't. He was able to sleep comfortably on his back or on either side of his body.

The circus billed Lentini as "the Three-Legged

Wonder." At the peak of his career he weighed 175 pounds, and physicians estimated that the partial twin joined to his body accounted for about twenty-five pounds of his weight. Lentini said he ate about 15 percent more than the average man to provide the nourishment needed for the extra leg.

For years Lentini had a home in Wethersfield, Connecticut. He married and became the father of three sons and a daughter, all of them typical, healthy children. He died in 1966, a showman to the very end.

Myrtle Corbin: "The Four-Legged Woman from Texas"

Myrtle Corbin (see photo insert), who for many years was active with carnivals and circuses, including Ringling Brothers, went Frank Lentini one leg better. Myrtle was known as "the Four-Legged Woman from Texas." In a typical photograph we see her seated, her skirt raised to her knees. She has two normal-sized legs—but between them dangle two others the size of a small child's. On both her small pair of legs and her normal pair Myrtle wears matching shoes and socks.

Myrtle had part of a twin's body joined to the lower part of her own body. According to circus handouts, she was the possessor of two sets of sexual organs. She was married and became the mother of five children. The circus said that three were born from one body and two from the other. Myrtle was remarkably fertile for one who was so strangely formed.

other showman failed the sizes. When they began to ap-
in ...ne ...screep... ...
in th... ...
Sit... t...

3

Millie-Christine:
The Two-Headed Girl

"I contracted to bring her to Cleveland," Frank
M. Drew, an old-timer in the dime-museum business
reminisced many years afterward. "She was to have so
much a week and her hotel and traveling expenses. I
took her over to the old Kennard House and the
manager started an argument. He said as two mouths
had to be fed I would have to pay two board bills. That
opened the question, and when she left town the ticket
agent compelled me to pay two railroad fares. She was
an expensive proposition. . . .

"She had four arms and four legs. When it came
time for the instrumental music she could play a simple
thing with two hands or she could play an intricate
composition with four hands. Great girl she was." (See
photo insert.)

It was classic American frontier humor, right in
the Mark Twain tradition. But the public, avid for
wonders, was eager to believe that the black Siamese
twins were a single person.

"The Two-Headed Girl," Drew, Barnum, and

other showmen billed the sisters when they began to appear in dime museums and circuses in the second half of the nineteenth century. And the posters showed a single torso with two heads and two arms coming out of an elegant party frock; from the petticoat peeping out decorously below extended four legs. The pictures were far from accurate—although the sisters were joined together in a much more intimate way than their contemporaries, the original Siamese twins.

Chang and Eng were already well-known figures in show business when Millie and Christine came into the world. The girls were born in Columbus County, North Carolina, on July 11, 1851. Like their parents they were slaves, the property of a man named McCoy. The mother, a woman of thirty-two, named Monimia, had a large pelvis; the twins reportedly weighed seventeen pounds, but the birth was not a difficult one.

Joined at the Base of the Spine

The little girls were joined together at the base of the spine, so that the buttocks of one pressed against those of the other. They possessed a common anus and a common vulva. The bodies were not exactly parallel; one inclined slightly to the left, the other to the right. As sometimes happens with Siamese twins (although it did not with Chang and Eng), their hearts were on opposite sides of their bodies. Below the point of juncture they had a common nervous system. Otherwise they were complete, symmetrical, separate individuals, each with two arms and two legs. In photographs in which the twins are facing you, Millie is the girl on the left.

The Slaves Are Sold

Shortly after Millie and Christine were born, they and their parents were sold. Several more transfers took place, and the girls were separated from their family. Obviously their value as natural curiosities was recognized and it was high; in later years it was said that their final purchaser, J. P. Smith, paid thirty thousand dollars for them. They were still only infants. Smith, a warm-hearted man, also bought up the rest of the family and reunited them.

According to the girl's "official" story in a booklet sold in connection with their appearances, Smith was a "Southern gentleman from the country." However, he was interested in exhibiting the little tots and he took them on a tour of the Gulf States. He advertized them as "the North Carolina Twins" or "Double-Headed Girl."

In New Orleans the management of the twins was turned over to a professional showman, who was to receive a percentage of the receipts. The children's mother traveled along to take care of them.

Kidnapped

The exhibitor recognized that he was on to a good thing. He decided to make it even better. When business called Smith back to North Carolina, the showman decamped with the twins, leaving their mother behind.

For nearly two years the kidnapper dragged the girls around the country, showing them to small private audiences; they were stolen property and he didn't dare to exhibit them publicly. Then he sold them to another promoter, who took them to Philadelphia. There the two little black waifs, friendless and far from home, were exhibited at a museum run by Colonel Wood on Chestnut Street near Sixth.

A Valuable Property

Millie and Christine were a rare and a valuable property. A visitor to the museum, hearing they had been born in the South, decided to try to get control of them. Going to the authorities, he said the twins were slaves and had been brought to a free state, where they were unlawfully being deprived of their liberty. Before the law could take action, however, the girls were bundled aboard a ship headed across the Atlantic.

On Trial

Smith, the children's legal owner, by now had traced them. He followed them across the ocean, taking Monimia, their mother, along.

Unlike the United States, Great Britain didn't recognize the right of one person to own another—slavery had been abolished there in 1833—so Smith couldn't claim Millie and Christine as his property. But their mother could claim them as her children. Smith instituted a suit in her behalf.

The man who had brought the children to England had no intention of giving them up without a struggle. He hired a black woman to pose as their mother. Well rehearsed though her testimony was, it lacked the simple, truthful ring of Monimia's plea for her children. But Monimia's sobs said even more than her words. When the trial closed, the little girls, who had been denied the warmth of a mother's arms for half of their short lives, finally felt it again.

Never a Quarrel

Millie and Christine, only four years old, were one of the main attractions of the season when they were exhibited in 1855 as "the United African Twins" at the Egyptian Hall in London. Dr. H. F. Ramsbotham examined them.

"The children," the doctor noted, "stand not quite back to back, but rather sideways, so that they are able to place their arms around each other's neck, and give each other a kiss; but they cannot walk side by side. When lying, one reclines upon her back, and the other upon her side . . .

"They run about with amazing ease and activity," he went on. "Their dispositions are both very amiable, although one is milder than the other in temper, the little one having the most 'pluck,' and their intelligence is equal to, if it does not exceed, that of most European children of the same age.

"They play together with their toys; they seldom

have contrary wishes, and although there are at times little tiffs between them they have never been known to have a downright quarrel."

A Visit to the Queen

During the twins' stay in England the queen, Victoria, who often showed a special sympathy for Very Special People, asked that the sisters be brought to her. Wrapping her babies up against the fog, their mother took them to Osborne House, the queen's elegant mansion on the Isle of Wight.

Victoria and the rest of the royal family were fascinated by the clever prattle and the antics of the two strange little girls from the South. When they left, they carried with them priceless mementos of their visit.

Their "White Ma"

Back in the United States again, Smith continued to exhibit the girls. From their "white ma," as they called Mrs. Smith, they learned to read and write, as well as to sing and dance. The children were becoming full-fledged performers.

During the Civil War, Smith died. The war's end left his widow in straitened circumstances. Legally the girls were now free to go their own way. But they felt a deep loyalty to the Smith family. With Mrs. Smith as their guardian, they returned to the exhibition circuit.

The ex-slaves were a top drawing card now. They or their guardian collected as much as six hundred dollars a week. "We are *interested* pecuniarily in the 'show,' " they said, "and are daily receiving and putting away our share of the proceeds."

"The Two-Headed Nightingale"

The twins spent a good part of their lives on tour, appearing with circuses and museums, including Barnum's. They were attractive, intelligent dark-skinned girls with curly hair, and were on the short side. On the stage they danced and skipped rope; also, according to an old program, there was "experimenting with the girls by a committee selected from the audience." They had good voices (sometimes they were billed as "the Two-Headed Nightingale"). One was a soprano, the other a contralto, and they sang popular songs, accompanying themselves on guitars.

You can't hear the girls sing anymore—but you may be interested in the lyrics of one of their songs because it captures so well the spirit of their show and of their times:

> *It's not modest of one's self to speak,*
> *But daily scanned from head to feet*
> *I freely talk of everything*
> *Sometimes to persons wondering.*
>
> *Two heads, four arms, four feet,*
> *All in one perfect body meet;*
> *I am most wonderfully made,*
> *All scientific men have said.*
>
> *None like me, since days of Eve—*
> *None such perhaps will ever live;*
> *A marvel to myself am I,*
> *As well to all who passes by.*
>
> *I'm happy, quite, because I'm good;*
> *I love my Saviour and my God;*
> *I love all things that God has done,*
> *Whether I'm created two or one.*

At Barnum's Museum

We have an account of the twins written by a visitor who saw them at Barnum's museum in 1866, when they were fifteen years old. "They are in excellent health," he said. "Their combined weight is one hundred and fifty-nine and a half pounds. They are well formed; they resemble each other very much; their complexion is that of the fair mulatto; their features and expression are rather pleasing; they are very cheerful and intelligent; fond of reading; sing very sweetly, and converse modestly and fluently. They dance a schottische gracefully, and run with remarkable celerity. In running or walking they advance the inner limbs together, (being the right of one and the left of the other) and they bring forward the other limbs, which touch the floor simultaneously. They can walk quite readily with their outer limbs alone, by holding up the inner ones; in which case the right and left outer limbs are moved alternately, as in a single individual . . .

"The inner limbs are a little shorter than the outer ones," the visitor observed. "The result is that in standing the outer feet rest firmly on the floor, while the inner ones merely rest upon the front parts, .the heels being elevated. . . . Christina . . . is somewhat larger and stronger than Millie. Christina lifts Millie when she stoops, and walks or runs with her with great ease; no pain or strain is experienced at the seat of the junction. Millie, being weaker, cannot perform the same feat with her sister. .-. . They present every indication of attaining advanced life."

"Two Hearts That Beat As One"

Tours took the twins to Europe again in 1873 and 1885. Queen Victoria received them with great warmth. Then they returned to the United States. In the early 1900s Millie and Christine retired to Columbus County, where they had lived with their parents and their fourteen brothers and sisters. They moved into a ten-room house, which they filled with the treasures and souvenirs they had gathered during their many years in the theater. Countless visitors called on them. The twins had good hearts and they gained a wide reputation for their charitable acts. In 1909 their home burned down and they moved into a six-room cottage.

For a long time Millie had been ailing with tuberculosis. On October 9, 1912, she died. Christine knew at once what had happened. In seventeen hours she, too, was gone.

The sisters were buried in a churchyard not far away. Engraved on their tombstone were these words:

"A soul with two thoughts. Two hearts that beat as one."

4

The Tocci Brothers:
The Two-Headed Boy

Almost every American city of ten thousand or more had its own dime museum around the turn of the century. In 1891 the sensation they featured was the twins were from Italy, and people queued up across the country to get a look at them. "The Two-Headed Boy!" screamed the posters. "The Blended Twins!" "More wonderful than the Siamese Brothers—more interesting than the Millie-Christine Sisters!"

It was no exaggeration. In many ways the Tocci Tocci twins from Italy, and people queued up across other Siamese twins. The simple fact that they were alive was extraordinary.

The Toccis were virtually a single body with two heads. Each twin possessed his own had and arms and part of a chest—but below the sixth rib they formed a single body. They shared a single abdomen, a single set of sexual organs, and two legs. They had individual backbones, which united in the lower back, and three buttocks.

The twins were born in Turin, Italy, on July 4,

1875. One was baptized Giovanni Battista, the other Giacomo. Their mother, Antonia Tocci, was a strong, healthy woman of nineteen who went on to bear nine normal children.

Signor Tocci, a workingman of thirty-two, felt heartsick when he saw the strange heirs his signora had presented him with. His feelings soared skyward, however, when he discovered the babies were worth their weight in million-lira notes. The twins were only a month old when they were bundled off to the Royal Academy of Medicine in Turin to be weighed (they weighed eight pounds together), measured, studied, and exhibited. It was only the first stop in a sideshow career that would take the twins to the major cities of Europe. Everywhere they created a sensation.

Unable to Walk

Each of the boys had control of only the leg on his side. The result was that they could not coordinate the movements of their legs and were unable to walk. In addition, Giacomo's foot was abnormal in shape, so he couldn't rest it flat on the ground. Both legs were weak, and the boys needed support when standing.

Each twin had control of his own two arms and could move them freely. However, because their torsos merged below the shoulder their inner arms were very crowded. The boys were often pictured in a pose with the inner arms held straight up, one against the other, the hands grasping a little nosegay overhead. They readily learned how to write and draw, one using his left hand, the other his right.

Independent of Each Other's Moods

Giovanni Battista and Giacomo, despite their extraordinary handicap, were lively, alert, and eager to please. There was nothing unpleasant about their appearance. They were fair-skinned, with brown hair, and their natures were gentle. When they were small, observers were struck by their remarkable independence of each other's moods or actions. Giacomo might be wide awake and playing with a toy while Giovanni Battista was sound asleep. Giovanni Battista might be crying his heart out over some little frustration while Giacomo was gurgling and in the best of humors. Both were fond of music. In the course of their travels the youngsters learned to speak some French and German and were happy to chat with strangers.

In 1891 the twins, then sixteen, were brought to the United States on tour. They were promoted as "the Greatest Human Phenomenon Ever Seen Alive." The conservative *Scientific American* came close to agreeing. They were, it commented, "probably the most remarkable human twins that have ever approached maturity." Reportedly the Toccis earned a thousand dollars a week during their American tour.

The Twins Downhearted

Money, of course, isn't everything. Charles E. Davis, an old-time sideshow buff, saw the twins in Allyn Hall, a dime museum in Hartford, Connecticut, and talked to them through an interpreter, They spoke to him without reserve, telling him that they minded their condition very much and that they frequently felt discouraged and downhearted. He described them as "pathetic." He noted that the boys were able to sit down or stand up by themselves but were unable to "walk a step." After they returned to Italy they took up residence in a villa in Venice, and refused to exhibit themselves again.

It is good to be able to change from this somber note to a much more cheerful one. The Tocci twins, it turns out, were the inspiration of one of the classics of American literature, Mark Twain's *Pudd'nhead Wilson*.

Mark Twain and the Two-Headed Boy

Twain published *Pudd'nhead Wilson* serially in 1893–94. He developed the novel from a story he had been working on which he called "Those Extraordinary

Twins." "I had seen a picture," he wrote in his preface to that work, "of a youthful Italian 'freak'—or 'freaks'—which was—or which were—on exhibition in our cities—a combination consisting of two heads and four arms joined to a single body and a single pair of legs—and I thought I would write an extravagantly fantastic little story with this freak of nature for hero—or heroes . . ." Included in the text of "Those Wonderful Twins" in an old authorized uniform edition of Twain's collected works is a "made-up" picture which shows the humorist studying some posters. One of them portrays a human oddity with two heads and bears the words "Wonderful Twins."

The Teetotaler and the Drunkard

Twain made the twins in his story Italian and named them Angelo and Luigi. He put them through a series of bizarre adventures in which he exploited the contrasts of character in the two young men joined in one body. As he'd done in his humorous sketch "The Siamese Twins," discussed in our chapter on Chang and Eng, he made one twin into a teetotaler and the other a drunkard. One of the climaxes of the story hinged on the fact that the twins had kicked a man and were brought to trial for assault—but no one could say which twin had actually done the kicking. A lawyer named Pudd'nhead Wilson defended the twins, who were eventually exonerated on the grounds that the guilty party could not be punished without also punishing his innocent brother.

An Arrangement for Walking

Twain may well have heard of the difficulty the Tocci brothers had in walking. He solved the problem for his fictional twins by giving them a marvelous power. For one week one of the twins had complete control of the two legs. The following week the other twin took over. And so they alternated from week to week. This arrangement was not a matter of choice or will but had been ordained by God.

It's interesting to read Twain's explanation of the logic of this arrangement. In the story, Angelo and Aunt Betsy are talking. Angelo says: " 'And it stands to reason that the arrangement couldn't be improved. I'll prove it to you. If our legs tried to obey two wills, how could we ever get anywhere? I would start one way, Luigi would start another, at the same moment—the result would be a standstill, wouldn't it? . . .

" 'We should always be arguing and fussing and disputing over the merest trifles. We should lose worlds of time, for we couldn't go downstairs or up, couldn't go to bed, couldn't rise, couldn't wash, couldn't dress, couldn't stand up, couldn't sit down, couldn't even cross our legs, without calling a meeting first and explaining the case and passing resolutions, and getting consent. It wouldn't ever do—now would it?' "

How It Feels to Be a Siamese Twin

The brothers, in Twain's story, are very different individuals, just as the real Tocci twins were. With his artist's imagination, Twain could sense what it must feel like to be a Siamese twin, and to wish for freedom. One of the passages he wrote on this subject is especially eloquent:

"At times, in his seasons of deepest depressions, Angelo almost wished that he and his brother might become segregated from each other and be separate individuals, like other men. But of course as soon as his mind cleared and these diseased imaginings passed away, he shuddered at the repulsive thought, and earnestly prayed that it might visit him no more. To be separate, and as other men are! How awkward it would seem; how unendurable. What would he do with his hands, his arms? How would his legs feel? How odd, and strange, and grotesque every action, attitude, movement, gesture would be. To sleep by himself, eat by himself, walk by himself—how lonely, how unspeakably lonely! No, no, any fate but that. In every way and from every point, the idea was revolting.

"This was of course natural; to have felt otherwise would have been unnatural. He had known no life but a combined one; he had been familiar with it from his birth; he was not able to conceive of any other as being agreeable, or even bearable. To him, in the privacy of his secret thoughts, all other men were monsters, deformities: and during three-fourths of his life their aspect had filled him with what promised to be an unconquerable aversion. But at eighteen his eye began to take note of female beauty; and little by little, undefined longings grew up in his heart . . ."

"I Took Those Twins Apart"

As Twain continued to write, his original idea changed from a farce to a tragedy. He developed two separate stories which were all tangled up, and he carried the manuscript back and forth across the Atlantic several times before he could decide what to do with it. Finally he pulled out the farce about the Siamese twins and left the tragedy. "Also I took those twins apart," Twain wrote, "and made two separate men of them." So the Tocci twins are still remembered in the characters of Luigi and Angelo in *Pudd'nhead Wilson* but now they are run-of-the-mill identical twins. In "Those Extraordinary Twins," the farce which Twain extracted from the novel, we can still see his original comic intent.

The Tocci twins dropped out of sight long ago. They did not do so however, without making a splash. It was reported in the French press that—although they possessed only a single set of genitals—they had gotten married to two separate women! French wags, both medical and literary (including the celebrated author Pierre Louÿs) had a field day speculating on the implications of this union. The great teratologist Marcel Baudouin theorized that each of the twins was the owner of one of their testicles. The biologist Maurice Gille wondered who would be the father if one of the wives bore a child, and how the inheritance would be divided if there were several children. But what actually became of the twins and how they fared in their marriages remains dark. And so, reader, if you possess knowledge of their later lives (they were still alive in 1912, reportedly), please inform the author, so he can write the conclusion of the strange story of Giovanni Battista and Giacomo Tocci.

5

Violet and Daisy Hilton: Sold into Slavery

Two of the most successful—and beautiful—Siamese twins of modern times were Violet and Daisy Hilton. (See photo insert). They were what doctors call "pygopagi"—a pair of twins joined at the buttocks. The bones of their lower spines and hips were fused to each other and the twins shared the same blood circulation.

"We found out when we were little," said Daisy, the blond sister, "that if one of us wanted to go one way, and another pulled in another direction, nobody got anywhere. I think there are lots of other people who ought to learn that lesson."

Another extraordinary lesson that the girls learned was that each could dissociate herself from the experiences and feelings of her sister—even when that sister was making love.

Violet, the brunette sister, was married to Jimmy Moore, a dancer, in the Texas Cotton Bowl in 1936. Afterward she faced a barrage of questions from reporters, who wanted to know what it was like to have her sister along on her honeymoon.

"It's merely a matter of psychology," Violet answered. "When the proper time comes for it, Daisy and I just get rid of each other—mentally."

Both of the sisters had many romances, and plenty of occasion for blanking each other out mentally. Violet once reminisced about Daisy's love affairs. "Sometimes I quit paying attention," she said, "and didn't know what was going on. Sometimes I read and sometimes I just took a nap. Even before that, we had learned how not to know what the other was doing unless it was our business to know it."

Not many normal people are so successful in shutting out of their thoughts a person with whom they are obliged to spend a great deal of time. Daisy was married once to Buddy Sawyer, a nightclub master of ceremonies. After ten days the new husband moved out permanently.

"Daisy is a lovely girl," Sawyer said, "but I guess I just am not the type of fellow that should marry a Siamese twin. . . . As far as being a bridegroom under such conditions is concerned, I suppose I am what you might call a hermit."

Treated Like Slaves

The Hilton sisters, for years, were among the highest paid of nightclub and vaudeville performers. They were in show business almost before they were out of diapers. Yet for the first twenty-three years of their lives they received hardly a penny of their earnings. They were kept under a control as taut as slaves were and treated like chattels.

The Hilton girls were born in Brighton, the famous English seaside resort, on February 5, 1908. Their name, originally, wasn't Hilton. Their mother, Kate Skinner, was a barmaid, and she bore the babies out of wedlock. An unmarried woman didn't have need of a baby—much less two, and Siamese twins at that. The sisters were two weeks old when their mother sold them to Mrs. Mary Hilton, a midwife. As soon as the girls could talk, she taught them to call her "Auntie." They were trained to address her husband as "Sir."

Troupers at Three

Auntie had only one interest in little Violet and Daisy—making money out of them. She taught them, or had them taught, how to recite, read, and sing when they were very young. At three years of age they were already traveling with the Hiltons and their daughter, Edith, and performing at circuses, carnivals, exhibitions, fairs, bars. At four they were taken on a tour of Germany. At five they were traveling through Australia. When they were eight they were brought to the United States. Life, for the motherless twins, was a succession of dingy rooms in boarding houses or crowded little cabins on shipboard.

Violet was taught to play the piano, Daisy the violin. Auntie was determined to make them profitable prodigies. One day she saw the little girls stand on a chair, make it rock till it turned over, and then do a flip in the air and land on their feet. She added dancing to their endless music lessons.

A young man taught the twins how to do "The Black Bottom." His name was Bob Hope. Others whom they found friendly early in their theatrical careers were Harry Houdini and Sophie Tucker. But the Hiltons kept them isolated from outsiders. They didn't want them to have friends, and rarely allowed the girls out of their sight. Violet and Daisy learned to bow to Auntie's wishes unquestioningly. If they didn't, they later told Ethelda Bedford, a reporter, they knew Auntie's murderous belt buckle would come swishing through the air at them. . . .

Threatened and Terrified

Not long after Auntie lost her fifth husband, her daughter, Edith, gained her first. This was a young man she had met when the twins were playing in a circus in Australia, where he sold candy and balloons. So again there was another "Sir" to threaten and terrify the children.

The girls were looking forward to the day when they would be eighteen years of age. Then they believed they would have the right to seek out legal aid and gain their freedom from their guardians. Auntie, who was getting rich from their efforts, made very sure that they had no money of their own. Well, almost no money. In one way or another, Daisy had managed to accumulate a half dollar and Violet a quarter. These coins they kept carefully hidden away. They were the twins' "freedom fund."

The Death of Auntie

In Birmingham, Alabama, Auntie, then over sixty, passed away. The girls were taken to the funeral parlor to pay their last respects. In their pockets they clutched their coins. They had only one idea in mind—to run away. For, although they had always feared the dead woman, they feared her son-in-law even more.

Violet and Daisy looked at the waxlike face in the coffin. Auntie had never loved them. She had exploited them for her own profit—and the future promised to hold only more of the same. One sister nudged the other. "Let's run!" she said.

But the girls had hardly taken a step when they felt Sir's heavy hands on them. Their chance at freedom, if it ever existed, had slipped away. . . .

That evening Sir told the twins that he and Edith were their new guardians. Auntie had willed the girls to her daughter and her son-in-law, along with her other earthly possessions. They had no hope of escape. Edith and her husband slept in the same room with them and never allowed them a moment of privacy.

Breaking into the Big Time

Life was a constant push to break into the big vaudeville circuits and the big money, with Edith and her husband driving the sisters constantly. In 1924 the girls, moving with the times, were playing the saxophone, like their idol, Rudy Vallee. "We are our own jazz band," the fifteen-year-olds told an interviewer. "For quite some time we have been studying music via the saxophone and we have now reached the point where we can make the big horns moan and whine and laugh and cry and gurgle. It's lots of fun making them do stunts, and especially when there are two of us so that one can supply what the other misses."

By the time the girls reached their seventeenth birthday they were headliners in vaudeville, playing the Loew and Orpheum circuits and earning thousands a week. They had also begun to look into their mirrors and see more than children's faces gazing back at them. Men, they found, were interested in them in spite of their handicap. While waiting to go on stage there were warm glances, handclasps, whisperings. But always their guardians were right behind them, herding them from the theater back to their hotel room. They were forced to go without makeup, to dress alike, and do their hair like young girls.

Harry Houdini's Secret

In moments of depression—and such moments came frequently to the girls, who were only too aware how different they were from everyone else—they would remember the advice that Harry Houdini had given them in brief chats they had had together.

Houdini, born Erich Weiss, was the master escape artist of all time. He had learned how to liberate himself from anything—handcuffs, straitjackets, or sealed chests under water—and made a handsome living doing so. Houdini had known hard times and suffering, and he took a special interest in the pretty, hard-working, but often sad-faced twins.

"Girls," Houdini had said to them, "character and concentration will accomplish anything for you. You must learn to forget your physical link. Put it out of your mind. Work at developing mental independence of each other. Through concentration you can get anything you want!"

Taking Houdini's advice to heart, each girl taught herself to concentrate and blank the other out. Each learned to live in a world entirely her own—although she was linked as tightly as ever to her sister.

One of the twins' few other friends—at least they thought he was a friend—was William Oliver, who worked as advance man for their act, traveling ahead and arranging publicity. Once he asked them to autograph a picture for him so he could give it to his wife. They were pleased. "To our pal, Bill, with love and best wishes from your pals, Daisy and Violet Hilton," they wrote, and thought no more about it.

The Twins Strike

When Violet and Daisy were playing in Newark, New Jersey, a critic complained in his review that they were still dressed like children, their heads loaded with demure curls. They showed the review to Edith. That day they were finally allowed to pay their first visit to a beauty parlor and have their hair cut. They began to stand up increasingly for their rights. They insisted that they needed to have a room of their own. They told Edith and her husband that they had made many thousands of dollars for them and they would like to have bracelets. Almost meekly, their guardians gave in.

Sued for $250,000

The girls were twenty-three years old when a bombshell struck. Newspaper headlines shrieked the news that Violet and Daisy Hilton were being sued for a quarter of a million dollars by their advance man's wife, Mrs. William Oliver, who named them as correspondents in a divorce suit. The twins were too stunned to comprehend. They had never even been alone with her husband. All they had ever done was give him a photograph with an innocent message. A message that did mention love, however. . . .

The twins needed legal advice, and Edith's husband drove them to the office of his lawyer, Martin J.

Arnold. The case astonished the attorney as much as it
had the girls. They assured him that they had only had
business dealings with Oliver. But the attorney sensed a
special restraint in their manner with their guardian
present. He asked to be left alone with them. Their
guardian refused to leave the room at first, but finally
he walked out.

No sooner were the girls alone with Arnold than
they told him, "We're almost slaves. Please help us to
get free! You must help us!"

For an hour Violet and Daisy poured out their
hearts to the attorney. Their hour of freedom had
struck. He accepted them as his personal clients. He assured them that the divorce suit was a fraud—and he
also intended to enforce their rights against their so-
called guardians. The girls, after all, were no longer mi-
nors. . . .

Escape

After their interview, Edith's husband took Violet
and Daisy for their usual music lesson. But from there,
by arrangement with their attorney, they went directly
to the San Antonio Hotel, where a room was engaged
for them.

At the hotel, for the first time in their lives the two
sisters discovered the meaning of freedom. As guests of
their lawyer, they enjoyed the rich thrill of doing anything they wanted to. They had flowers and candy.
They ordered different dresses—avoiding the matching
ensembles they had been forced to wear. They went to
beauty parlors. They telephoned some of the men with
whom, until that day, they had been able to do little
more than exchange glances. They saw anyone they
wished.

A Sensational Trial

Finally the girls' suit against their "guardians"
came to trial. "Siamese Twins Unfold Tale of Bond-
age," the headlines said. "Earned Thousands and Never

Collected a Dollar." Through their attorney the girls demanded an accounting of the money they had earned over the years. They also requested an injunction forbidding their "guardians" from interfering in their lives anymore.

The trial was one of the most sensational of its day. At its conclusion, all contracts between the twins and Edith and her husband were dissolved, and the girls were awarded one hundred thousand dollars. At last the road lay open before them. They could lead their own lives.

Hollywood

In 1932, shortly after they'd won their freedom, Violet and Daisy went to Hollywood to act in the film *Freaks*. They lived in their own apartment and traveled to the studio in their own big black sedan.

"We don't mind having people stare at us," Daisy said. "We're used to it. We've never known anything else. We're happier now than we've been for a long time because we're entirely on our own. We can do as we please, go where we please and think what we please. It's so good to be free!"

Romances of the Siamese Twins

It was hard for the girls to realize they could go out with anyone they wanted to. In the theater Daisy had been exchanging glances—for years, it seemed to her—with Don Galvan, a guitar player. Now at last they could be alone together.

But, of course, they could never be completely alone. This story of the couple's first kiss comes to us not from Daisy but from Violet.

"When Don came to see my sister," Violet said, "he just stood there gazing at her. A big thrill ran through both of us. At that time I had not yet learned how to will myself to be immune to my sister's emotions. Later on each of us acquired the ability to blank out the other in romantic moments.

"This was our first real-life romance, and it intoxicated both of us. I was as anxious for Daisy to experience her first kiss as she was herself. Then Don held out his arms to her. She moved closer—and he kissed her on the forehead!

"Our first kiss was a little disappointing to both of us. Don was of the old world and he didn't believe a man should kiss his lady-love except on the forehead, until they were engaged."

Don's engagement to Daisy didn't last. He wanted her to leave the theater and go to live with him and his family in Mexico. But Daisy felt it would be unfair to Violet to make her leave show business and the only world she knew.

Daisy broke off another engagement because she suddenly realized that her young man talked to her only on the telephone most of the time. She decided that any man who needed to hide behind a telephone was hardly cut out to be the husband of a Siamese twin.

Violet became engaged to Maurice Lambert, her orchestra leader. But when he sought to obtain a marriage license, he was turned down. One after another, twenty-one states told him the marriage would be contrary to morals and public policy. In the end his love died of frustration.

Eventually Violet married James Moore in Texas, one of the states Lambert hadn't tried. That marriage, performed in 1936, at the Texas Centennial Exposition, was one in name only, she said later. It was undertaken for the sake of publicity, and it paid off. After some years it was annulled. In 1941 Daisy married Harold Estep, whose stage name was Buddy Sawyer, but that marriage, as we saw earlier, was over almost before it began.

Hard Times

Violet and Daisy, at the peak of their careers, were said to be earning five thousand dollars a week. They were starred in a film called *Chained for Life*. At one time they lived in Pittsburgh and owned a hotel there.

Then the girls must have fallen on hard times. In 1960 they were said to be operating a fruit stand in Florida.

Some years later the sisters were in Charlotte, North Carolina. They worked at two weighing counters in a suburban supermarket.

One morning in early January, 1969, the twins failed to report to work. They were missing the next day and the next. The police were called. They drove to the sisters' apartment.

When the officers gained entry, they found Violet and Daisy inside. They were lying on the floor, joined in death as they had been in life. They had died, it was said, of complications of the Hong Kong flu. They left no known survivors.

6

The Biddenden Maids, Radica-Doodica, and other Remarkable Siamese Twins

We have been seeing and hearing less and less about Siamese twins, ever since it became possible to separate most of them and unfashionable to exhibit them. The physical connection between the great majority—over 90 percent of them—is fairly superficial. It consists of cartilage or tissue that joins them at the base of the spine, the thighs, the head, chest, legs, or arms. Operations on these twins are usually successful. However, separating those who share body organs, an abdominal tract, or blood vessels poses a much more serious problem. Some years ago Dr. Frederick J. Bailey, then deputy health commissioner of Boston, estimated that one set of conjoined twins occurs in the United States in every 250,000 births. Most are stillborn.

The past was prolific in Siamese twins. Greek medical writers mentioned them hundreds of years before the birth of Christ. Cicero told of the birth of a girl with two heads in ancient Rome. The names of quite a number of these twins have gone down in history. The

Biddenden maids were celebrated in older times. In the nineteenth and twentieth centuries, as we've seen, Siamese twins achieved great popularity on the stage. Among the most remarkable were two exquisite little girls from India known as Radica-Doodica, the exotic (and erotic) Rosa-Josepha Blazek, and the Godino brothers.

The Biddenden Maids

In England, the earliest Siamese twins who lived to adulthood were two sisters said to have been born in 1100. Known as the Biddenden maids (they lived in Biddenden, Kent), the girls were named Eliza and Mary Chulkhurst and were the children of well-off parents.

Old pictures show the two young women joined together at the hip and shoulder. They have four legs but only two normal arms; the inner arms appear to grow into each other. It's been suggested that the pictures are misleading and the girls actually did have two inner arms; however, because each placed her arm over her sister's shoulder, much as Chang and Eng did, the arms appear fused in these crude representations.

In 1134 one of the girls died. The doctors, according to tradition, proposed to separate them at once by surgery. The survivor refused. "As we came together, we will also go together," she is reported to have declared. In six hours she joined her sister in death.

Now comes the most memorable part of the Biddenden story. In their will the maids are said to have bequeathed twenty acres to their parish, providing that the rental be used to make cakes with their images imprinted on them, which were to be distributed each Easter Sunday to strangers in the town. The rental was also to provide loaves of bread and cheese to be given to the poor. In 1875 a writer reported that the cakes, two by four inches, were made of simple flour and water. The images of the maids were primitive in character and made with a boxwood die cut in 1814. The impression bore the date 1100, the names of the girls, and their age when they died.

The distribution of the maids' charity, according to this writer, "used to take place in the Church, immediately after the service in the afternoon, but in consequence of the unseemly disturbance which used to ensue the practice was discontinued. The Church used to be filled with a congregation whose conduct was occasionally so reprehensible that sometimes the church wardens had to use their wands for other purposes than symbols of office."

However, the good work started by the maids did not stop. The author of this book has been in touch with the church at Biddenden. "Yes," says the Reverend Dr. C. J. Wayte in a recent letter, "the Chulkhurst charity is still going strong. It was merged several years ago to form the Consolidated Charity and is administered by Trustees. The dole you mention is distributed on Easter Monday from the old Parish Poor House.

"But, more importantly, help is given throughout the year to the elderly or those in need, and a grant was given toward the Village Hall building fund. . . Regarding the girls themselves I could not add anything to the published conjectures about their life."

Radica-Doodica

These beautiful little girls (see photo insert) were four or five years old when they were exhibited in Europe in the early 1890s. Dressed in exotic finery of their native land, with their dark eyes flashing, they appealed to everyone, and especially to every parent, who saw them. They seemed to be perfectly formed—except that they were joined front to front by a four-inch band of cartilaginous tissue, much as Chang and Eng were.

The girls were born in Orissa, India, in 1888. No sooner were they born than their lives were in danger. Their fellow villagers believed they were the incarnation of evil spirits, and the entire family was thrown into jail. However, the people came to their senses before anything serious happened. In 1892 the children appeared in France under the management of Captain Colman, a well-known showman.

Both Radica and Doodica were of normal intelligence. Sleeping required a special arrangement: one of the girls would lie on her back, the other on her side. When one child ate, the food appeared to satisfy the hunger of the other as well; if one was given medicine, her sister would also show its effects. Although the twins were well developed and in good physical health, during their first year in Europe they took sick and had to spend a considerable time in a Paris hospital. After they recovered, they were exhibited in England.

Later Doodica fell ill. Her condition was diagnosed as tuberculosis. An operation was performed and the twins were separated. Doodica died soon afterward. Radica survived her sister for two years, then also succumbed to tuberculosis.

Rosa-Josepha Blazek: the Bohemian Twins

"It strikes me as pretty sad," wrote Signor Saltarino, a circus authority at the turn of the century, "that when the two girls have a little tiff, more in fun than in earnest, one cries out threateningly to the other, "If you don't give me that, I'll have myself cut apart from you!"

No matter how much they might have wanted to, the Blazek girls (See photo insert) couldn't have been cut apart. When the twins were born, on January 20, 1878, and for many years afterward, medical knowledge had not developed far enough to permit such an operation. The girls, united at the pelvis and spine, shared the same anus and urethra. However, they did have separate rectums and vaginas. They were born at Skreychova, in Bohemia, Czechoslovakia. Their mother, twenty-two years old, had already given birth to a normal daughter. The twins were vigorous, healthy children. They quickly learned to coordinate their movements and went up and down steps without difficulty.

In 1891 the girls were exhibited in Paris and London. Josepha was the quieter of the two and was slower in her movements. Rosa was an easier talker and was stronger and more active than her sister. When the two walked, she was usually the leader. As we have seen in other Siamese twins, one could sleep while the other was awake.

Although the same blood coursed through the sisters' veins, one might feel perfectly healthy while the other was ill. However, if one took a medication, both twins showed a reaction to it.

In the 1890s, according to Saltarino, the twins were already thinking of marriage. It provoked him to some quaint thoughts that have the pronounced antifeminist flavor of the age of Victoria. He saw the girls as both marrying the same man. "We will not be able to blame the bridegroom," he said, "if he exhibits both of his wives for money. For he will have to provide double wardrobes; satisfy double appetites; fulfill double costly whims ... The future groom will have only one advantage over other men: he will have two wives—and only a single mother-in-law."

In April, 1910, when the girls were thirty-two years old, Rosa gave birth to a son in Prague and both sisters were able to nurse the child. It was said that the baby's father wanted to marry Rosa, but her parents would not consent. It was also reported that a court refused permission for the marriage to take place, holding that the man would actually be marrying two women rather than one.

Many stories were told about the Blazek sisters and their supposed romance, but it is difficult to sift the truth from the myths. The girls toured the United States in 1922. In Chicago they came down with a severe respiratory infection and they were admitted to the West End Hospital. Rosa's son, young Franz, was a constant visitor. The sisters died on March 30, 1922, leaving a fortune estimated at $200,000.

Macha and Dacha: the Russian Twins

Two girls similar to the Blazek sisters were Macha and Dacha, Russian twins, reported to be eleven years old in 1961. According to Robert Tocquet, in his book *Les Hommes-phénomènes,* the girls had two legs, plus a third one that was deformed and had a double foot. Each had control of the leg on her side, and either one could move the atrophied leg in the middle. They were at the Moscow clinic of Professor Anokine, a teratologist or specialist in human oddities, who hoped to make biologists of them.

The Godino Brothers

The Godino brothers, Simplicio and Lucio, were born in the Philippine Islands in 1908. They were joined at the base of the spine by a muscular ligament like the one that linked Chang and Eng. The boys were soon in show business, exhibiting in the United States. They were appearing at Coney Island at the age of eleven when the Society for the Prevention of Cruelty to Children objected that they were without proper guardianship. The youngsters had the good fortune to be adopted by Teodor Yaco, commissioner of the Philippines to the United States, and they received an excellent education in this country and their native land. Encouraged to develop their ability in sports, they became proficient in tennis, golf, and swimming.

When the boys were in their early twenties, they married two attractive Filipino sisters. After their honeymoon they told reporters they'd had an enjoyable trip and they found their physical juncture no problem, since all four young people liked each other.

The brothers and their wives went into vaudeville and became headliners. Then, in November, 1936, at the age of twenty-eight, Lucio came down with pneumonia. Simplicio, of course, had to lie next to his seriously ill brother, although he didn't show a symptom.

One night the healthy brother awoke with a deep feeling of unease. "I was drowsing," he told newsmen, "not expecting anything, when all at once a feeling came over me that I can't describe. It was just a—a sensation. . . . I leaned over to speak to Lucio about it. As I did so, I touched his body. It was cold. I rang the bell. When the nurse came I told her my brother was dead."

It became urgent to perform an operation to separate the living twin from the dead one. Plastic surgery was performed so Simplicio could function on his own. The operation was declared a success. Things looked bright for the survivor, but he suddenly began to lose ground and the doctors discovered he had cerebrospinal meningitis. In eleven days he was dead.

Doctors felt Simplicio should have survived. They found a psychological explanation for his contracting the meningitis and succumbing to it. They pointed out that it was Lucio who had always led the way; Simplicio was the follower. Unconsciously, they said, Simplicio had given up the fight to stay alive. He had always been backing into life and could not stand the idea of turning around and facing it alone.

PART 2

ARMLESS AND LEGLESS WONDERS

7

Carl Unthan:
The Armless Fiddler

"Bravo!" "Bravo!" "Bravissimo!" A storm of applause and enthusiastic outcries rocked the Dianasaal, the concert hall in old Vienna. The conductor, Johann Strauss, bowed until his back ached.

But not all the applause was for the famous maestro. A new performer, Carl Unthan (see photo insert), had just made his debut with the orchestra. He was only twenty, but he played the violin, many in the audience said, *"wie ein Engel"*—like an angel. With his soft eyes and gentle, spiritual face he looked like an angel, too. The spectators had not been able to take their eyes off him all evening.

Had it really happened? Had that beautiful young man actually drawn such exquisite music out of his violin—*with his toes?*

It couldn't be true. Yet the audience knew it was. They had watched the young man seat himself and slip his feet out of his shoes. His jacket was draped over his shoulders, so they hadn't realized at once that he had no arms. His violin was tied to a stool in front of him.

He had raised his feet. The spectators saw that the lower part of his socks was cut off, and his toes exposed. He placed the toes of his right foot on the strings on the upper part of the instrument. With the toes of his left foot he grasped the bow, gave it a musicianly flourish, and drew it across the strings.

Others who lacked arms and performed feats of dexterity or strength in circuses or vaudeville were billed as "armless wonders." Unthan, because of his unique ability with the violin, was to gain fame as "the Armless Fiddler." One of the greatest showmen of his time, he was to win the applause of millions of music lovers and theatergoers on three continents.

For the armless prodigy, that day in Vienna was the happiest he had ever known. It was certainly far, far happier than another one twenty years earlier—the first day of his life.

"Let Me Hold a Pillow over His Face!"

Carl Unthan was born on April 5, 1848, in Sommerfeld, East Prussia. Holding up the red-faced, crying infant she had just ushered into the world, the midwife screamed in horror. Never in the many years she had practiced her profession had she seen such a disheartening sight. For instead of arms the tiny creature was waving short little stumps.

The midwife put down the child. "Herr Unthan!" she called. *"Kommen Sie mal her!"* She gestured frantically toward the squirming little figure. "It's hopeless." Her voice dropped to a whisper. "Let me hold a pillow over his face. God will forgive me. . . ."

"That would be murder." Herr Unthan picked up his baby boy gently and carried him to his wife. She was barely conscious. *"Sieh, Liebchen. . . .* He has no arms."

She saw, and wept.

Herr Unthan shook his head vigorously. *"Nein, nein!* We are not murderers. This is our child. God gave him to us and He will not abandon him."

Why Children Are Born Without Limbs

Little Carl, like the other Very Special People whose stories are told in this section, was the victim of a birth defect. What factors cause a child in the womb to develop without arms or legs, or both, medical science cannot always say. Often the condition is due to an abnormality of the chromosomes—the minute units that transmit the human heritage from parents to children. Or it can be the result of an infection of the mother, especially during the early weeks of pregnancy. German measles can wreak havoc on the developing embryo.

Birth defects can also be caused by a drug the mother has taken. In our own day, thalidomide—a drug intended to help expectant mothers sleep soundly—was given to the world before it had been tested adequately. The result was a nightmare. In Great Britain and Germany alone, over three thousand children were born deformed, many of them without limbs.

Three Rules to Grow By

Carl grew rapidly into a healthy, vigorous little boy. Relatives and neighbors were often moved to tears when they saw the armless child. They fondled him and clucked over him with sympathy.

Herr Unthan became aware of what was happening. His face grew dark.

"If people show the boy they feel sorry for him, he'll feel sorry for himself," he roared to his wife. "Self-pity can destroy him!"

And he laid down the first of three iron rules that were to guide Carl's early life.

"No one is ever to show pity to the boy!" he thundered.

On that anvil Carl's character was hammered out.

Often the little boy wore shoes and socks, as befitted the son of a schoolmaster. Whenever he wanted something, his mother, anticipating his wish, rushed to give it to him. Carl was one year old when his father became aware that the armless boy was reaching with his feet for things he wanted, if he was barefooted. And Carl's mother heard his father frame what was to be the second rule:

"Don't put shoes and socks on the child!"

Allowed to crawl around with bare feet, the little boy used his toes more and more. He developed unusual dexterity with them. His thighs and legs grew noticeably more powerful and flexible than those of other children his age.

One night the family was seated at dinner. Frau Unthan passed a bowl of oatmeal down the table. As the bowl went by Carl, he reached out a foot and dug his toes into the cereal. He brought a footful to his mouth. He licked his toes contentedly, wreathing his mouth with the oatmeal.

Carl's mother rushed to wash his foot and his face, bringing a spoon to feed him. Everyone else was eager to help.

But not Herr Unthan. He brought his hand down hard on the table and announced his third rule:

"Let Carl do as he wants! Anyone who helps him will have me to deal with!"

It was a Prussian household in the old style; father's word, God's word. No one dared to disobey the three commandments, no matter how sorry they felt for the child.

Guided by the rules his father had laid down, Carl, without arms and hands, began to do innumerable little things for himself that other children depend on their mothers for. If he didn't succeed at first, he kept trying. And trying. He learned early in life something that many other people never learn—the art of being infinitely patient.

The Climb up the Ladder

The child started to walk late. He was two years old when he abruptly picked himself up off the floor and marched out into the street. Other armless people report similar experiences. He started to play with the other children of the village. He taught himself to take part in their games, using his feet in place of the arms he had been denied.

Carl was still a small child when he saw a house being put up nearby. Working men were clambering up and down a ladder. He watched them and envied them, as a little boy will. When the men went away he saw his chance. He seated himself on the ladder, his back to it. He looked up. Then he placed his feet on the bottommost rung, gave his body a shove upward, and found himself on the next rung. Another shove and he had moved up another rung. Rung by rung, the boy tirelessly pushed his way up.

Seated at the top of the ladder, Carl looked down with pride at the many rungs over which he had traveled so slowly and laboriously. He was filled with excitement.

Although he did not realize it at the time, that climb up the ladder was a symbol of the kind of life he was going to lead, of the kind of person he was becoming. He simply refused to be kept at the bottom of the ladder by an accident of birth.

The Secret Scholar

The house in which Carl's family lived was attached to the schoolhouse where Herr Unthan taught. The little boy used to creep into the back of the classroom when school was in session and hide. There, without being seen or heard, he could see and hear everything. And he could learn. He got a little slate for himself and, clutching it with the toes of one foot, he wrote on it with a piece of chalk held by the toes of the other. By the time he was six years old and his father enrolled him in the school, he had already taught himself how to read and write.

Learning to Swim

Nearby was a pond where the Sommerfeld boys swam in warm weather. Carl envied them. He could do almost everything else they did—why couldn't he learn how to swim?

One day the armless boy decided to try. Walking into the water, he took a deep breath, till his lungs were full of air. Slowly, he leaned backward till his upper body was resting on the water. At the same time he raised his feet to the surface and began to beat them up and down. Instantly his head went under the water. Gasping and coughing, the boy regained his footing. Then he started all over again.

Before that summer came to an end, Carl was lying on the surface and propelling himself all the way across the pond with rapid, regular strokes of his little legs.

Carl Helps

All the other children in the family had chores to do and the boy without arms didn't want to be left out. It was a thrilling moment for him when his father hung a small basket around the boy's neck, gave him some money, and sent him off to Weeskenitt, a mile away, to buy fish for the family's dinner. The sympathetic fisherman gave him the fish at a bargain price and he started back home. The day was hot and the fish was heavy; the string of the basket cut into his skin. Carl's neck was chafed and he was tired when he walked through the doorway with his burden. But he was smiling.

Bringing home the fish was only one of the boy's chores. He taught himself to polish shoes with his feet, and delighted in shining the entire family's footwear spanking bright.

Although Herr Unthan was a teacher he was also a farmer, and Carl took his place with the rest of the family working in the fields. In the springtime he tramped behind the plough and shoved manure into the long furrows, using his bare left foot instead of a rake, as the others did. When the vegetables were ripe, he helped to gather them. Resting his weight on his right foot, he thrust his left into the soil and pulled the potatoes up, one by one.

Undressing Without Arms

Many tiny tasks that the normal child does without a second thought can loom like a mountain before the child who has no hands. Take undressing. The day that Carl succeeded in undressing himself was one he remembered all his life.

One evening the boy decided he was just too big to let himself be undressed by his mother anymore. He was wearing a jacket, and sitting down, he used his toes to pull it over his head. If you think that's easy, try it sometime for yourself.

His trousers came next. They had buttons, and opening them was the problem. Pulling in his stomach to gain some slack, he inserted his big toe next to the topmost button and tried to force it open. Finally he succeeded. Then, one by one, he pulled the rest open, always working with his toes. Getting to his feet, he wiggled until the trousers fell.

When he had finished, his clothes were hanging neatly over the back of the chair.

Dressing himself was considerably harder and took him longer to master.

A Thin Skin Becomes Thicker

At bottom, handicapped people are usually far more sensitive than those who have all their faculties. The handicapped are always being reminded that everybody else has something that they don't—and that, as a result, they're not as good as others are.

It took Carl a long while to develop a realistic acceptance of his lot. He was still a child when his little brother died and he was assigned the mournful task of writing invitations to the funeral. Again and again people looked into the dead boy's casket and said, "The dear Lord has certainly taken the wrong one this time." Each remark, each reminder of his plight, was like a sharp slap in Carl's face.

But with time he learned how to take such slaps. And not to feel them too much.

First Violin Lessons

The armless boy loved music. Others around him were given violin lessons, but playing a musical instrument seemed to be something a child with his handicap could never learn to do.

Carl disagreed. Borrowing a violin, he tied it down to a stool in the kitchen. Then, seating himself, he took up the bow with his left foot. With his right he began to "toe" the strings, while he scraped the bow back and forth across them.

To the rest of the family it sounded like two angry cats. They held their hands over their ears and groaned. To Carl, however, it was melody, or the beginning of it. He had taken a position at the bottom of the ladder of music. With infinite patience he would get to the top.

Carl was about ten when he began to study the violin by himself. He practiced so long and so hard that his knees ached. Little by little he began to make progress. One day, Herr Unthan in the next room, pricked up his ears: Could that be his little armless rascal producing that sweet melody? The boy was given lessons.

At sixteen, Carl was sent to the conservatory. Excitedly, he studied the theory of music, the aesthetics, the history. And he practiced. Hour after hour, day in, day out. Endlessly. Exhaustingly.

His First Concert

Finally—Carl could hardly believe it—he was giving his first concert. The pieces he played were far from easy, but the violin sang under his bow. When he finally put it down, people crowded around to congratulate him. They were eager to shake hands with the talented young musician. But it was his foot that Carl held out to them!

One concert led to another. The youth was soon being hired to perform for money. Soon he was traveling to other cities to give performances. People, he discovered, had heard many fine violinists, but never one who played with his toes. They were willing to pay handsomely for the privilege.

An Emergency

One evening Carl was in the middle of a performance—the hall was crowded—when one of the worst things that can happen to a violinist happened to him. The E-string snapped on his violin.

A long, drawn *oh-h-h* of sympathy rose from the audience.

Jumping up, the young man ran over to his violin case, took out another string, and deftly substituted it for the broken one with his toes.

The audience, which had been watching in complete silence, broke out in cries of astonishment.

The intent young musician raised his big toe to his lip. "Hush!" he said.

If he had needed to win his audience, that spontaneous, utterly natural gesture would have won it. It was a long time before the spectators allowed him to resume the concert.

Unthan had discovered that he could entertain an audience by doing other things than playing for it. He began to introduce other features into his performance—things that showed his dexterity with his toes. Soon he was signed to a long-term contract and was winning acclaim in all the great cities of Europe.

Encounter with the Police

In Saint Petersburg Unthan was given an ovation. But after the performance he almost ran into trouble. Walking off the stage, he found the chief of police waiting for him.

"You didn't actually play that violin with your feet," the chief charged. "You're a fraud. A real violinist with hands was playing for you backstage."

"Well, sir, come and see for yourself."

Unthan led the chief of police to his dressing room. He fastened a violin to a stool and sat down before it. The bow was poised in the toes of his left foot, over the strings. The skeptical frown on the chief's face had not lightened.

Music began to come from the violin. The police chief's dark look dissolved in a glow of wonder. Then his body stiffened. He snapped to attention. Unthan was playing the Russian national anthem.

Unthan on Horseback

The violinist's career took him to England. From there he went to the United States, where he appeared in vaudeville. He toured Cuba. In Mexico the distances between cities were vast and there were no trains or coaches available. Unthan and his companions were told they had to travel on horseback. The musician had never ridden a horse by himself, but he was ready for the challenge.

"I buckled a soft leather strap around my neck," he said later. "Taking the reins, I made a slip knot with a thin string and tied the reins to the strap. All I had to do was lean my head forward and I was able to grasp the reins with my teeth. In this way I could control the horse if he started to get frisky. Most of the time I could guide the animal by pressing against his flanks with my thighs or by talking to him.

"What if I should get knocked off or fall off? I didn't have to worry about being dragged along, because the string would break."

An Extraordinary Performance

Unthan toured South America and then returned to Europe. By now he had developed a highly unusual and entertaining act. Here's what it looked like to one spectator.

"At the start of his performance, Unthan slipped into his morning coat. Then with a skill and speed astonishing for a man without arms, he showed how he performed the duties of the perfect host. He lit cigars. He pulled a cork out of a bottle. He filled glasses with wine. He cut a cake. He shuffled cards and dealt them out. He did fantastic card tricks.

"Next he gave one of his fine performances on the violin. He had learned to play the cornet with considerable virtuosity, and now he performed a piece on this instrument. Picking up a rifle with his feet, he began to shoot at some very small targets on the stage. He never missed.

"It was an extraordinary performance. And he did it all with his toes."

Typing with His Toes

The entertainer's other accomplishments were innumerable. He wrote a "hand" so elegant that it never ceased to surprise people who received letters from him. He taught himself to type. His technique was his own—it was the two-pencil rather than the two-finger method. Sitting down on a chair in front of the stool on which his Woodstock typewriter rested, he picked up a pencil in each foot. Then he would strike the keys with the pencils' rubber ends.

Unthan sharpened pencils by holding a knife between the big toe and its neighbor on one foot, the pencil with the other. It was remarkable to see him adjust his watch with his toes or insert a collar stud in his shirt. And visitors often gasped when the armless man opened a door for them. His shoe was loose; he simply slipped his foot out of it (the toes were bare) and seized and turned the doorknob with his toes.

The Armless Man Marries

During a long appearance in Prague, Czechoslovakia, Unthan met a young lady named Antonie Beschta who sang in the Court Theater. The armless young man was immediately taken with Fräulein Beschta. Her sister was also a singer, and Unthan proposed that the three should team up. The girls accepted, and they went on a concert tour that proved successful. Then Unthan proposed to Antonie that she should team up with him for life. She agreed.

A Demonstration for the Scientists

In Berlin, Rudolf Virchow, one of the most celebrated scientists of the age—we'll encounter his name again and again in these pages—invited five hundred physicians and scholars to a demonstration of Unthan's skill at a meeting of the Anthropological Society. To this distinguished audience Virchow pointed out the extraordinary development of the violinist's toes and the unusual degree to which he could spread them out and bend them. In addition, Unthan had developed an exceptional capacity to turn his upper thighs in the hip joints—even more than a professional contortionist could.

Rescuing a Drowning Woman

Unthan by now was a worldwide celebrity. Gerhart Hauptmann, the famous German novelist, had met him and introduced him as a character in a novel. He was invited to come to Sweden and act in a film.

In Germany the violinist was featured in another film called *The Armless Man*. In the climax, he saved the heroine from drowning. It was an unusual scene. The young woman sank beneath the water. With his knee Unthan pushed her back to the surface. Then he fastened his teeth on the back of her blouse. Turning on his back, he propelled himself to the shore with her by kicking his legs. Of course it was only a film script—but few who knew him doubted that the armless prodigy could do as much in real life.

He Serves His Country

When World War I broke out in 1914, Unthan was in his sixties. He was eager to serve his country. As the casualties mounted, the German Army found a place for him. He was sent to hospitals, where he lectured soldiers who had lost their arms or hands about how they could train their legs and feet to take over. Artificial limbs were coming increasingly into use. It isn't surprising that Unthan opposed them. He thought they were difficult to use, if not downright painful.

Paris Nov. 23d 1893

Messrs. Koster, Bial & Co. New York.

Gentlemen

I received both your cable & letter, containing contract & I must say that you show such a considerable amount of "enterprising pluck" as to astonish me to perplexity.

My performance has been seen here & in London by F. F. Cooney, John D. Hopkins & various other American Managers, & every one of them was afraid to introduce me in the U.S. "for fear of feet", so that I had come to the conclusion those useful lower members must have been rather neglected by the U.S. Public to cause such an animosity. — Well, I shall come & see myself, & I trust that I'll do like Cesar: vene, vidi, vici. I wish & hope that the New York Public will reward your courage & flock in by thousends to see my act. you fully deserve it.

Most faithfully yours

C. H. Unthan

Written by the foot of Carl Unthan

The armless man gave performances of dexterity with his feet much like those he'd given on the stage.

The soldiers were as delighted as his civilian audiences had been. Probably his demonstrations had little educational value; not many amputees could have emulated him, for he had been developing his skill since infancy. Still, his cheerful, constructive attitude toward his situation made many an embittered amputee realize that life could be worth living even without arms. Kaiser Wilhelm, who had a withered arm, was present at a shooting demonstration Unthan gave at the Royal Hospital in Dresden. Wilhelm was so impressed that he took home as souvenirs two bullets that the old performer had fired. For his services in the war Unthan was decorated.

Before he passed away in 1929, Unthan told the story of his life in a book. With his inextinguishable sense of humor, he called it *Das Pediskript*—"the pediscript," since it was written by foot rather than by hand, as a manuscript is.

In the front of his book Unthan placed a motto. It sums up his life—and his message to all who have to bear the same kind of burden he did:

"Where there's a will there's a way."

8

Tripp and Bowen: on a Bicycle
Built for Two

You could hardly believe your eyes.

Two dignified middle-aged men, neatly dressed in
business suits and wearing bow ties and felt hats, were
riding a tandem bike. But the man who sat on the front
seat steering the bicycle was only half a man. He had
no legs. The man on the back seat, pumping the pedals
with easy vigor, had no arms. (See photo insert.)

A legless man and an armless man, riding a bicycle
built for two. Each possessed what the other lacked.
They made a perfect team for a tandem.

The two dapper riders—Charles Tripp, "the
Armless Wonder," and Eli Bowen, "the Legless
Wonder"—were among the most popular figures in
American circuses and carnivals for many years. Noth-
ing like that duo had ever been seen on a tandem be-
fore, and nothing has ever been seen since.

Both Tripp and Bowen were noted for their ready
sense of humor; their witty exchanges were classic. One
of their favorites, which hinged on their peculiar handicaps, will be remembered as long as they are.

Addressing his legless friend, Tripp used to say: "Bowen, watch your step!"

And Bowen never failed to shoot back to the armless Tripp: "Keep your hands off me!"

Charles Tripp: "the Armless Wonder"

Tripp was born on July 6, 1855, in Woodstock, Canada. A beautiful, normal baby, there was only one thing the matter with him—he had no arms. Like Carl Unthan, born just a few years earlier, he had to train his feet and toes to do the work of hands and fingers or be a helpless dependent for the rest of his life. With the encouragement of his parents, he learned to feed himself and dress and undress himself. He learned to write a clear, legible "hand," holding the pen between his toes. (Later, samples of his writing were in great demand among circus audiences.) Eventually he was holding the handle of a straight razor between those powerful toes and shaving himself.

How to Overcome a Handicap

Often a person who has a serious shortcoming will put forth almost superhuman effort to overcome it. Do you remember the ancient Greek orator Demosthenes? "He had," said Plutarch, his biographer, "a weakness in his voice, a perplexed and indistinct utterance, and a shortness of breath, which, by breaking and disjointing his sentences, much obscured the sense and meaning of what he spoke." But Demosthenes was determined to overcome this handicap. He put pebbles in his mouth and went out to the seashore, where he raised his voice over the waves, day after day, to strengthen it. He declaimed while running up a hill. He shut himself up in his study to practice, and shaved one side of his head bare so he wouldn't dare to stop working and go out of doors.

In the end, he not only conquered his handicap—he became the most celebrated orator in a nation of orators.

Feet Become Hands

Charles Tripp was cut out of the same durable cloth. Lacking arms, by ceaseless effort he taught himself to do the things that people usually needed a pair of arms to do—as well as things most people with arms were unable to do. He acquired tools and learned how to use them with his feet. He became an expert with the brace and bit, the chisel, hammer, saw, screwdriver. Because his will was strong and his wish was great, his feet became hands for him. He developed into a skilled cabinetmaker and carved and inlaid exquisite designs on the things he made.

Young Tripp, with his incredible feet, was the talk of his hometown. Neighbors said he should join a show and give demonstrations of his skill.

In time the youth heard of P. T. Barnum, the American showman. Barnum's name, in the seventies, was known around the world; it had even entered foreign languages as a synonym for "showman." "As a discover and exhibitor of 'freaks of nature,' " says Earl Chapin May in his *The Circus from Rome to Ringling,* "no country has known his equal in harvesting fame and fortune, nor has any museum proprietor or manager excelled him in acquiring and sponsoring novelties."

As a novelty, Charlie Tripp believed he was as unusual as any. Why shouldn't he go to New York and offer his services to P. T. Barnum? The teen-ager talked over his notion with his parents and they fell in with it.

In P. T. Barnum's office

In 1872, when Tripp arrived in New York, he was just a country boy seventeen years of age. He felt alone and friendless in the big, alien city. Finding out where Barnum's museum was, he went to look him up.

The desk that Barnum sat at was more beautiful and ornate than any Tripp had ever seen before. The youngster could feel the film of perspiration on his face. Looking at the imposing figure sitting opposite him, he found he had forgotten every word of the speeches he had been rehearsing since he left Woodstock.

"Now, my boy, take it easy," Barnum said. "What can I do for you?"

The young Canadian finally found the words he had been groping for. Slipping his feet out of his shoes, he gave Barnum a demonstration of some of the astonishing things he had trained himself to do. Barnum hired him on the spot.

Tripp stayed with Barnum for many years. He toured the world three times with Barnum and Bailey and Ringling Brothers, and appeared with many other amusement enterprises. Always eager to demonstrate what he could do with tools, he became known as the handyman of the circus.

Tripp married late. For the last fourteen years of his life he traveled with the big carnivals. "That was the only way that we could be together," his wife wrote. "I always sold tickets on some of the rides."

On January 26, 1939, in Salisbury, North Carolina, Tripp succumbed to pneumonia. He was eighty-four years old. The following day the *Salisbury Evening Post* published an editorial about him.

"He never let the words 'I can't' enter his vocabulary," the newspaper said, "and the fine accomplishments and achievements despite handicaps should be a challenge to those of us who possess all our faculties.

"He was a real hero in every sense of the word and overcame odds in life that would have submerged many a man with less determination and spirit."

Eli Bowen: "the Legless Acrobat"

He was one of the handsomest men in show business. He had large piercing eyes, a magnificently shaped head covered with dark brown curls, a long drooping silken mustache, a firm chin. His shoulders were massive and his arms superbly developed.

But, as Eli Bowen used to say, "I don't have a leg to stand on."

Born on October 14, 1844, in Richland County,

Ohio. Bowen was one of ten children. The others were completely normal. For some unknown reason—a genetic slip, a disease his mother had or a drug she took during pregnancy—he was born without legs. Two feet of different sizes grew directly out of his hip joints.

Just as Charles Tripp made his legs serve him in place of arms, Eli Bowen made his arms do the work of legs. He was already managing by himself in childhood. He could even get about without legs. He did this with the aid of wooden blocks held in his hands, using the larger of his feet.

Touring at Thirteen

Bowen was only thirteen when he entered upon the life of what used to be called an "exhibitionist." He traveled with Major Brown's Colosseum, an old-time wagon show that toured the inland country and stopped at small towns. The year was 1857. Long, long afterward he remembered it well; he could always recall the excitement of moving constantly to new towns, the thrill of being on exhibition, and how hard it was to fall asleep at night. But he soon settled down to the life of a traveling showman.

Over the years Bowen toured with many different shows whose names have passed into history: Forepaugh, Pullman Brothers, Campbell's Circus, and others. In 1869 he went to England with the Greatest Show on Earth, and again in 1897. He became close friends with Charles Tripp, and he and the armless man used to divert each other and their audiences with their clever banter. When he was in his twenties he married Martha Hain, an attractive young women of sixteen, who bore him a large, healthy family. He made his home in Ogden, California.

Stunts on a Pole

In a sideshow, Bowen was often billed as "the Legless Acrobat." Not only did he do tumbling tricks, but he also performed on a pole.

Climbing up the pole—remember, he had no legs—Bowen would swing his body around in a series of remarkable semi-circles. Then, as a pamphlet he sold in the circus tells it, "lowering himself partially on the pole, he will suddenly, by a movement at once daring and full of grace, skill, and agility, hold himself aloof from the pole, simply holding on to it by the upper right hand lowered against the pole."

This feat would always bring down the house. While the audience was still applauding, Bowen would swoop downward unexpectedly and knock the cap off a boy who had come in too close to the pole. Every attitude, every posture he took was said to be the picture of power and grace.

Bad Boys Beware

Bowen, according to his old friend Charles E. Davis, was not overfond of boys. They tended to be too full of mischief for him, especially as he grew older. Davis described a typical gambit of Bowen's with a boy one day when he was with the circus in Hartford, Connecticut.

"The air in the sideshow tent was stifling. Bowen was squatting on his pedestal. His sharp eye picked out two small boys working their way through the crowd toward him. Pulling a red bandanna out of his shirt pocket, he placed it between the toes of one of his feet.

"Bowen noticed the boys had seen the action, and he shut his eyes. Well, they were almost shut. He appeared to be dozing peacefully. One boy nudged the other and reached his hand out for the bandanna.

"All at once, as fast as lightning, Bowen's foot shot out. So did the end of the handkerchief, which whipped across the boy's cheek. The boy let out a shriek of pain, clapped his hand to his face, and disappeared into the crowd with his friend. The spectators exploded in laughter.

"The incident seemed to put old Eli in a better humor. A slow smile spread across his wrinkled features."

Another time a youngster asked Bowen how or by

what accident he had lost his legs. The old performer was annoyed.

"Why," he said, "my legs were shot off."

"Shot off!" the youngster exclaimed. "But how did you save your feet?"

"Well, they were fastened back on, partly by thread and partly by cement."

```
=□□===□■===□■===□□===□□===□■===□□□=
```

9

Kingston, Kobelkoff, and Other Wonders

```
=□□===□■===□□===□□===□□===□□===□□=
```

William Kingston: a Successful Farmer

Although many armless or legless wonders have gained a livelihood as entertainers or artists, some have succeeded in the ordinary occupations of everyday life. One of the most remarkable of these people was William Kingston, an armless farmer, who lived in Ditcheat, Somerset, England.

We gain a fascinating picture of the things that Kingston could do and how he did them from a letter that the Methodist clergyman John Wesley received in 1788 from a man named Walton.

"I went with a friend to visit this man," wrote Walton, "who highly entertained us at breakfast by putting his half-naked foot upon the table as he sat and carrying his tea and toast between his great and second toe to his mouth, with as much facility as if his foot had been a hand and his toes fingers.

"I put half a sheet of notepaper on the floor with a pen and ink-horn; he threw off his shoes as he sat, took the ink-horn in the toes of his left foot and held the pen in those of his right ... He then wrote three lines as well as the most ordinary writers and as swiftly ...

"He cleans his own shoes, his knives, lights the fire and does almost any other domestic business as well as any other man.

"He is a farmer by occupation and milks his cows with his toes, makes his hencoops, cuts his hay, and binds it up in bundles.

"He goes to the field, catches his horse, saddles and bridles him with his feet and toes. If he has a sheep among his flock that ails anything, he can separate it from the rest, drive it into a corner and catch it when nobody else can. He is so strong with his teeth that he can lift ten pecks of beans with them, and can throw a great sledge-hammer as far with his feet as other men can do with their hands.

"In a word, he can nearly do as much without, as others can with their hands."

Marc Cazotte: the Italian Dwarf

One of the most famous armless and legless people of the eighteenth century was Marc Cazotte, who performed feats of extraordinary agility.

Cazotte was born in Venice in 1741 as Marco Catozze. He had several brothers who were all normal. At the end of each of his very prominent shoulders he had a well-formed hand. Attached to his buttocks were badly shaped feet. He stood only two feet six inches high.

A versatile and gifted showman, Cazotte traveled throughout Europe. When he was younger he traveled on horseback; a specially constructed saddle made it possible for him to hold his position on the horse. He was a good walker in spite of his abnormal feet.

Since his hands were so far from his mouth Cazotte had a hard time feeding himself. To overcome this handicap, he developed his bottom jaw so he could lower it to an unusual extent and thrust it forward. To pick up objects that were some distance away he had a hollow tube made about three feet in length. Inside it was a metal rod with a hook at the end of it. Cazotte was able to catch the things he wanted with the hook and pull them up the tube.

The little man finally settled in Paris, where he appeared under the name of Pépin. He was also known as "the Italian Dwarf." He died at the age of sixty-two, and his skeleton was preserved at the Musée Dupuytren.

A contemporary of Cazotte's, Matthew Buchinger, the German dwarf, was also similarly handicapped. That didn't keep him from gaining a Europe-wide reputation as a performer and marrying four times. His story is told later in this book.

Armless Artists: Ducornet and Aimée Rapin

Art is superb therapy for handicapped people of all kinds. People who lose their arms often take it up. Frequently they hold the paintbrush in their mouths. Some, however, have trained their feet to hold the brush and work with the skill of hands and have achieved lasting reputations in art. One of the most noted of these was the French historical painter César Ducornet.

The son of poor parents, Ducornet was born in Lille on January 10, 1806. The child had no arms. Otherwise his body was finely formed, except that on his right foot he had only four toes. The space between the big toe and the next one was greater than normal. Picking up pieces of charcoal from the floor and holding them in the space between his toes, he did rough sketches on the wall. They showed such promise that he was given training in art, and eventually the city sent him to Paris to study.

Developing considerable skill, Ducornet became a successful painter. One of his outstanding works was a picture eleven feet high depicting Mary Magdalene at the feet of Jesus after the resurrection. The French Government purchased the painting and presented it to the city of Lille. Other noted paintings of Ducornet's are *Repentance* and *Christ in the Sepulchre*. He died in Paris in 1906.

Another proof that determination and love of art can overcome the greatest obstacles was provided by a Swiss girl, Aimée Rapin, who made her home in Geneva. Like Ducornet, she was born without arms and yet could wield her pencil or brush with astonishing skill.

As a small child, Aimée discovered she could use her feet to make up for the hands she lacked. One day her mother took her for a walk in the garden. Mme. Rapin was surprised to see her little girl suddenly kick off her shoes. With her left foot Aimée picked a flower and with the toes of her right foot she plucked its petals. After this the mother did everything in her power to help her child develop suppleness in her feet, making sure her toes were not cramped or confined by shoes and socks when they didn't have to be.

Aimée showed a remarkable talent in drawing and painting, and after she finished her regular schooling her parents sent her to art school, where she achieved an outstanding record among her normally equipped peers. The ease and deftness with which she worked, holding her pencil or brush between her big toe and the next one, bordered on the miraculous. Her skill as a portraitist was in great demand in the 1890s.

Kobelkoff: "the Human Trunk"

At least as impressive as Carl Unthan was another performer who was often seen on the European stage at about the same time. This was Nikolai Vassilivich Kobelkoff. In France he was known as *l'homme-tronc*—"the human trunk"—for he lacked both arms and legs.

Born in Troizk, Russia, in 1853, Kobelkoff was the fourteenth child of completely normal parents. His brothers and sisters were normal also. At first his mother was so unhappy about her unfortunate child that she tried to keep outsiders from seeing him. Eventually she had to bring him out-of-doors. When the superstitious peasants glimpsed the armless and legless little boy they crossed themselves.

Kobelkoff grew into a powerfully built, muscular man with a short, thick neck. In place of limbs he had only stumps, but he was able to use them with remarkable effectiveness, thanks to the guidance of a humane clergyman who supervised his education. When he appeared in the theaters of Western Europe in the 1870s he gave the public an unforgettable demonstration of what a human being can accomplish through endless, bone-wearying patience.

In his actions Kobelkoff made particular use of his right arm stump, which contained some eight inches of bone. He picked things up with his teeth and then used this stump in conjunction with his chin, his cheek, or his shoulder. He made, so to speak, a crude pair of tongs or pincers, which enabled him to do seemingly incredible things. His bed, the size of a cradle, was only sixteen inches from the floor, so he could get into it and out of it unaided. To move around, he used a child's three-wheeled wagon.

In the theater, when the curtain rose, Kobelkoff would be seen sitting in front of a table on which were spread out the objects he used in his act. Picking up a penholder with his teeth, he placed it between his right stump and his cheek. Next he dipped the point in an inkwell and wrote his name in a good "hand" on pieces of paper, which were distributed to the audience. Then he picked up a paintbrush and sketched some objects on paper. His drawing was highly competent.

The way Kobelkoff ate was something to see, as he demonstrated it on the stage. Taking a bottle, he pulled out the stopper and poured some of the contents into a glass. He placed the glass on his stump and raised it to his lips and drank. He picked up a spoon, thrust it into a dish of food, and brought it to his mouth. He used a fork the same way. In a time when heavy watches were worn on gold chains, he still managed to tell the time. He pulled his watch out of his pocket, placed it on his stump, pressed the catch, snapped open the lid, and read out the time. Then he returned the watch to his

pocket. He was equally handy with a pistol. Not only
did he pick up the gun, load it, and fire it—he also
unerringly shot out his target, a candle flame. He must
have been able to make himself useful around the
house, for he was able to thread a needle with his lips
and stump.

The human trunk was an acrobat, too. He would
jump to the floor from his chair and bounce up and
over, landing upright on his shoulders and the back of
his neck, facing in the opposite direction. Then, with a
powerful thrust, he turned himself over, landing in his
former position. He also doubled as a strong man. Inviting a person of average weight to come up on the
stage, he extended his stump and asked the man to
stand on it. Then Kobelkoff lifted him up.

When the Russian half-man was touring Austria,
he met and fell in love with a young woman, Anna
Wilfert. Their wedding, in 1876, was one of the most
unusual ones on record. The veiled bride walked
solemnly to the altar—carrying her groom in her arms.
At the end of the ceremony the groom put the ring on
his new wife's finger with his teeth. He himself had no
hand on which to wear his wedding ring; he carried it in
a little leather pouch around his neck. It was a happy
marriage that, over the years, produced eleven normal
children, six of whom reached maturity.

The human trunk was an intelligent and cultivated
person. Like Unthan, he published his memoirs. He
performed before all the crowned heads of Europe. For
a while he toured with a traveling show of his own.
When he passed away in January, 1933, he was the
owner of a show in the Prater, Vienna's historic amusement center. He was buried in the city's Central Cemetery, in a child's coffin.

Tommy Jacobsen: Armless Pianist

If Carl Unthan were alive today, he could make a
unique concert duo with Tommy Jacobsen. For Jacobsen plays the piano with his feet just as Unthan did the
violin.

Jacobsen, billed as Tommy "Toes" Jacobsen, is a popular British entertainer. He performs in nightclubs and has appeared on the British Broadcasting System's "In Town Tonight" show. Seated on a special stool that brings the entire keyboard within reach of his toes, he plays with what has been described as pianistic wizardry. On his right leg he wears a wrist watch, on one of his toes a ring.

Actually, playing the piano is Jacobsen's second career. His first one was sign painting. Born in 1921 in Newport, England, he was sent to a special school for handicapped children when he was seven years old. There he was taught to use his feet the way other people use their hands and instructed in the craft of painting signs. He also learned how to play the xylophone and the piano.

For the first months Jacobsen did fine as a sign painter, but then he began to show strange symptoms. Doctors diagnosed it as lead poisoning. The lead was in the paint he worked with, so he was compelled to abandon his occupation. He thought of his love for music. At a time when there was a diminishing demand for live musicians, Jacobsen's extraordinary skill won him a secure and permanent place in the profession. He is married and the father of a completely normal daughter.

Toes, incidentally, are not the only organs a person without hands can use to play the piano. In the eighteenth century there was a beautiful French girl born without arms and legs who still managed to turn in a striking performance on the piano. She did it *with her nose*.

Johnny Eck: Legless Runner

"Legs? What do I need them for?" Johnny Eck, "the Living Half-Boy," said to an interviewer in 1932. "If you have legs you have to have pants—and if you have pants you have to keep them pressed. To ask me if I'm sorry I have no legs is like asking an Eskimo if he's sorry he never tasted an artichoke.

"I may be half a boy but they can't slip me half a salary."

Johnny Eck (see photo insert) didn't miss his legs because he'd never had them—and he had learned so beautifully to get along without them. He was an expert swimmer and diver. He was a tightrope walker and a juggler. He composed music and conducted an orchestra. Most incredible of all, he was an excellent dancer.

On his hands of course. For his torso ended just where his hips should have been. Johnny, a native of Baltimore, was born on August 27, 1911. Delivered with him was a perfectly normal twin brother. But Johnny? The doctor doubted that he would live through the day. For he was, as one writer put it, "a veritable human fraction . . ."

But Johnny did live. By the time he was a year old, like other children, he was walking. Walking in his own fashion. It took perfect balance, but the little boy had that in every sense of the word. He grew into a remarkably charming, cheerful boy. He went to grade school and high school with his brother. Often he rode in a kiddy car, pushing himself along with his hands. An outstanding student, he won award after award. In drawing and music he was especially proficient. He learned to play the saxophone and clarinet like a professional.

Johnny began to make public appearances at fourteen. People found his performances as appealing as his radiant smile. Soon he was performing with traveling shows. Sometimes he posed on the stage with his brother. The two young men, standing side by side, almost looked like carbon copies of each other. But Johnny, perched on a pedestal, was only eighteen inches tall—less than a third of his brother's height. He weighed only fifty-seven pounds and ate just a small part of what the average person does.

In the winter, Johnny had his own twelve-piece orchestra in Baltimore, which he conducted. The group performed for nightclubs, cabarets, and dances.

Johnny had a handicap, but, as with so many other Very Special People, it was the making of him. It helped him develop a courageous, cheerful disposition. In time it was to put him into motion pictures. He played in a number of films, among them *Tarzan* and Tod Browning's *Freaks*. Theaters where *Freaks* was shown gave out a button with a picture of Johnny. If you could find one, it would be a collector's item today.

Although Johnny was always moving about on his hands, his palms weren't nearly as hard and tough as you might have expected them to be. In his pocket, when he was sitting, you could see a conspicuous bulge. It was made by a heavy pair of gloves. As soon as he wanted to go somewhere he would take out the gloves and pull them onto his long, strong hands. They were his "hand shoes." With them on, he could run faster than the average man with legs is able to.

Prince Randian: "the Living Torso"

Prince Randian, who came from British Guiana, had neither arms nor legs. In his performances he wore a one-piece woollen garment that covered him like a sack. All you could see was his swarthy head and his tiny sack-covered torso.

A famous figure in sideshows, Randian (his name also appeared as Randion) was reportedly brought to the United States by P. T. Barnum in 1889. For forty-five years he appeared in carnivals, circuses, and dime museums. He was married, had five children, and was proud of his many grandchildren. Like Johnny Eck, he played a role in the MGM film *Freaks*. He died at the age of sixty-three.

Randian used to move about by wiggling his hips and his shoulders. His sinuous movements resembled those of a snake or a caterpillar, earning him the billing of "the Snake Man" or "the Caterpillar Man." He was also known as "the Living Torso." He had taught himself to write, holding a pen or pencil with his lips, which served him as fingers. His most famous trick was rolling a cigarette with his lips. He was able to shave by fixing the razor in a wooden block.

The box in which Randian kept his smoking

materials and the other paraphernalia for his act, he claimed, had been built by him, using a saw, knife, and hammer. He also said he had painted it, holding the brush with his teeth, and even fixed a lock on it.

"Someday," Randian used to say, "I'll build myself a house."

Prince Randion, Barnum Protege, Dies After Show

Was Billed as 'Armless and Legless Wonder' 45 Years

Prince Randion, who has been billed in side shows for forty-five years as "the armless and legless wonder," died at 7 o'clock last night soon after he had given a performance in Sam Wagner's Fourteenth Street Museum, 122 East Fourteenth Street. He was sixty-three years old.

The Prince was brought to the United States from the Demerara district of British Guiana by the late P. T. Barnum in 1889. He appeared first in Huber's Museum, which occupied the present site of Luchow's restaurant. Later he was with Barnum's "Greatest Show on Earth." He had a bag of tricks, of which the most popular was rolling a cigarette with his lips. He used to show his audiences how he shaved with his lips, by fixing the razor in a wooden block.

His wife, Princess Sarah, four daughters and a son, survive. The Prince and Princess lived at 174 Water Street, Paterson, N. J.

PART 3

THE HAIRY PEOPLE

10

Mme. Clofullia

The star of one of the most successful exhibitions ever staged by P. T. Barnum, prince of showmen, was Mme. Fortune Clofullia. She was a personable, good-looking young lady, with a difference. She had a six-inch beard. (See photo insert.)

Over the years bearded ladies were to become a staple feature of the sideshow, but in 1853, when Barnum unveiled Mme. Clofullia to the public in his American Museum in New York City she was a distinct novelty, and people came from far and near to see her. Adding to the uniqueness of the spectacle, she sometimes appeared with her son, Albert. Little Albert, then under a year old, was an attractive, completely normal baby, except that he was covered with hair and sported a light beard about half an inch long.

The "Bearded Lady of Geneva," as Mme. Clofullia was billed, was born Josephine Boisdechene on March 25, 1831, at Versoix, Switzerland, near the city of Geneva, according to the pamphlets she sold in connection with her public appearances. Her parents

were overjoyed when she came to join them eleven
months after their marriage—but their happiness
turned to concern when they noticed that little Josephine's face and body were covered with heavy down.

The family doctor was reassuring. After examining
the child carefully, he promised the apprehensive
mother and father that the unseemly hairy growth
would disappear in a few weeks. Every baby, he
pointed out, was born with a downy covering; Josephine's was simply somewhat darker and longer than
usual.

The weeks dragged by for the worried parents.
Every day, when the baby was dressed, diapered, or
bathed, they examined her minutely for signs that the
doctor's prognosis was being fulfilled. They couldn't be
sure at first, but to their troubled eyes it seemed that
the down, instead of disappearing, was growing darker
and longer. The weeks became months and finally the
anxious parents could no longer delude themselves. The
down on their daughter's body had become hair.

Deeply disturbed, M. and Mme. Boisdechene
called the family physician in again. He examined the
baby from the crown of her head to her feet and
fingered the hair that covered the little body. Then he
shook his head.

"This case is too extraordinary for a simple country doctor like me to pass judgment on," he said. "I can
only recommend that you consult the physicians of the
faculty of Geneva."

Geneva, on the southwest shore of beautiful Lake
Leman, has been a scientific center for centuries. Confident that its medical professors could shed some light
on their daughter's condition, M. and Mme. Boisdechene hurriedly made an appointment with them.

But the distinguished physicians of the faculty
turned out to be just as mystified as the village doctor.
After a thorough examination of little Josephine they
confessed that they had never encountered a case like
hers before.

"It will be necessary to wait till your child is seven
or eight years old," the senior member of the faculty

said, "before we can form a final opinion about her condition."

The Doctors' Verdict

Eight years is a long time to wait. For M. and Mme. Boisdechene they could not have been very happy years. It is a strange experience for parents to pat their little daughter on the cheek and have to wonder whether she isn't a son after all . . .

By Josephine's eighth birthday the hair growth on her cheeks and chin had reached a good two inches in length. Her father and mother, refusing to give up hope that the doctors would find a way to restore their little girl to normalcy, took her to consult the medical faculty again.

The physicians were less than helpful. They could merely confirm what M. and Mme. Boisdechene could see only too well for themselves: their daughter definitely had a *beard*.

"Surely there is something that can be done for our poor little girl," the parents pleaded. "At least we can call in a barber and have him shave the growth off."

The doctors felt the child's whiskers.

"The growth is exceptionally thick," the senior physician observed. "If it were shaved off or cut, it would only grow longer. It would get tougher, too. I advise you to leave well enough alone."

Bearded Women in History

Although the doctors who examined Josephine Boisdechene could do nothing to help her, her condition was not an unfamiliar one. Bearded women have been known through the ages. They have played a prominent role in folklore, religion, history, and the theater.

In the fifth century before Christ, Hippocrates, the Father of Medicine, described a woman who grew a beard after she entered her menopause. The ancients held bearded women in awe, believing that they possessed special gifts and could even be oracles of the gods. Herodotus tells of a priestess of Athena who grew a beard whenever her people were in danger.

In the Middle Ages and afterward bearded ladies declined in popular esteem and were held to be witches. But one Spanish nun who had a beard was sainted. This was Saint Paula the Bearded. According to church tradition, a wicked young man was pursuing her and she prayed for help. Instantly a beard grew on her face. When her would-be attacker beheld her changed appearance he turned his attention elsewhere.

Perhaps the most distinguished bearded lady in history was Margaret of Parma, regent of the Netherlands. Margaret was a woman of masculine abilities and her beard was a source of delight to her; she thought it made her look more like a ruler. She had her doctors prepare special concoctions that supposedly would be of benefit to her whiskers. A bearded woman fought in the army of Charles XII of Sweden as a grenadier. When she was captured by the Russians she became a favorite of the czar's. She was said to be very attractive.

In the Renaissance, bearded ladies discovered that they could make a living—often a handsome one—by exhibiting themselves. Over the years many famous bearded ladies have appeared on the stage. We shall meet the most notable of them in these pages: Julia Pastrana often called the ugliest woman of her time; Annie Jones, who traveled with Barnum and Bailey; Catherine Delait, France's best-known bearded lady; Lady Olga, Stella MacGregor, and some others. We shall also encounter some Very Special People who have been entirely covered with long hair and who are taken to be specimens of Darwin's missing link.

What Makes a Bearded Woman?

All of these unusual people were human beings like the rest of us, with one basic difference: excessive hairiness. Medical science calls this condition hirsutism, hypertrichosis, or polytrichosis. Sometimes, as we shall see, the condition runs in families. It can simply be due to a genetic or hereditary factor which emerges from time to time. This seems especially likely when a bearded lady gives birth to a bearded child.

Usually, hirsutism can be traced to an abnormality of the endocrine glands. The endocrines are glands that manufacture hormones. These chemical messengers are poured directly into the blood stream and have a significant effect on the chemistry and activities of the body. The ovaries, for example, are endocrine glands. In addition to producing eggs, they manufacture sex hormones which prepare the woman's body for her female role in life. Under abnormal conditions, however, the ovaries may produce an excessive amount of *male* hormones. These can cause a woman to lose her female curves and take on male characteristics—develop a beard and a deep voice, and cease menstruating. An abnormality of the pituitary gland can have the same effect.

Frequently, excessive hairiness and other signs of masculinity can be traced to the adrenal glands. These are two small endocrine glands, each situated on top of one of the kidneys.

Actually, an adrenal gland is a gland inside a gland. The inner part is called the medulla and the outer part the cortex. Each part has its own secretions. The medulla produces the familiar adrenalin, which speeds up your heartbeat and increases your body's capacity for exertion in an emergency.

The cortex secretes the hormone we are concerned with here—androgen, which gives the male his masculine characteristics—and sometimes gives them to the female.

According to Dr. Hugo H. Young of Johns Hopkins University, before a baby is born it has an intermediate region between the medulla and the cortex. In the normal female embryo, this zone disappears early. But under unusual circumstances the zone may persist. It may even enlarge or develop large tumors. The result is an abundance of hair on the face and body of the girl infant at birth.

Sometimes the same condition occurs abruptly in adults when they develop tumors on the adrenal glands. This disorder, known as adrenal virilism, can be corrected by removal of the tumors.

With all these possible causes, the wonder is that we don't have more bearded ladies than we do. The fact is, they have become rarer and rarer as we have found out more about the endocrine glands. The bearded ladies of today can usually remove their unwanted facial adornments by undergoing a gland operation, by taking hormone therapy, or having the hair roots of the beard removed by electrolysis.

Josephine Boisdechene lived before any of these scientific facts were known. She was destined to become one of the most celebrated bearded ladies of two continents.

A Bearded Schoolgirl

Bearded or not, young Josephine had to have an education. M. and Mme. Boisdechene sent her off to boarding school. They faithfully followed the doctors' advice about not allowing her beard to be cut. By the time she was fourteen it was some five inches long. Its texture was soft and silky—probably not much of a consolation to an adolescent girl who was beginning to think about boys.

At about this time Mme. Boisdechene passed away, leaving three younger children who needed to be cared for. M. Boisdechene had no choice but to withdraw his daughter from the boarding school to look after them. At Versoix, the neighbors barely noticed Josephine's beard, having known her since childhood.

To strangers, however, this full-bosomed girl, of middling height, with her silky dark brown whiskers and long hair, was an unusual sight. They never failed to ask about her history. Word of the bearded girl of Versoix spread rapidly through the countryside. Not many months had passed before showmen from nearby cities were calling on her father and offering to engage Josephine to appear on the stage.

Boisdechene, a solid, respectable Swiss farmer, was appalled by the idea of having his daughter make a public display of herself. One after another, he turned the showmen's proposals down. This only seemed to whet their interest and their offers improved. Boisdechene began to listen to them more attentively.

Josephine on the Stage

Finally, in 1849, a showman from Lyons made Boisdechene such a handsome offer that he found it impossible to resist. He put his younger children in boarding schools, leased his farms, and went on tour with his daughter.

Josephine made her first public appearance in Geneva. Large crowds turned out to look in wonderment at the gentle, handsome girl with the beard. It was trimmed in the latest style and somehow it gave her a special dignity—almost an air of majesty.

Next the Boisdechenes toured Lyons and other cities in France. Josephine's contract was for a year. When it expired, her father decided against renewing it. He had been studying the techniques of showmanship and wanted to try his hand as Josephine's manager for a while. They continued the tour on their own.

Love Comes to the Bearded Lady

In matters of the heart, bearded ladies are usually just as susceptible as their beardless sisters. At Troyes, Mlle. Josephine made the acquaintance of M. Fortune Clofullia, Jr., a good-looking young man who was acquiring a reputation as a landscape painter. Josephine was interested in painting, and Clofullia was interested in Josephine; he offered to give her watercolor lessons. She made progress under his instruction in more ways than one. By the time the Boisdechenes' three-month stay at Troyes came to an end, Fortune Clofullia had proposed to Josephine and she had accepted him. And so the traveling twosome of father and daughter became a threesome.

Josephine and the Emperor

M. Boisdechene wanted to exhibit his daughter in Paris. If she could be accepted there, she could succeed anywhere. At the French capital leading doctors were invited to examine the bearded lady. They found her case as impressive as previous examiners had—perhaps even more so, since her beauty had ripened with the years—and their report quickly made her reputation in the city. The nobility thronged to see her. Louis Napoleon, soon to assume the title of Napoleon III, emperor of France, summoned her to his palace at the Tuileries and lavished princely gifts on her.

"Her Breasts Are Large and Fair"

Paris had been conquered. But what about London? The Great Universal Exposition was about to be held there and the city would be full of tourists; no doubt plenty of money could be earned by a bearded lady. Soon Josephine and her companions were crossing the choppy waters of the English Channel.

In what was becoming a regular operating procedure, prominent doctors and surgeons were invited to examine the new marvel from abroad at a London hospital. Dr. Chowne, a well-known physician, signed a certificate that assured Josephine's success in the English capital. He declared:

> I have this day seen, professionally, Josephine Boisdechene, and, in relation to the legal question referred to me, hereby certify, that although she has beard and whiskers, large, profuse, and strictly masculine, on those parts of the face (the upper lip excepted) occupied by the beard and whiskers in men, and, although on her limbs and back, she has even more hair than is usually found on men, she is without malformation. Her

breasts are large and fair, and strictly characteristic of the female.

W. D. CHOWNE, M.D.
Charing Cross Hospital, Sept. 22, 1851.

The bearded lady remained in London for over a
year. She was the talk of the town: upwards of eight
hundred thousand people paid to see her—or so her
agent declared—and she was lionized by the city's
dignitaries.

A Bearded Mother

Three months after the physical examination that
made her reputation in England, Mme. Clofullia had to
call on the services of the medical profession again. On
December 26, 1851, she gave birth to a daughter. The
little girl was devoid of the heavy down that had covered her mother when she was born.

Probably at the request of the bearded lady or her
manager, the physician who delivered the child supplied
an affidavit of the birth. In the document, after af-
firming the delivery, the doctor went on to declare, "I
consider the mother one of the most remarkable freaks
of nature ever witnessed. She has abundant beard and
whiskers; the descriptions of her, as shown by the public prints, are strictly correct." Doubting Thomases
were always appearing who asserted the bearded lady
was not all that she was advertised to be. Showing the
skeptics a row of medical certificates might not be as
convincing as allowing them to pull her whiskers or examine her more intimately—but it was a lot easier on
the bearded lady's dignity, not to mention her chin.

Mme. Clofullia's daughter lived for only eleven
months. But the bereaved parents were not childless for
long. Six weeks after the first child's funeral the
bearded lady gave birth to a son. Again the attending
surgeons provided an affidavit of the birth, certifying
that they had delivered "Madame Fortune (the extraordinary whiskered lady) ... of a very fine nine
months' male child." And inevitably they included a

phrase that has the quaint but purposeful ring of one of the advertising posters of the day: "We can further add, that we consider Madame Fortune as one of the most strange productions of the human female we ever beheld."

If Mme. Fortune was "one of the most strange productions of the human female," little Albert, as his parents called him, was an equally strange production of the human male. His face and body were covered with soft light hair. M. and Mme. Clofullia were not, however, as dismayed as her parents had been when she was born. A bearded lady, they had discovered, could make a handsome living. Certainly a bearded little boy had possibilities . . .

Enter P. T. Barnum

A few months later the Clofullias, Albert, and M. Boisdechene were aboard the steamer *City of Manchester*, bound for Philadelphia. An American showman had made the bearded lady a good offer to tour the United States. In New York City Mme. Clofullia was introduced to P. T. Barnum. The great showman recognized at once that here was a Very Special Person almost made to order for him. Americans, he had proved in his exploitation of General Tom Thumb, found his human oddities doubly fascinating when he billed them as coming from abroad—and here was an attractive bearded lady with a convincing Swiss French accent! Her beard looked convincing, too. But first, to satisfy himself that it was as real as it appeared, he asked his visitor to submit to an examination by a battery of doctors. Mme. Clofullia didn't mind—she was used to it—and the examination turned out as could have been predicted. Barnum, "who never shrinks before any sacrifices to please the public," as his advertising declared, made Madame Clofullia an offer she could not resist and she was soon attracting big crowds to his American Museum.

Little Albert made his debut with his mother, drawing the oohs and aahs of the country visitors who filled the showplace daily. In keeping with the religious leanings of the day, Barnum called the boy "the Infant Esau"—after the son of Isaac and Rebekah, who, the Book of Genesis relates, at birth was covered "all over like a hairy garment." The name, over the years, was applied to a number of other bearded children.

The Bearded Lady and Women's Lib

The press, like the public, was intrigued by Barnum's bearded lady and devoted considerable space to her story. Women's lib was far from unknown in that time. In fact, an active struggle for women's rights was in progress and the spectacle of a female with a beard inevitably made male journalists think of it. In 1851, only two years before Mme. Clofullia arrived in the United States, Amelia Jenks Bloomer, advocating greater freedom for her sex, had shocked the country by appearing in public in a short skirt and trousers. They were quickly named bloomers after her. Commenting on the bearded lady in a page-long article, *Gleason's Pictorial Drawing Room Companion* declared: "Here is a member of their sex who out-Herods Herod; not content with claiming the right to vote, and lay siege to our nether garments (à la bloomer), our beards are actually in jeopardy. Heaven forfend!"

The Bearded Lady on Trial

Not all of the visitors to the American Museum were favorably impressed by Mme. Clofullia. One of them, after paying his twenty-five cents to gain admittance, studied the bearded lady from various angles and decided that she was a fraud. This man, William Charr, took his dissatisfaction to the police. He complained that Mme. Clofullia was actually a male trying to pass as a female.

The case against Barnum and his bearded lady came to trial in the Tombs Court in July, 1853. On the witness stand, Charr reiterated his charge that he had been defrauded of his twenty-five-cent admission fee by the bearded lady. "She and Mr. Barnum are humbugs and ought to be dealt with according to law," he claimed angrily.

The situation was tailor-made for Barnum. Into court he marched with an impressive array of documents and witnesses. First he swore that to the best of his knowledge Mme. Clofullia was a member of the female sex. Then he placed in the hands of the judge an impressive affidavit. It was signed by three doctors. In their statement the physicians affirmed that:

(1) It was possible for a woman to have a beard.

(2) They had examined Mme. Clofullia and she was indeed a woman.

(3) Mme. Clofullia's beard was genuine.

Fortune Clofullia, Jr., also appeared on her behalf. He swore that he was the bearded lady's lawful husband and had been married to her for three years. He also declared that she was the mother of two children, and that one of them was still living.

M. Boisdechene took the stand. He declared that he was the father of Mme. Clofullia. She was not his son, he pointed out, but his daughter, and M. Clofullia was her lawfully wedded husband.

Just in case any doubt might still remain about the true sex of Mme. Clofullia and the genuineness of her whiskers, Barnum had asked Dr. Covil, a physician on the staff of the Tombs, to examine the bearded lady. In his affidavit, the doctor stated that he had conducted his examination with the assistance of a matron and that "both are convinced that, in spite of her beard, she is a woman."

The evidence in favor of Barnum and his bearded lady was overwhelming, and the judge dismissed the charge of fraud. Press reports on the case had drawn a large throng of curiosity seekers to the Tombs, and they trailed the witnesses out of the courtroom. In the following months the interest aroused by the trial caused a literal flood of twenty-five-cent pieces to pour into the cashboxes of the American Museum.

Not long after the trial of the bearded lady an editor reported he had heard that Barnum was actually the instigator of the suit. He had put William Charr up to suing him for fraud in order to win some free publicity for his show. The report sounded plausible enough, for if the showman had wished, presumably he could have kept the case out of court simply by furnishing Charr with the same kind of evidence he provided for the judge.

But then some of the three and a half million people who reportedly paid admissions to enter the American Museum during the nine months Barnum exhibited the bearded lady might have spent their money somewhere else.

11

Annie Jones: the Bearded Girl

"Annie Jones, the Bearded Girl," proclaimed the colorful poster in front of Barnum's museum in downtown New York City. She was no more than a baby when the great showman placed her on exhibition in 1866. Thirteen years earlier Barnum had exhibited Madame Fortune Clofullia and her bearded little boy, Albert. When Barnum heard from his agents that they had discovered a baby girl with whiskers in the mountains of southwestern Virginia, he began to envision a repeat of his earlier triumph.

Annie (See photo insert) was born on July 14, 1865, at Marion, in Smith County, Virginia. At birth her face was covered with heavy down and she had long hair. She was the only one in her family—which eventually included seven brothers and sisters—to show this peculiarity. "We called her Esau, on account of her hairy growth," her Bible-reading mother recalled long afterward.

When Mrs. Jones first saw her hairy baby daughter, she burst into anguished weeping. Her suffering, however, was considerably relieved when she read Barnum's message urging her to bring her child to New York so he could exhibit her. The showman's invitation worked like magic on the minds of Annie's humble parents. His name was one of the most famous in the United States. Many considered him and President Lincoln the outstanding Americans of the century. Dressing up the little girl in her holiday best and throwing some belongings into a carpet bag, her mother headed for New York City.

Barnum's showplace, the American Museum, had burned down the previous year—only a day before little Annie was born. The loss cost Barnum hundreds of thousands of dollars. Never daunted, he had speedily leased an old building on Broadway, between Spring and Prince streets, and stocked it with new wonders. Annie was destined to be one of the most wonderful of them.

The portly showman nodded approvingly as the mother undressed her baby and showed him that her little shoulders, as well as her face, were covered with heavy hair. He soon had a three-year contract ready for Mrs. Jones to sign. It provided, she recalled later, $150 a week, a considerable sum in those days, for the privilege of exhibiting her daughter in his museum. Barnum had come a long way since his struggling beginnings in the 1840s, when he engaged the minuscule Tom Thumb for only three dollars a week.

The Bearded Girl Kidnapped

At first Barnum billed little Annie as "the Infant Esau," just as he had Mme. Clofullia's son. The bearded girl was an instant success, and her mother remained in New York to take care of her. However, just as Mrs. Jones was getting used to life in the Big City an emergency arose at home in Virginia, compelling her to return. She left her daughter in what she thought were competent hands.

Not long afterward Mrs. Jones was handed a message that filled her with terror. Little Annie, the

message said, had disappeared. So, too, had a man
named Wicks, a phrenologist. (Phrenology, greatly in
vogue in those days, was a pseudoscience that pretended to reveal a person's character and abilities by a
study of the shape of his skull.)

Mrs. Jones took the first train she could get to
New York. P. T. Barnum, greatly concerned for the
safety of the child, had launched a wide search for her.
But months passed and the child could not be found.

A Court Suit to Recover Little Annie

Finally, six months after Annie's disappearance,
she was reported to be in upstate New York. When
Mrs. Jones arrived there, she discovered that Wicks was
about to exhibit her daughter at a church fair. The
phrenologist denied that Mrs. Jones had any claim to
Annie and refused to surrender her.

There was nothing to do but take the case to
court. In the courtroom, Wicks still maintained the
child was his. To determine to whom Annie belonged,
the judge didn't have to go to the lengths that King Sol-
omon did when he pretended he was going to divide a
child in two and give half of it to each of the two
women who claimed to be its mother. The judge simply
kept Annie in a side room during the early portion of
the hearing. Then he went out and brought her into the
courtroom.

The little bearded girl looked at the dark, solemn
chamber and the strange grownup figures sitting on the
benches. One face looked familiar.

"Mama! Mama!" she screamed. She tore herself
free from the judge's hand and ran to her mother's outstretched arms.

When the judge beckoned, Mrs. Jones carried the
little girl forward and placed her in the witness chair.

"What is your name, little girl?" the judge asked.

"Annie Jones," the child answered. Then, in re-
sponse to his questions, she told him her mother's name
and her grandfather's name. If Wicks, the phrenologist,
was still in the courtroom, he had stayed too long.

In the Sideshow

Annie and Mrs. Jones returned to the Barnum museum. Over the years other attempts were made to kidnap her, for she was a valuable property, but none succeeded. When she grew too big to be called "the Infant Esau" Barnum billed her as "the Bearded Girl" or "the Child Esau." We gain a picture of Annie—no doubt a somewhat promotional one—from a pamphlet that was sold at Barnum's "Great Moral Exhibition," as he called his show. She was about five years old at the time.

"This strangely interesting little girl," the booklet said, ". . . has sparkling black eyes, magnificent Persian lashes, an intelligent look, a lustrous head of hair growing well down on the forehead, a marvelous endowment of fine silken beard, whiskers, and mustache; while her entire person, from head to foot, is literally covered with a mass of long delicately fringed hair . . .

"Never, since the first begotten of Rebekah, more than 3,700 years ago, has there been known an instance of a mere child, and a female at that, who at the age of five years, supported such a marvelous development of mustache and side whiskers as appear upon the cheeks of this remarkable little prodigy. . . . She is otherwise . . . amiable and winning in manners, kind and affectionate in disposition, tractable and confiding in her ways, and altogether as other little girls of her age . . ."

Photographed by Mathew Brady

A photograph of Annie, taken at about this time by Mathew Brady, America's premier photographer of the Civil War era, who made so many fine portraits of Abraham Lincoln, shows Annie with a massive mustache and a beard of patchy whiskers about two inches long. She is wearing a simple taffeta plaid dress and has a ribbon in her long flowing hair. Her shoulders are exposed, as are her arms and legs; her arms appear notably hairy. The expression on her little face is a solemn, brooding one. It must have felt strange to be a pretty little girl . . . with whiskers.

By the time Annie reached her sixteenth birthday she had a silky, dark brown beard about six inches long. Otherwise she was a woman in most respects. Her voice, soft and feminine, provided a startling contrast to her masculine profile and hairy arms.

As Annie matured, her billing was updated again: "the Bearded Girl" became "the Bearded Lady" or "Esau Lady." Barnum began touring the country with the Greatest Show on Earth in those years and Annie traveled with it. When the season came to an end and the circus went into winter quarters Annie began a second season of her own. She was in great demand among the proprietors of dime museums and she would appear on their premises during the cold months. In the spring she rejoined the circus.

Two Marriages

Annie was scarcely sixteen years old when she secretly married Richard Elliott, one of the barkers with the show. (Circus people call them "talkers" or "lecturers," never "barkers.") Although her mother called it a "bad match," the marriage lasted fifteen years—until 1895, when Annie divorced Elliott. Later she married William Donovan, a wardrobe man with the Barnum show. By now Annie had a big reputation, and the couple decided she might do better on her own, so they left the circus and sailed to Europe.

Europe turned out to be as rewarding as they expected. Annie was hailed everywhere, and she made a lot of money. (Like other canny people, she invested it in real estate—in her case, in Brooklyn, where her mother had relocated.) Her tour took her as far as Saint Petersburg, Russia, where she appeared before the czar and the members of the royal family at the imperial palace.

From Russia Annie went to Germany and then to France. In Germany she was presented to the emperor, Wilhelm II, who gave her a handsome gift. In Italy she met the king and his daughter. Artists were struck by the thoughtful, spiritual look on Annie's bearded face and asked her to pose for paintings they were making of Jesus, according to her mother's recollection.

"The Charm of a Society Dame"

People who got to know Annie were impressed by the breadth of her cultural background, which she had acquired in good part by reading during the long pauses between appearances on the platform. "She possessed," said W. Buchanan Taylor, a London theater manager, "all the charm of a society dame and much more erudition. She was familiar with most of the classics and read the poets." Her accomplishments included playing the mandolin and other musical instruments.

Annie had a small hand and a shapely foot. With her beard covered up, she was an attractive woman. She concealed it when she was going about her everyday business away from the sideshow. The trick she used for this purpose was an interesting one. First she wrapped up the beard and tied it in a roll under her chin—much like the knot of hair that women used to wear on top of their heads. Then she tied a band of black cloth around her chin and fastened a heavy veil over her entire face. To passers-by she looked like a woman who had wrapped herself up to protect her nose and throat from the wind.

For several years Annie traveled about Europe, exhibiting and meeting the diademed heads of Europe. This happy, successful period came to a sudden end when Donovan, her husband, died. Annie found it impossible to continue her tour without him. The Barnum and Bailey Circus was in Europe and she got in touch with them. Barnum himself was long gone—he had passed away in 1891—but the manager cheerfully welcomed her back into the fold. She was, after all, one of the best-known bearded ladies of the age.

Annie's reunion with the circus was a joyful one. She had many old friends there. Her warmth and eagerness to help were as proverbial in the circus as her skill with her needle. Whenever she came down from her platform after a show she had a steady stream of callers, including many who wanted to chat with her and circus hands who knew they could rely on her to sew on a button or put a patch in a pair of trousers. And she enjoyed hearing herself called by her familiar name, Jonesy, once more.

Consumption

Annie had developed a bad cough. It continued to get worse, until it became so serious she was compelled to leave the circus. She went to a hospital in Paris. After six weeks her condition appeared improved and she was discharged and caught up with the circus. But at Nîmes she had a relapse—a serious one. She had to leave the show.

Annie appeared in the doorway of her mother's house in Brooklyn in May, 1902. She unwrapped the veil with which she always covered her face and beard when she was going and coming. Her mother was struck by her pallor and her thin, drawn features.

"I have consumption, Mother," she said. "I don't think I'll last longer than when the leaves start to fall."

Her words were prophetic. On October 22 she passed away. She was buried in Evergreen Cemetery in Brooklyn.

Few people have spent as much of their lives in show business as Annie Jones did. She was thirty-seven years old when she died—and she had been summoned to New York City and fame by Barnum when she was just a nine-month-old in her cradle.

12

France's Most Celebrated Bearded Lady

The name of Annie Jones lingers on only in the memory of a handful of sideshow buffs. But the case is far different with another bearded lady, Clementine Delait. A few years ago, at her birthplace, Thaon-les-Vosges, a small town in Lorraine, in northeastern France, a museum was opened in her honor. She is considered France's most celebrated bearded lady.

Clementine Delait was born in 1865, the same year as Annie Jones. History gives us no inkling that she ever considered going into show business as a young person. She was more interested in following the normal life of a woman, for she showed a beardless (shaven) face to the world. In due time she married M. Delait, who kept a café in the town. In between fulfilling her duties as a responsible wife and mother and earning a reputation as a fine needlewoman, she helped her husband at the bar of the café.

On a spring holiday, M. and Mme. Delait went to Nancy, a big city not far away. There they joined the happy crowds at a fair.

A sideshow caught their eye and the Delaits went in. They were duly impressed by the demonstrations of strength by the strong man and the strangeness of the "cannibals" from Africa. When they moved on to the next performer, at first there did not seem to be anything exceptional about her. Then Mme. Delait stopped suddenly in her tracks and gasped.

There, but for the grace of her razor, stood Mme. Delait herself!

The *artiste* came forward so the visitors could get a better look at her whiskers. After a careful examination, Mme. Delait concluded they were rather sparse. Why, if she herself were to stop having the barber apply his razor to her face. . . .

The following evening the café was crowded with patrons who kept talking of the big event of the month, the fair at Nancy. Many of them had been there. They were full of the wonders of the sideshow, and especially of the bearded lady. She was truly one of nature's prodigies, they said. Of course, everyone had seen old women with slight mustaches or a few hairs on their chins. But a young woman with a full beard!

Mme. Delait was serving at the bar.

"I don't think her beard was so full. As a matter of fact, it was rather on the skimpy side."

"Ah, no, Madame. It was extraordinary. A long beard—why, it reached almost to the lady's chest."

"Nonsense!" Mme. Delait cried. "It wasn't a real beard at all. Why, I could raise a better beard myself . . . if I wanted to."

"Yes, she could," her husband chimed in.

A Historic Wager

The customers sitting at the tables came up to join the discussion at the bar. The argument became increasingly heated. Some, who knew that Mme. Delait shaved, offered to bet that she could grow a more impressive beard than the one on the woman in the sideshow. Others swore that the café proprietor's wife could never produce a hairy growth that would bear comparison.

Mme. Delait was caught up in the excitement of the argument. She whispered to her husband. He nodded.

"I'm willing to bet five hundred francs that I can raise a better beard than that . . . that . . . impostor," she said.

"Taken!" cried one of the men at the bar. The others cheered. Bets and counterbets were made all over the small café.

"A Faultless Chestnut in Color"

Mme. Delait watched the stubble growing on her cheeks. Day by day it became longer. "I saw my beard filling out," she reminisced afterward. "I was filled with pride and joy. The hairs were a faultless chestnut in color, just like the hair on my head. They were soft and on the wavy side."

Each night the habitués of the Café Delait watched the whiskers increasing on madame's face. They speculated on their length. They asked madame the latest measurement. When she told them, those who had wagered against her declared she was exaggerating.

One evening, however, madame appeared at the café and the dispute could continue no more. She had a full-fledged beard. No one could question that it was longer than that of the bearded woman at the fair. By acclamation, she was declared the winner of the bet.

And Still the Wonder Grew

For days the town buzzed with the news that Delait's spouse had sprouted a good-sized beard which put that of many a man to scorn. Word spread to the neighboring towns. People from all over the *département* came to see if the story they had heard about the bearded lady was true. They came from as far as Nancy . . . Paris . . . Bordeaux . . . Lyons . . . Marseille.

The facts were incontrovertible, and madame

speedily became a celebrity. If she ever thought of returning to her former shorn state the hordes of new patrons that the beard brought to her husband's café would have dissuaded her. Business was booming as never before. Delait had to hire extra help. And everyone who came into the café insisted on seeing and speaking to madame.

What the Doctor Found

Mme. Delait took pride in her new role as a bearded lady. In contrast to some of the other women encountered in these pages, she displayed her hairy appendage without shyness or reserve. She toyed with it not the way a man does, but in a charming, coquettish manner, when talking to customers.

To satisfy skeptics that she was everything she was reported to be, Mme. Delait visited an eminent physician, who gave her a physical examination and declared that she was a normal woman in every respect but the obvious one. She was photographed, and her picture was circulated through the country. The picture showed her with her hair pinned up elegantly, her thick beard extending downward over a capacious bosom. Her image engraved itself on many a Frenchman's heart. And at least one—a resident of the town—had it tattooed on his chest.

Café of the Bearded Lady

Delait was making a small fortune with the increased business. Recognizing that he owed his rise in the world to his wife, he changed the name of his café from the Café Delait to what everyone was already calling it—Café de la femme à barbe ("Café of the Bearded Lady").

In 1926 Delait passed away. No longer bound to Thaon, Mme. Delait began to travel, with her daughter as a companion, and to exhibit. She became a popular figure on the stages of Paris and London. Immigration control officials, busy stamping passports, must have looked up with surprise when they saw that hers, under "Distinguishing Characteristics," said "Has a beard"—and found that it was true.

Clementine Delait's claim to fame was her whiskers, and she took pride in them. Before she died, in 1939, she asked that the words "The Bearded Lady of Thaon" be incised on her tombstone. Thirty years later Thaon-les-Vosges paid her full honors by dedicating a museum to its most famous daughter.

13

Some Modern Bearded Ladies

Ringling Brothers' Lady Olga

A bearded lady who is well remembered by frequenters of circuses and dime museums was Lady Olga. Olga sported a thick growth of whiskers that hung down her chest thirteen and a half inches. It was not the longest female beard in history—some bearded ladies have claimed that their beards grew down to their knees when they stopped trimming them during an illness—but it was unquestionably a "meal ticket," as she called it. Every night, before turning in, Olga used to twist and plait her beard so it would curl more luxuriantly. She also had a large mustache whose ends hung mournfully downward. Except for her unusual hairy growth, Olga's appearance was quite feminine and her manner ladylike, in keeping with her professional name.

In her later years, after her hair turned gray, Olga let her beard grow shaggy and go untrimmed. But in her salad days, during the Gaslight Era and later, when there was a cult of the beard even more than there is today, she had her whiskers carefully barbered in the most fashionable modes.

Few sideshow personalities have appeared before the public as long as Lady Olga. She was first exhibited when she was four years old. Sixty-five years later she was still going strong. In between, she had appeared with Ringling Brothers, Barnum and Bailey, Hagenbeck-Wallace, Forepaugh-Sells, Royal American Shows, and many others. In 1932 she acted in Tod Browning's film *Freaks,* where she naturally played the role of the bearded lady.

In April, 1938, Ringling Brothers opened in New York. Olga, then in her sixth year with them, was asked if she would join the Easter Parade on Fifth Avenue.

"I most certainly will not parade on Fifth Avenue," she replied. She stroked her beard. "Somebody might mistake me for a Supreme Court judge." She reflected for a moment. "But I might give my beard some extra curling for Easter."

That was Olga's last year with the circus. The union was conducting a campaign to organize Ringling Brothers, and Olga, a rock-ribbed conservative, was opposed to unions. When the circus was struck in Scranton, Pennsylvania, she was greatly upset and decided it was time for her and Ringling to part. Besides, she was approaching her seventieth birthday. For years the circus kept asking her to return, but she always turned a deaf ear to their offers.

Olga on the Platform

Olga settled down in New York City. There she appeared from time to time at Hubert's Museum, once a landmark on West Forty-second Street, and, during the summer, also at a dime museum in Coney Island.

On the sideshow platform Lady Olga, with her long gray beard, was a commanding presence. She stood five feet five inches high and exuded a quiet, almost aristocratic dignity in her black gown. A large Spanish comb sparkled in her bobbed gray hair. The "professor," as the sideshow barker is sometimes called, would invite the audience to ask her questions during her brief appearances.

"How long have you had a beard?" a curious spectator would ask.

"When I was born, I had down all over my cheeks and my chin. By the time I was two years old I had a beard." Her voice was deep and solemn and she spoke with a southern drawl.

"Do any other women in your family have beards?"

"No. I had three sisters but I'm the only one with a beard."

When a member of the "tip"—the carnival word for audience—dared to ask her about her personal life, she would ignore him. Her private life was strictly private. If someone persisted with personal questions, he would learn that Olga, for all her ladylike bearing, had a tongue second to none in sharpness.

A Troubled Childhood

Lady Olga was born Jane Barnell in Wilmington, North Carolina, in 1871. Her father, George Barnell, a Jew from Russia, was a repairer of wagons by trade. Her mother was part Irish, part Indian. From the moment she was born, Jane, with her down-covered face, was recognized as an oddity.

As in other cases we have seen, the down showed no signs of disappearing. By the time Jane reached her second birthday she already possessed the makings of a beard. Her mother, who was not an educated woman, was sure someone had put a curse on the child. Jane's father was less troubled by her appearance and treated her with greater affection than her mother did.

A Performer at Four

Jane was just a tot when her father had to go out of town on business. He stayed away a long time. In the interim a circus pulled in to Wilmington. It had only six wagons, drawn by oxen, but it traveled under the ornate name of the Great Orient Family Circus. Jane's mother took the child to the circus—and came home without her.

The family that ran the circus had dark skins. Jane thought they were foreigners. Everyone had a part in the show. The sons did tricks on the tight rope; the daughters entertained the public with dances; the mother was a snake charmer. But they didn't have a bearded lady—or bearded girl—and so they took Jane under their wing and treated her with affection.

When Jane's father got home from his business trip she had been gone for weeks. Frantic, he appealed to the police for help in finding his missing daughter, and North Carolina and the surrounding states were scoured for her. But Jane and the Great Orient Family Circus had vanished.

In an Orphanage

In one of the large cities of the South the circus troupe sold their wagons and embarked for Europe. Jane, starlet of the ensemble, was taken along. On the Continent the troupe signed up with a circus and went on tour. While the circus was appearing in Berlin— Jane was about five at the time—she came down with a serious illness. The Great Orient Family, despairing for her life, took her to a hospital. By the time she recovered they had left the city and she ended up in an orphan home.

One day the little bearded girl was summoned to the orphanage office. In one way or another her father had finally located her and he was waiting in the office. For the lonesome child there was an unforgettable reunion, and Barnell took her back to the United States. Jane did not go to live with her unloving mother again, but with her grandmother, on a farm in North Carolina. Here she fed the chickens and did all the other chores required of a farm girl. When she reached the age at which boys begin to shave, she did, too. But her beard required a great deal more shaving than theirs.

The Circus Calls

A neighbor of Jane's grandmother was a farmer named William Heckler. For part of the year Heckler was a professional strong man with a circus. He informed Jane that her beard was nothing to be ashamed of and that, instead of shaving it off, she could allow it to grow and cash in on it.

Life on the farm was less than exciting for Jane, and Heckler's arguments carried conviction. She allowed him to introduce her to his friends in the John Robinson Circus. In 1892 she went to work for them. She was twenty-one years old.

For Jane, the circus opened up a whole new world. Color, noise, excitement surrounded her. She began to keep company with a musician who played in the band and discovered that, with the right man, a beard was no barrier to true love. The couple was married and had two children. Neither of the children lived very long, and then her husband passed away too.

For Jane, circus life lost its glitter after the death of her mate. She became restless and drifted from one circus to another. She married another circus man but the romance was ill-starred; her husband lost his life in an accident.

Jane's third marriage was not a happy one. It ended in divorce. But she still believed in love, and she found it a year later with Thomas O'Boyle, a circus clown. O'Boyle, some twenty years Jane's junior, worshipped her. They were married in 1931. Later he became a barker and took a job at Hubert's Dime Museum when Jane began appearing there.

In a recent letter to the author, Johnny Eck, the famous Half Boy whose story was told earlier in these pages, related some of his memories of Lady Olga. "Of all the sideshow people assembled for Tod Browning's *Freaks*," he wrote, "it was Lady Olga who was attracted to me like a magnet. No, it was not a case of love at first sight but rather an honest, warm, and affectionate feeling toward me. I admired her. I was just twenty years old and I'm sure she must have been twice my age.

"It was Lady Olga that never let me go before the cameras until she had carefully combed my hair, straightened my tie, and given me her final blessing.... I was the only one who could command—and get—a private dressing room, other than Daisy and Violet Hilton. The rest of the group settled in one large building with long benches and tables ... Talcum powder hung in the air like a pink fog. It was Lady Olga who would tap gently at my door and say, 'Come, little John, everything is so clear now, the chickens are gone and the smoke powder has blown away.' "

Tips from a Bearded Lady

When the film *Freak*s appeared in 1932, Olga gave some tips to the public about how she kept her beard in prime condition.

"Every woman who is lucky enough to have a beard should learn how to take care of it," she declared.

"Never use too hot a curling iron on the beard. It makes the hair brittle, and destroys the fine sheen that has made the beards of the followers of the House of David famous." (The House of David is a religious sect that wears beards and gained fame for its bearded baseball team.)

"In fact, I spent a week learning the secrets of beard beauty culture from them, and took a post-graduate course, so to speak, in Moscow....

"Wash the beard in warm milk once a week. It keeps the lustre and color perfect.... Also, avoid eating Chinese noodles if you want to keep a good beard looking really nice."

No Lady Bluebeard

In her long career as a sideshow performer Olga changed her professional name several times. First she was Princess Olga. Later she altered her billing to

Madame Olga. Finally she settled on the more distinctive title of Lady Olga.

Once a showman with ideas seriously proposed that she dye her beard blue.

"Then," he said, his eyes sparkling, "we can give you a wonderful billing. We can call you 'Olga, the Lady Bluebeard.' "

For a few moments Olga forgot her customary dignity. The showman never dared to repeat his suggestion after that.

Grace Gilbert: "The Girl with the Golden Whiskers"

Old-timers still recall another famous bearded lady of the circus, Grace Gilbert. Grace was born at Kalkaska, Michigan, in 1880, the daughter of a farmer. At birth, her entire body was covered with red hair. When she was still quite young she was more than earning her keep. She was billed as the "Woolly Child" and also, inevitably, as "the Female Esau."

As Grace grew taller her beard grew longer. Eventually it was quite luxuriant. She presents a quaint picture with her heavy mustache, side whiskers, and beard, her full feminine tresses arranged attractively on top of her head.

Grace's beard, light brown, was six inches long. At one point in her career she bleached it with peroxide and her name appeared on sideshow posters as "Princess Gracie, the Girl with the Golden Whiskers."

Grace traveled with Barnum and Bailey and other circuses for many years. In the winter season, when the circus closed down, she would return to her father's farm. She was heavily built, and according to legend she was able to perform a man's work on the farm. Old circus buffs also say that when the roustabouts were erecting the sideshow tent she would take up a sledge and give them a helping hand. Yet, like other bearded ladies, she was famed for her ladylike refinement and her skill with needlework and spent much of her spare time making lace.

Most of the bearded ladies in show business get married, and Grace was no exception to the rule. Her husband was a successful Michigan farmer. She died in 1925.

Stella MacGregor

Bearded ladies are becoming scarcer in circuses and carnivals. Medical science has found ways to cure many of the conditions that cause hirsutism. But the ladies with the chin adornments can still be found. Some of them, as always, are not genuine females but men who dress up as women. Some of them are homosexuals or transvestites—men in "drag." Others have genuine beards but are hermaphrodites. But the real bearded lady—the lady who has an authentic beard yet in other respects is a normal, feminine woman—is a rare article today.

One genuine bearded lady who can still be seen when the carnival comes to town is Stella MacGregor. Mrs. MacGregor, an attractive woman who has been married two times, was traveling most recently with Colonel Jerry Lipko and his trained chimpanzee act. She has lovely brown eyes and a brown beard that she keeps trimmed to a neat, conservative length.

Mrs. MacGregor was born in Battle Creek, Michigan. She is in show business because it gives her that freedom she needs and she loves the colorful, changing life of the midway. She has tried other careers, including a military one, as a WAC. Later she studied nursing at Kalamazoo College Hospital. When nursing lost its appeal she attended the University of Michigan, where she took a master's degree. Her field of specialization was gifted children. She published some original papers on the subject, and for a while she was a teacher.

It was her beard, however, that was to be her destiny. Whatever profession she followed, the beard made problems for her. It just grew too rapidly. Almost every time she looked at it, she needed a shave. And shave it she had to, five times or more a day, just to keep up appearances.

When she worked in a hospital, for example, she was continually obliged to make up pretexts so she could slip out of a patient's room and give her cheeks and chin a quick going-over with a razor. Naturally she was acquainted with many doctors and they tried to help her overcome her condition. But no matter what quantity of female hormones they injected or prescribed, her beard kept coming back as heavy as ever.

Things weren't any better for Mrs. MacGregor when she turned to teaching. Every couple of hours or so she had to dash out to her car, plug in an electric razor, and remove the bristly stubble that kept pushing up on her face. Having a lady teacher with whiskers was a source of constant amusement to the children in her classroom.

Eventually Mrs. MacGregor decided that the strains and restrictions imposed on her by the beardless life were just too oppressive. She resolved that, for her, there was only one way out—to let her beard grow and join a sideshow. In the free-and-easy life of the circus and carnival she was at last able to be herself and find fulfillment. Neither of the men she married, however, was in show business.

There are plenty of bearded-lady stories but few can cap some of the true-life experiences this charming bearded lady relates. Like many others who don't want their chin growth to draw attention to themselves, she is likely to cover her face with a heavy veil when she goes out. Twice in banks she has been stopped by sharp-eyed guards who detected her beard and jumped to the conclusion that she was a gunman about to pull off a robbery.

Using a public lavatory has also posed special problems for Mrs. MacGregor. Once a man waiting for his wife, who was in the ladies' room, noticed that a bearded figure in a dress was about to push in the door and he flung himself at the intruder. It must have come as a considerable shock to him to learn that although the beard was one a man could have been proud of, its owner had every right to be on the premises.

14

The Hairy, Hairy People

There are entire races of people that are hairier than others. The Ainus of Hokkaido, in northern Japan, and the aborigines of Australia provide notable examples. At different times and places individuals have also turned up whose bodies are covered with an extraordinary growth of hair. Often their faces are so overgrown they're compared to terriers, poodles, or other animals. In circuses and carnivals they've traveled under such names as "the Dog-Faced Boy" or "the Lion-Faced Man." German scholars, who have studied these oddities intensively, call them *Haarmenschen* ("hairy people"). In the dim past, it's possible that people with abnormally hairy faces gave rise to legends of human beings who could turn themselves into wolves and other kinds of beasts.

At Castle Ambras, near Innsbruck, in the Austrian Tyrol, there is a painting made in the 1500s that depicts a family of hairy people. The father is standing on one side, the mother is seated on the other, and in between are the couple's two children. Nothing is especially unusual about the mother's appearance; she's a normal-looking, neatly groomed, well-dressed lady. The face of the father, however, including his forehead, is covered with hair. The children look like miniature versions of their father.

Barbara Ursler

A celebrated hairy person who lived about a hundred years later was Barbara Ursler of Augsburg, Germany. Several contemporary pictures of her have survived. In them we see Barbara's entire face covered with a dense growth of hair.

Georg Seger of Nuremberg has left a description of Barbara. "She had then been married for over a year and was childless," he noted. "Her whole body and face were covered with blond, soft curling hair and she had a thick beard that reached to her waist. Long blond locks grew from her ears."

Barbara was married to a man named Vaubeck. According to some accounts, he had used the wedding ring as a means of getting control over the hairy lady so he could put her on exhibition—a story we encounter repeatedly with bearded women. Vaubeck traveled as far as England with his wife and is said to have found his career as a showman highly profitable.

Already the Very Special People were being trained not just to appear as curiosities before the public but to provide entertainment for it as well. In one old woodcut, Barbara is shown playing a stringed instrument, like a zither.

For three generations a family in Siam (or Burma) produced hairy people, who became objects of interest after they attracted notice early in the nineteenth century. The "Sacred Hairy Family of Burma" was exhibited in the United States long afterward. It is possible that Krao, who was a familiar sight in circus sideshows a generation ago, was a relative of this family.

Krao: "Darwin's Missing Link"

Krao (See photo insert) was first exhibited in Europe in the early 1880s, after being brought from Siam. She was then about six years old. Coming under the management of Farini, a well-known London showman, she was later taken to the United States.

H. Kaulitz-Jarlow, a corresponding member of the Institution Ethnographique, has provided a "scientific" description of Krao at age six. It was the heyday of the controversy over Charles Darwin's theory that man was descended from ape-like creatures (Darwin never said man was descended from apes themselves) and his followers were constantly hoping to turn up a creature intermediate between man and the apes. To some, Krao appeared to be just what they were looking for.

In his description, Kaulitz-Jarlow highlighted those features of Krao that he considered particularly simian. "Thick, jet-black smooth hair covers her head and reaches far down her back," he said. "It forms a virtual mane on the back of the neck. Her eyes are shadowed by wide, silky, shiny eyebrows. Her pupils are sparkling and dark black." Hair, he observed, covered her body from the top of her head to her feet. He went on to point out in detail how closely her facial structure resembled that of the gorilla.

Little Krao's character, this writer reported, was amiable; she had an easily satisfied, cheerful disposition. She liked to play and was grateful when attention was paid to her. "If she is annoyed," he said, "her wild nature at once comes to the fore; she throws herself to the ground, screams, kicks, and gives vent to her anger by pulling her hair in a very peculiar way." Presumably these were also supposed to be apelike characteristics. In America, Gould and Pyle, two well-known physicians and scholars of the time, reported in their *Anomalies and Curiosities of Medicine* that Krao had extraordinarily prehensile (grasping) powers of the feet and lips.

Krao, in spite of these curious descriptions, was simply one of the hairy people. A picture of her at sixteen shows her with long hair, hairy legs and arms, and a mustache and beard. But, aside from these peculiarities, she was unquestionably a human being and unquestionably a woman. A well-read person who spoke several languages, Krao was one of the stars of the Ringling Brothers and Barnum & Bailey Circus. She died in New York on April 16, 1926, at the age of forty-nine.

Jo-Jo the Dog-Faced Boy

In 1884 Barnum brought to the United States another of the hairy people. This was Fedor Jeftichew, known as "the Russian Dog-Faced Boy." (See photo insert.) He was sixteen years old. Fedor's father, Adrien or Andrian, a Russian peasant, was also covered with hair, especially on his face, and was often compared to a poodle. He was exhibited in the major cities of Europe as *l'homme-chien* ("the man dog").

For their promotional literature Barnum's publicity men concocted a romantic tale of Fedor's origin calculated to intrigue even the least imaginative. Thirteen years earlier, the story ran, Fedor had been found living with his father in the forests of Kostroma, in central Russia. A hunter had tracked them to their cave. The father and son subsisted upon wild berries and small game, which was killed with stones and clubs. Returning to his village, the hunter gathered a party, returned to the cave, and succeeded in capturing the wild pair.

"The father was extremely savage," Barnum's booklet declared, "and resisted capture in every way in his power.... The father ... could not be civilized, and as the child was very small, nothing could be discovered about the mother's descent."

Other accounts suggest that the boy was born in Saint Petersburg and toured with his father until the elder Jeftichew passed away at the age of fifty-nine. They had been studied by Rudolf Virchow, the German scientist. After noting that hypertrichosis tended to run in families, Virchow observed that "if someone

were to breed these people he could develop a race
which would present an entirely different appearance
from the rest of mankind."

Fedor, or Jo-Jo as he was professionally known,
resembled his father quite closely. An amiable young
person, when he appeared in New York starting in
1884, he was attractively costumed in a uniform like
that of the Russian cavalry of the time, and held
himself in an erect military manner. From his neck up,
of course, he looked less like a cavalryman and more
like the Beast in the tale of Beauty and the Beast. Here
is how a reporter of the New York *Herald Tribune*
(October 13, 1884) described him:

"Jo-Jo's appearance certainly bears a strong resemblance to that of a Skye terrier. His face is
completely covered by a thick growth of silky yellow
hair, which is specially abundant on each side of his
nose. Here there are two little tufts, like a terrier's whiskers, while his mild, hazel eyes have a remarkably canine expression. . . . The luxuriance of his hair offset
by the scarcity of his teeth. Of these he has only four,
two in the upper jaw and two in the lower. Although
the hair is most abundant on his face, his whole body is
covered with a scattered growth."

Jo-Jo spoke Russian and German tolerably well
and already knew a few words of English when he arrived in the United States. (Later he learned to speak
English as fluently as Russian.) His manager made
much of his resemblance to a dog and said that when
Jo-Jo was angry he snapped and barked. In public Jo-
Jo would oblige by snapping or growling, but his behav-
ior suggested more the astute playfulness of a born performer or one who had been well coached, rather than
any canine tendencies. Certainly the enjoyment with
which he autographed his picture in flowing letters was
thoroughly human.

Jo-Jo was billed as a "ward" of the Russian Government and he traveled in the company of a Russian
couple. For many years he was a familiar and popular
figure in the circus.

Lionel the Lion-Faced Man

Lionel the Lion-Faced Man, who was widely exhibited in Europe and America, was possibly the hairiest man in history. A great growth of shaggy hair six inches long almost blanketed his head. His nose, forehead, cheeks, and ears were all covered. His gray-green eyes peered out with seeming ferocity through the bewildering matting of hair. He possessed a considerable mane, so that the comparison to a lion was inevitable.

Lionel's real name was Stephan Bibrowsky, and he was born in Wilezagora, Poland in 1890. He was the fourth of six children, and his parents were normal. His mother hadn't been frightened by a lion shortly before he was born, nor, for that matter, had she ever left her native village. But circus publicity was later to declare the opposite—that she had seen his father torn to pieces by a lion, and the sight marked the unborn child in her womb.

A German impresario named Meyer discovered Lionel when he was four years old and took him to Germany. He was soon a celebrity throughout Europe. Brought to America in 1901, for five years Lionel was a featured attraction with Barnum and Bailey. Then he returned to Germany.

When Lionel was about sixteen he was playing in the Passage-Panoptikum in Berlin, where human oddities were exhibited and accepted an invitation to allow himself to be studied by members of the Berlin Society for Anthropology, Ethnology, and Prehistory.

According to a report prepared by one of the society's members, Von Luschan, Lionel's head was so covered with hair that not even a tiny patch of skin was visible. He did not have a beard, head hair, eyebrows, or even eyelashes in the ordinary sense; his head was blanketed with hair, but hair that was incredibly thick and had grown to a remarkable length. Tiny hairs grew by the hundreds out of his nostrils and ear openings, a common finding in people of this type.

Lionel had only two teeth at the time, one in the

upper jaw and one in the lower. Earlier he had possessed two more, but these he had lost. Jo-Jo the Dog-Faced Boy had also possessed only four teeth and Julia Pastrana, according to some reports, also had an abnormally low number of teeth. This is another common characteristic of the hairy people. Dentists call the condition "partial anodontia." It often occurs in connection with other abnormalities.

Abnormally hairy persons like Lionel or Jo-Jo are extremely rare. It was Von Luschan's considered opinion that only one is born in about every billion births (*Zeitschrift für Ethnologie,* May, 1907).

Lionel continued to exhibit himself extensively in Europe. He came back to the United States in 1923. One place where he appeared was Coney Island. Millions of Americans saw him there. He had mastered a wide variety of gymnastic skills and developed his physique to a remarkable degree. He weighed about 156 pounds and stood five feet seven inches. Traveling in different countries, he had become fluent in five languages.

A favorite question of any audience, looking at Lionel's astonishing hair-covered face, was this one: "Couldn't you shave the hair off your face and look like the rest of us?"

Lionel's reply, in good colloquial English, was fairly predictable. "Of course—but why should I punch a meal ticket full of holes?"

Lionel was one of the higher-paid Very Special People of his time. It was reported that he earned five hundred dollars a week. He never married. In 1931 American newspapers said he had died in a hospital in Berlin.

15

The Long-Haired Ones

Louis Goulon and His Beard

Bearded ladies have always had to face competition from members of the opposite sex. In that competition the ladies have not stood much of a chance, for men are favored by nature in their chin adornments. Although male beards are making a comeback today, rarely are any seen that come close to matching the records of a few generations or a few decades ago.

A man named Louis Goulon, who was an iron worker at Montluçon, in central France, was reported on good authority to have a beard eight feet three inches long. Goulon was already shaving seriously at age twelve, but his mustache and side-whiskers grew so rapidly it was impossible for him to keep them under control. By the time he was fourteen he had a beard over a foot long, covering his chest. It had tripled its length when he reached his twentieth birthday. Nor had it stopped lengthening when he was in his sixties. In a photograph taken toward the end of the last century, he was shown holding his beard with one hand to keep it from sweeping the floor. Seemingly, the beard wagged the man and not vice versa.

Goulon never exhibited his beard in public, although he was often urged to. A person who did, however, was Adam Kerpfen of Chicago. In the 1870s Kerpfen toured Europe. His beard had then reached a length of nine feet six inches.

Longest Beard on Record

But these monumental beards of yesterday seem small by comparison to what may be the longest one on record. This beard is preserved at the Smithsonian Institution in Washington, D.C. It belonged to Norwegian-born Hans Langseth, who lived in the United States during the last fifteen years of his life. When Langseth passed away in 1927, his beard had reached the unprecedented length of seventeen feet six inches!

The Longest Mustache

Credit for growing the longest mustache in history belongs to a resident of Uttar Pradesh, India, named Masuriya Din. In 1962 Din's mustache measured fully eight feet six inches long. When held up at each end, it looked like a length of rope attached to his head, except that it was considerably thicker close to his face.

Long Hair

If men have excelled in the long-beard and long-mustache department, you might expect women to win the laurels for the longest growths of head hair. A number of ladies were celebrated during the 1890s and the early decades of this century for their massive tresses before the bobbed-hair style took over. One of these women was a Miss Jane Owens, whose lengthy locks would have been capable of keeping her warm if she had worn only them and nothing else. They measured eight feet three inches.

The Seven Sutherland Sisters

The seven Sutherland Sisters, all of whom had hair that reached to the ground, enjoyed an international reputation for many years. Women, especially, found these long-haired beauties fascinating. The sisters had excellent voices and they used to give concerts that were well attended. But their hair was their main attraction. In the 1880s they toured with Barnum and Bailey, billed as "The Longest Hair in the World." The combined length of their tresses was said to be thirty-six feet ten inches. (It is exceptional to find hair longer than three feet in a woman.)

The seven sisters—Sarah, Isabella, Naomi, Mary, Grace, Dora, and Victoria—hailed from Lockport, New York, where their father had a farm. They lived in a simple long cabin and helped with the farm chores till their long hair attracted vaudeville and circus impresarios to their door. They were already famous when it was suggested that a hair tonic named after them and endorsed by them could be a great success.

A company was set up to manufacture the tonic. A photograph of the seven young women, all decorously seated, with their exquisite hair running down to the floor, became the registered trade mark of the Seven Sutherland Sisters' Hair Grower and Scalp Cleaner. Demand for the tonic kept growing and in a few years the sisters' earnings amounted to a million dollars.

The seven ladies did not give up their personal appearances for a while. In the 1890s they built a great home where their father's small log cabin had stood. It was an elaborate rococo structure with verandas and turrets. They also built a large mausoleum.

Only two of the sisters married. The first of the seven died in 1895. Over the years, demand for the tonic began to dwindle. Extravagance ate up most of the sisters' fortune. The last of the Sutherland sisters, Grace, passed away in 1946. The mausoleum was so crowded by then that there was no room for her and she was buried in an unmarked grave in the family plot.

Hair Twenty-Six Feet Long

Although great attention focused on the Sutherland Sisters, their hair was not much longer than seven feet or so. In 1949, according to the *Toronto Morning Star,* in a monastery in India, a man was found whose hair was an astonishing twenty-six feet long. He was a swami or Hindu religious teacher named Pandarasannadhi.

Woman with a Mane

A most unusual case of hairiness was displayed by Bella Carter, an attractive young American woman. Bella was exhibited in the United States and Europe around the turn of the century as "the Lady with a Mane." Out of her back, between her shoulders, grew a reddish-blond mane. It was over a foot and a half long and was as soft as the hair on the young lady's head, which was a dark blond. She wore a gown with a low back to afford a clear view of this unusual phenomenon. Presumably the mane grew out of a large mole.

PART 4

THE LITTLE PEOPLE

16

The Amazing Career of General Tom Thumb

Charles Sherwood Stratton, better known as General Tom Thumb, was the most famous midget in history. (See photo insert.) He brought delight to twenty million people, young and old, around the world. He sang, danced, and charmed his way into the hearts of the most important personages of his day—including Queen Victoria, King Louis Philippe of France, Queen Isabella of Spain, the Duke of Wellington, Abraham Lincoln, and a host of others. In the process the little man accumulated a fortune that enabled him to indulge a passion for full-blooded racehorses and yachts.

Tom Thumb was made by P. T. Barnum, who figures so large in this book. But it can almost as accurately be said that Tom Thumb made P. T. Barnum.

When Barnum discovered Tom Thumb, the showman had already built a reputation by exhibiting a curious assortment of oddities. One of the most notable of these was Joice Heth, an old black woman, whom he presented to the public in 1835 as George Washington's nurse. She was then said to be 161 years old and

Barnum had the papers to prove it. After her death, he released her body for an autopsy. Unfortunately, it revealed that she was not over eighty.

Another exhibit that lured hordes of people through the doors of Barnum's American Museum at Ann Street and Broadway in Manhattan was the Fejee Mermaid. Naturalists said it was a fake, but the public gazed at it in goggle-eyed belief. This blackened, monstrous figure had an agonized expression on its face. To skeptics it seemed to consist of the upper half of a monkey joined to the bottom half of a large fish.

But the success of these strange exhibits, although considerable, was small compared to the reception accorded General Tom Thumb. Handsome, lively, and talented, the tiny man—he was just a young boy at the start—brought millions of dollars into Barnum's coffers.

Barnum Finds Tom Thumb

Barnum was thirty-two years old when he discovered Tom Thumb. In November, 1842, the showman spent a night at Bridgeport, Connecticut, with his brother, Philo T. Barnum, who managed the Franklin Hotel. Barnum, always on the lookout for a new oddity for his American Museum, which he had then owned about a year, had heard about a remarkably tiny midget in the town, and asked his brother to bring him to the hotel.

Tom Thumb, when Barnum first set eyes on him, was five years old. "He weighed less than sixteen pounds . . . ," the showman recalled later, "but he was a perfectly formed, bright-eyed little fellow, with light hair and ruddy cheeks and he enjoyed the best of health. He was exceedingly bashful, but after some coaxing he was induced to talk to me, and he told me that he was the son of Sherwood E. Stratton, and that his own name was Charles S. Stratton."

The Baby Stops Growing

Charles Sherwood Stratton had been born in Bridgeport on January 4, 1838, the son of a carpenter.

Oddly enough, he was a big baby: he weighed nine pounds two ounces at birth. For a while he continued to develop at a normal rate. At five months he weighed fifteen pounds two ounces and was two feet one inch tall. Then his parents noticed that he did not seem to be growing anymore. At the end of a year his weight was exactly the same and so was his height. When the distracted Strattons showed Charlie to the doctor, he could offer them little hope that the child would ever grow to normal height.

Nor did he. When Charlie, at age five, was introduced to Barnum, the boy had not grown an inch. Apart from his small size, however, he was a completely normal child. Barnum, with his showman's eye, at once saw the tiny boy's potential, and he approached the parents. He said that he wanted to hire Charlie as an experiment for four weeks at three dollars a week, to appear at his American Museum. All travel expenses and board for the boy and his mother would be paid by Barnum.

Barnum's American Museum

Mrs. Stratton and her son arrived in New York on Thanksgiving Day. Barnum's American Museum was located in what is downtown Manhattan today, but then it was the heart of the city. Nearby were City Hall, Delmonico's elegant restaurant, and the Astor House. The museum, five stories high, was decorated on the outside with banners, posters, and paintings of animals.

To Mrs. Stratton's astonishment, Barnum's handbills were advertising her son as "General Tom Thumb, a dwarf eleven years of age, just arrived from England." The showman had craftily added six years to the boy's age. He had decided that if he revealed the child's real age, some people might object that it was too early to tell he was actually a dwarf. For most of Charlie's life he was to be represented as being six years older. (The error is still perpetuated in some books.)

The choice of the name Tom Thumb was pure inspiration. The original Tom Thumb, well known from nursery tales, was a "doughty knight" of King Arthur's court who stood an inch high, rode on a mouse instead of a horse, and fought battles with cats and spiders. Placing the imposing rank of general before the name served to make it even more comical.

An Apt Pupil

Mrs. Stratton and little Charlie were lodged with Barnum's family next door to the American Museum. Barnum snatched every free moment he could find to prepare his tiny protégé for his big role in the museum's show. He taught him songs and jokes, and how to pose and strut. The child, thrilled by the attention he was receiving and the colorful costumes Barnum provided for him, was indefatigable, and the pair worked together day and night. "I was very successful," Barnum commented, "for he was an apt pupil with a great deal of native talent and a keen sense of the ludicrous. He made rapid progress in preparing himself for such performances as I wished him to undertake and he became very much attached to his teacher."

Before General Tom Thumb appeared on the stage, Barnum, who appreciated the value of publicity, made the rounds of newspaper editors' offices with the midget on his shoulder. The tiny boy, no bigger than a doll, was deposited on their desks, where he recited, danced, and sang to his heart's content and to the vast amusement of the newsmen. James Gordon Bennett of the *Herald* described him as a "comic little gentleman ... certainly the smallest specimen of a man we have ever seen."

Tom Thumb Performs

The little general's "levees" or performances at the American Museum were an instant success. Barnum, an incorrigible punster, probably wrote many of Tom Thumb's lines. Occasionally he appeared on the stage with the boy.

"I am only a Thumb," the general would say, "but

a good hand in a general way at amusing you, for though a mite, I am mighty." When Barnum, in order to show how much tinier the general was than a small child, asked for a little boy to come up on the stage for a moment, the general said, "I would rather have a little miss."

A little girl was brought up from the audience. Seated next to the twenty-five-inch-tall Tom Thumb, she almost looked like a giantess by comparison. Then Barnum asked him:

"Well, General, how do you progress with your courtship?"

"First rate, sir," Tom Thumb replied.

"Is the little miss in any wise bashful?"

"A little, sir."

"Well, you must endeavor to encourage her as well as you can."

"I'll try, sir."

And with that the general reached his little face upward and kissed the girl, while Barnum's lecture hall rang with laughter and applause.

A Celebrity Overnight

New Yorkers and their cousins from the country flocked to see Barnum's new star. One visitor to whom we owe an interesting word picture of the midget was Philip Hone, former mayor of New York.

"General Tom Thumb (as they call him)," wrote Hone in his diary on July 12, 1843, "is a handsome, well-proportioned little gentleman, lively, agreeable, sprightly, and talkative, with no deficiency of intellect. . . . His hand is about the size of a half dollar, and his foot three inches in length. In walking alongside of him, the top of his head did not reach above my knee. When I entered the room he came up to me, offered his hand, and said, 'How d'ye do, Mr. Hone?', his keeper having apprised him who I was."

Tom Thumb was the answer to a showman's prayer. His charm, his natural talent as a performer, his quick wit, and, above all, his diminutive size, made him a celebrity almost overnight.

The boy's contract soon ran out and Barnum reengaged him at seven dollars a week for a year. The Strattons were pleased—but not nearly as much as Barnum, who realized he had found a gold mine in the boy. Before the year was over he voluntarily raised the little general's salary to twenty-five dollars a week. Tom Thumb was sent on a tour and soon his fame had spread up and down the East Coast.

Farewell to America

With Tom Thumb's help Barnum had established his museum on a very solid basis. He had plenty of money in his pocket, and his adventurous spirit was eager for a new challenge. He had made the midget a popular figure in America. Why shouldn't it be possible to take him to the Old World and exhibit him to the millions there with equal success?

With Mr. and Mrs. Stratton (Charlie's father had agreed to accompany the party and sell tickets for his son's performances), a tutor, and a naturalist who worked at the museum, Barnum prepared to sail for England. When bad weather delayed the departure, Barnum, never one to neglect an opportunity, advertised that the public had a last chance to see the general. The eager crowds doubled. On January 19, 1844, Tom Thumb completed his last performance to a packed house only an hour before his ship was due to sail. Thousands of admirers crowded the dock to wave goodbye to their little favorite. As the vessel swung seaward the strains of "Home, Sweet Home," played by the municipal brass band, swelled on the breeze.

Concealed in a Shawl

In nineteen days Tom Thumb and his entourage arrived in Liverpool. Word of his coming had reached the city, and a crowd was waiting to catch a glimpse of him. Barnum was unwilling to let the boy be seen by anyone who had not paid for the privilege. Tom Thumb was carried from the vessel in his mother's arms, concealed in a shawl.

Disappointment

Barnum's first contact with English show business was a bleak disappointment. The proprietor of a Liverpool waxworks offered him ten dollars a week for the combined services of Tom Thumb and himself. Barnum declined the offer.

Next, an English gentleman told Barnum that the usual price for seeing giants and midgets in England was one penny. The standard admission charge at the American Museum was twenty-five cents. Barnum began to feel he had made a serious mistake in coming to England.

But the American was determined to succeed. "Never shall the price be less than one shilling sterling," he declared, "and some of the nobility and gentry of England will yet pay gold to see General Tom Thumb."

Barnum had hoped to present Tom Thumb to the young queen, Victoria, at Buckingham Palace in London within a week of his arrival. The English had a profound respect for royalty, he reasoned, and once the midget had been received by the queen all of London would be lining up to see him. But there had been a death in the royal family; any kind of entertainment at the palace was out of the question. So a hall was rented in Liverpool and Tom Thumb was presented in the roles that had brought him fame in America. The English found him irresistible, and when an offer of an engagement in London came, Barnum accepted.

Tom Thumb in London

In the English capital Tom Thumb scored less than a triumph. His contract soon ran out, but Barnum declined to renew it, confident that he could do better on his own.

Barnum had planned a strategy for the conquest of England. His first step was to rent a mansion in the fashionable West End and send letters of invitation to the nobility and to leading editors to call and meet the general. Before long, carriages marked with crests were lined up outside the mansion. Barnum and the general dined at the home of Edward Everett, the American ambassador. Delighted with Tom Thumb, the Everetts gave him many presents, and the ambassador promised to use his influence to have him presented to Queen Victoria.

A few evenings later the Baroness Rothschild, wife of the richest banker in the world, sent her carriage for Barnum and his protégé. At her mansion they were ushered up a broad flight of marble stairs, to find a party of at least twenty ladies and gentlemen waiting with the baroness. For two hours Tom Thumb kept the company in stitches. As the Americans were leaving, a well-filled purse was slipped into Barnum's hand. In his own words "The golden shower had begun to fall."

Buckingham Palace

The time now seemed ripe to present the general to the public. Engaging a room at the Egyptian Hall in Piccadilly, Barnum launched his advertising campaign. The public, which had been hearing about the midget's popularity with the aristocracy, rushed to see him. Tom Thumb played to one crowded house after another.

Some days later an elegantly uniformed officer of the Life Guards knocked at Barnum's door. Into his hand he delivered a note inviting Barnum and General Tom Thumb to appear at Buckingham Palace.

On the appointed evening, the two Americans arrived at the palace dressed for the occasion. They made a quaint pair, the six-foot-two showman and his tiny friend, dressed in their fancy court suits with knee breeches, white hose, and pumps. The Lord in Waiting gave Barnum a quick course in court etiquette. He was forbidden to address the queen directly; he could speak to her only through the Lord in Waiting. On leaving the

royal presence, the visitors were to back out, always
keeping their faces toward Her Majesty.

The Little General and the Queen

In the great picture gallery of the palace, the two
visitors found twenty or thirty members of the nobility
waiting expectantly. With Queen Victoria were her con-
sort, Prince Albert, and the Duchess of Kent. The party
was thrilled at the sight of the tiny creature striding
toward them. He looked, as Barnum put it, "like a wax
doll gifted with the power of locomotion." When he was
close enough, he made a deep bow. "Good evening,
ladies and gentlemen," he exclaimed in his high little
voice. The gathering burst into laughter.

Taking Tom Thumb by the hand, the queen led
him around the gallery. She was very curious about
Tom Thumb and plied him with questions. The boy's
replies kept the company laughing constantly. He told
the queen that her picture gallery was "first rate" and
he asked if he could see the Prince of Wales. Victoria
told him her son was already in bed, but the general
could see him another time. Then the midget gave a
performance of his best imitations, songs, and dances.
The company was ecstatic. For an hour he chatted with
Prince Albert and the lords and ladies.

Encounter with the Royal Poodle

Barnum had speedily abandoned the cumbersome
ritual for addressing the queen. When the time came to
depart, however, he resolved to follow the example of
the Lord in Waiting by backing away from the queen.
The tiny general did his best to imitate his friend. The
gallery was a lengthy one, but Barnum, with his long
legs, quickly covered most of the distance separating
him from the exit. Tom Thumb, however, with his
short legs, kept losing ground and, fearing he would be
left behind, he would suddenly turn around and run a
few steps toward the exit. Then he would turn back,
face Queen Victoria, and continue to back out. He did

this time and again—alternately turning and running toward the door, turning and backing away from the queen—while the gallery echoed with the laughter of the spectators. "It really was," Barnum wrote, "one of the richest scenes I ever saw."

What made the scene richer still was the presence of the queen's favorite poodle. The dog, excited by the sight of the running midget, began to bark sharply and took off after him. To a person of normal size the dog was just a noisy little animal, but to the tiny general it seemed a large and threatening beast. Startled, he abandoned all propriety and swung his little cane vigorously to make the poodle keep its distance. The queen and her companions laughed till the tears came to their eyes.

The following day all the London newspapers carried an account of Tom Thumb's performance at Buckingham Palace. (The account, distributed by a court official, had actually been written by the shrewd Barnum himself.) "His personation of the Emperor Napoleon elicited great mirth," the report said, "and this was followed by a representation of the Grecian Statues, after which the General danced a nautical hornpipe, and sang several of his favorite songs."

Tom Thumb and the Prince of Wales

The midget had won a place in Queen Victoria's heart, and she soon invited him back to the palace. This time Barnum and the general were received in a magnificent apartment. The general bowed respectfully to Queen Victoria.

"I think this is a prettier room than the picture gallery," he remarked. "The chandelier is very fine."

The queen smiled and took him by the hand. "General, this is the Prince of Wales."

"How are you, Prince?" He shook the three-year-old prince's hand and stood beside him. "The prince is taller than I am, but I *feel* as big as anybody." He began to strut up and down in his best comic style.

On a third visit to the palace King Leopold of Belgium was present. Tom Thumb entertained the party with one of his favorite songs, "Yankee Doodle." As after the general's two previous visits, a handsome sum of money was delivered to Barnum at the queen's request.

A National Celebrity

Barnum was doing a thriving business at the Egyptian Hall. Tom Thumb's three appearances a day brought in an average of five hundred dollars. In the bargain, the little general performed at three or four parties a week, for which Barnum collected eight to ten guineas each.

The midget's picture was frequently seen in the British press. The queen dowager presented him with a specially made little gold watch, which she hung around his neck with her own hands. *Punch* referred to him as the "Pet of the Palace." Children bought paper dolls representing Tom Thumb in the costumes he wore in his most celebrated roles. Musical compositions were dedicated to him and "The General Tom Thumb Polka" was played everywhere.

The Duke of Wellington, who had defeated Napoleon at Waterloo, came to the Egyptian Hall several times to see Tom Thumb. The first time he called, the general was playing Napoleon. Pretending to be wrapped in deep thought, the midget walked up and down the stage, taking pinches of snuff.

Afterward, Wellington asked him what he had been thinking of during his performance.

"I was thinking of the loss of the Battle of Waterloo," Tom Thumb replied.

This remark was repeated from one end of the country to the other. According to Barnum, it was worth thousands of pounds at the box office.

Tom Thumb's Coach

Of the innumerable gifts that Tom Thumb received, none meant more to him than the coach that Barnum ordered for him. Constructed by the queen's own carriage maker, it stood twenty inches high and was eleven inches wide. The wheels were red and white and the body a bright blue. Barnum had devised a coat of arms for the general which was painted on the doors. It portrayed the American eagle and the British lion supporting the Goddess of Liberty and Britannia, and it included the British and American flags and the motto "Go Ahead." The coach had silver hub caps, door handles, and lamp holders. Venetian blinds covered the plate glass windows and the interior was lined with yellow silk.

To draw the coach, Barnum obtained four perfectly matched tiny Shetland ponies, just thirty-four inches high. Two boys, dressed in sky-blue livery, served as coachman and footman. The coach and ponies cost a considerable sum, but they were to prove their worth. They traveled with Tom Thumb through Europe, and were one of his best advertisements.

Tom Thumb in France

After a long stay in London, Barnum took Tom Thumb on a tour of the English provinces. Then the midget and his party embarked for Paris.

Tom Thumb's success in France eclipsed all that had gone before. He was received at the palace of the Tuileries by the king, Louis Philippe, several times; the royal family of France, like that of England, made a pet of him. Valuable gifts were showered on him, including a brooch of diamonds and emeralds.

A major social event was to be celebrated on Longchamp Day, and Barnum obtained permission for Tom Thumb's tiny carriage to travel among the coaches of the court and diplomats. The crowds which packed the sides of the boulevards cheered wildly as the little general— *le Général Tom Pouce,* as the French called him—rode along in his coach, bowing left and right with all the aplomb of a conquering hero. At the Longchamp race track he was invited to join the royal family in their box.

Barnum had engaged the Salle Musard for Tom

Thumb to perform in. His popularity was so great that the hall was sold out for months in advance. "I was compelled to take a cab to carry my bag of silver home at night," Barnum wrote. Poems and songs were written about the midget. Children munched chocolate figures shaped like him. Plaster statues of him appeared in the shops. Snuffboxes with his picture on the lid were popular.

Coached in French, Tom Thumb performed for his audiences in their own language to tumultuous applause. The boy by now had developed into a capable actor and he appeared at the Théâtre du Vaudeville in Paris in a comedy called *Le Petit Poucet* ("Little Thumb"). In this play he went on a tour of France's major cities.

Further Successes in Europe

Next Barnum took his protégé to Spain. Queen Isabella, little more than a girl herself, received him at the royal palace and insisted that he come with her to see a bullfight. From Spain the American group went on to Belgium. Then they returned to London, where Tom Thumb appeared again at the Egyptian Hall. The roles the little man was seen in included Frederick the Great, Hercules, Samson, the Fighting Gladiator, and Cupid. By now he was one of the greatest celebrities in Europe, and larger crowds than ever before came to see him. Barnum had commissioned a play for him, *Hop o' My Thumb,* and he also acted in this.

A Tragedy

For one man Tom Thumb's good fortune spelled tragedy. Benjamin Haydon, a noted English painter, had rented a room in the Egyptian Hall to exhibit some of his pictures. Haydon was deeply in debt and he was hoping that his show would help free him from it. But the crowds preferred the little general's lively antics to historical paintings.

"Tom Thumb had 12,000 people last week," the

painter wrote in his journal. "B. Haydon, 133½, the ½ is a little girl. Exquisite taste of the English people." Later Haydon wrote: "They rush by thousands to see Tom Thumb. They push, they fight, they scream, they faint, they cry help and murder! and oh! and ah! They see my bills, my boards, my caravans and don't read them."

Having earned a grand total of seventeen or eighteen pounds—not much of a sum compared to the more than five hundred pounds that Tom Thumb was bringing in every day—Haydon closed his show and took his pictures home. Shortly afterward his daughter found him dead in his studio. He had slit his throat with a razor and then shot himself in the head with a pistol.

Who Supports Whom?

After closing in London, Tom Thumb and his companions went on a tour of the rest of England, as well as Scotland and Ireland. Always the showman, Barnum often told his patrons that his ticket seller was the father of Tom Thumb. As a result, Stratton was pestered with all kinds of questions.

One day an old woman asked Stratton, "Are you really the father of General Tom Thumb?"

"Wa'al," he replied with typical New England restraint, "I have to support him."

"I rather think," declared the lady with unerring accuracy, "that he supports you!"

Welcome Home!

In 1847, after three years in Europe, Tom Thumb returned to the United States and appeared in the lecture hall of the American Museum. The public found him more appealing than ever. He had left America, to quote Barnum, "a diffident, uncultivated little boy; he came back an educated, accomplished little man. He had seen much, and had profited much."

He also came back a rich little man. For the past two years Barnum and the midget's father had been dividing on an equal basis the money he brought in. Stratton had acquired a substantial fortune. After settling a large sum on the general, he invested the rest and built a mansion in Bridgeport. In 1852, the Strattons had a second son, who was of normal size, like their two daughters.

Later in 1847 Tom Thumb and his parents toured the United States with Barnum. President and Mrs. Polk entertained them at the White House. They also visited Cuba.

"Kissed Nearly Two Millions of Ladies"

People were constantly requesting the midget's autograph. In a letter to an Albany clergyman who had asked for it, the nine-year-old wrote, perhaps with a little help from Barnum:

"I have traveled fifty thousand miles, been before more crowned heads than any other Yankee living, except my friend Mr. Barnum, and have kissed nearly Two Millions of ladies, including the Queens of England, France, Belgium, and Spain.

"I read the Bible every day, and am very fond of reading the New Testament. . . . I adore my Creator and know that He is good to us all. He has given me a small body, but I believe He has not contracted my heart, nor brain, nor *soul*. I shall praise His name evermore.

"Time compels me to make this note *short* like *myself*."

In the Circus

Bitten by the showman's bug, Tom Thumb's father went into business with Barnum. In 1849 they organized Barnum's Great Asiatic Caravan, Museum and Menagerie. This was both a traveling version of Barnum's American Museum and the forerunner of what was to become "the Greatest Show on Earth." Tom Thumb traveled with the caravan during the four years of its existence. After the death of his father in 1855 he toured on his own, sometimes accompanied by his mother or another relative.

As a young man, the general continued to be one of the best-known figures in show business. During vacations in Bridgeport he stayed at his parents' home. Here he had an apartment of his own, furnished with small-scale furniture, which his father had built for him. Cupboards and doorknobs were carefully positioned for his convenience. He became a 32nd degree Mason, and regularly visited Masonic temples when he was on tour.

The General Rescues Barnum

In 1855, misfortune struck P. T. Barnum, then forty-five. He had endorsed notes for large amounts of money for a New Haven clock company, and when the company went bankrupt it dragged him down with it. His fortune and his possessions melted away rapidly.

But the showman had many friends. One of them was Tom Thumb.

"My dear Mr. Barnum," the midget wrote, "I understand your friends, and that means all creation, intend to get up some benefits for your family. Now, my dear sir, just be good enough to remember that I belong to that mighty crowd, and I must have a finger (or at least a thumb) in that pie. . . .

"I have just started on my western tour, and have my carriages, ponies and assistants all here, but I am ready to go on to New York, and remain at Mrs. Barnum's service as long as I, in my small way, can be useful."

Barnum declined the offer. But a year later he changed his mind and he asked his little friend to tour Europe with him.

In London Tom Thumb played to capacity houses. "The same rollicking, jolly little blade," a newspaper called him. He and Barnum toured the British Isles, France, and Holland. It was late 1859 before they came back to the United States. With Tom Thumb's help, Barnum was on his feet again.

In 1862 Tom Thumb was twenty-four years old.

A
Photographic Gallery of
Very Special People

Circus World Museum, Baraboo, Wisconsin

As a youngster, **Francesco Lentini** was so shocked
at what he saw in an institution for the severely handicapped
that he never complained about his third leg again.

P. T. Barnum and
General Tom Thumb.
The midget, who weighed
15 pounds and was 25 inches tall,
made millions for Barnum.

Extreme hairiness (called hypertrichosis) runs in families.
This hairy family, from Burma, toured the United States.

Eli Bowen and members of his family. He was known as "the Legless Acrobat."

Circus World Museum, Baraboo, Wisconsin

Hertzburg Circus Collection—S.A.P.L.

Eng and **Chang**, the original Siamese twins, were joined at the breastbone by a ligature.

George Auger, circus giant,
reportedly was 7 feet 11 inches tall. His fans included
Douglas Fairbanks and Charlie Chaplin (pictured with him).

Bartola and Maximo, "the Aztec Children," represented as the last of the Aztecs, were both undersized and retarded.

Hertzburg Circus Collection—S.A.P.L.

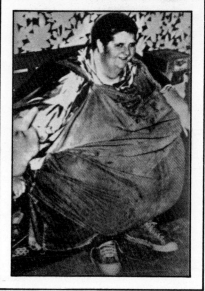

The heaviest man on record, **Robert Earl Hughes** weighed 1,069 pounds. He was buried in a coffin the size of a piano case.

Museum of the City of New York

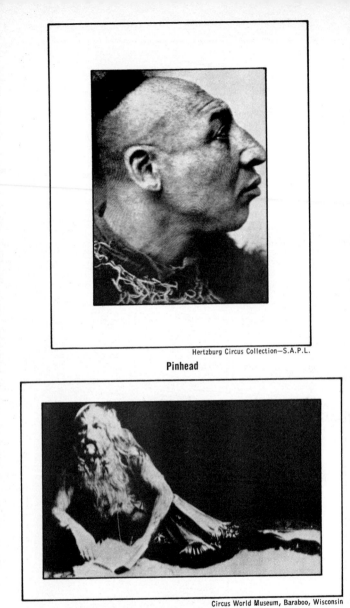

Pinhead

Long hair covered the entire body of
Lionel the Lion-Faced Man. He was born with just four teeth.

Julia Pastrana,
called "the Ugliest Woman in the World," was deformed and
covered with hair. She was a Mexican Digger Indian.

"The Skeleton Dude,"
James W. Coffey,
never married because
he couldn't find
"a lady who liked her
Coffey so thin."

The original Siamese twins, **Eng** and **Chang,**
with their wives and two of their twenty-two children,
in a photograph taken by Mathew Brady.

Mexican-born **Lucia Zarate,** smallest woman that ever lived, was under 20 inches tall, weighed 5 pounds.

Hertzburg Circus Collection—S.A.P.L.

Museum of the City of New York

Born without arms and legs, **Frieda Pushnick** was able to type and sew.

Museum of the City of New York

Bearded lady **Grace Gilbert** could swing a sledgehammer with the best of them.

The Elephant Man

This handsome midget,
General Mite, was only
22 inches high at age 14.

Radica and **Doodica** were
joined by a band of tissue.
When one took medicine,
the other felt its effect.

Circus fat man **David Navarro**
reached a top weight of
601 pounds. Many of these
pictures are from his collection.

Nikolai Kobelkoff,
armless and legless wonder, with his wife and children.

The Seven **Sutherland** Sisters had a total hair length
of 36 feet 10 inches. They were concert artists.

An accomplished acrobat,
Eli Bowen
had feet but no legs.

Charles Tripp, who used
his feet as hands, was known
as the handyman of the circus.

Tripp and **Bowen** used to go biking together for recreation.

The **Tocci** brothers
were two boys down to the sixth rib, but only one below.

Tom Thumb's wedding to **Lavinia Warren**
in 1863 pushed the Civil War off the front pages.
Commodore Nutt was best man.

Tom Thumb and his wife
in later years. He grew to a
height of 3 feet 4 inches,
weighed 70 pounds.

Lavinia Warren
with her second husband,
Count Primo Magri,
and his brother.

Alton Evening Telegraph

Giant of giants was **Robert Wadlow,**
shown with his brother. He was 8 feet 11.1 inches tall.

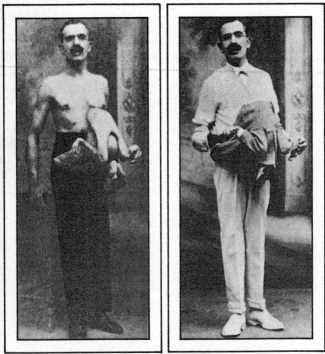

"Jacques" was the name **Jean Libbera**
gave to the miniature twin that grew out of his body.

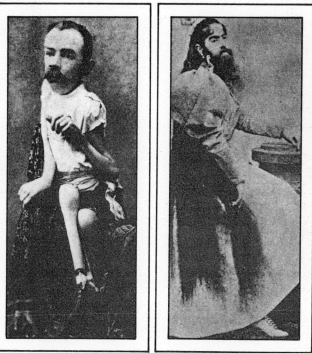

A popular human oddity
in old-time sideshows was
W. T. Sapp, "the Stone Man."

Mme. Clofullia
had to go to court to prove
she was a real woman
with a real beard.

Annie Jones, the bearded girl,
in a study by Mathew Brady.

Annie as a mature woman.
She had "the charm of
a society dame," married twice.

Not only a midget,
Carrie Akers
was also a fat lady.

Johnny Eck of Baltimore
was a well-known orchestra leader
and a movie actor.

A "half-and-half" (half-man, half-woman),
Bobby Kork packed a mean wallop.

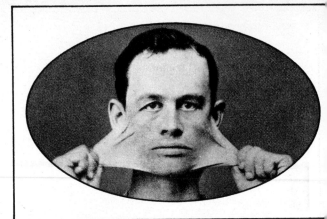

An elastic skin man. Such a person can pull
his skin out a considerable distance without feeling any pain.

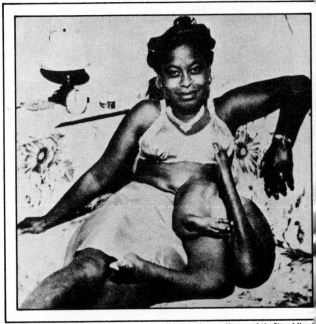

Betty Lou Williams, a shapely miss, was 19 years old
when she posed for this picture with her parasitic twin.

Annie Swan and
Captain Bates, tallest married
couple in the world.

Chang, the Chinese giant,
was 7 feet 8½ inches tall.
He settled in England.

Circus fat ladies
are often named "Jolly."
This one is **Jolly Nellie Terrel.**

Myrtle Corbin, who had two
lower bodies, bore three children
with one, two with the other.

Jo-Jo the Dog-Faced Boy
was covered with hair from head to foot.

Men fainted when
Grace McDaniels,
"the Mule-Faced Woman,"
removed her veil in
the sideshow.

Known as
"the Wild Men of Borneo,"
little **Hiram** and **Barney Davis**
beguiled the crowds
with their feats of strength.

The Saintly Giantess,
Ella Ewing, lived in a house
with 15-foot-high ceilings.

These Siamese twins, **Millie** and **Christine**,
were born into slavery. Later they earned $600 a week.

Pete Robinson,
circus living skeleton,
did a dancing act with his
467-pound wife.

Rosa-Josepha Blazek were born in Bohemia.
One gave birth to a child and both were able to nurse it.

Once popular vaudeville performers,
the **Hilton** sisters
were joined at the base of the spine.

Isaac Sprague and his family.
He weighed 52 pounds and
ate gigantic meals.

Tipping the scales
at 739 pounds,
Happy Jack Eckert
had difficulty walking.

An armless and legless wonder,
Matthew Buchinger
was married four times,
had eleven children.

Johnny, the Philip Morris midget,
with the tiny **Dancing Dolls** and the **Fischers,**
famed circus giants.

Laloo, from India,
had a small twin attached to
his breastbone. The twin
was dressed as a girl.

"Hopp the Frog Boy,"
Samuel D. Parks,
was happy with his dwarf wife.

Daughter of a Ringling Brothers fat lady,
Baby Ruth Pontico weighed 815 pounds.

Jack Earle, 7 feet 7½ inches tall,
a pituitary giant, weighed 4 pounds at birth.

The armless fiddler, **Carl Unthan**,
at the time he performed
in Vienna with Johann Strauss conducting.

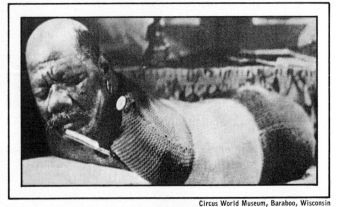

"The Caterpillar Man,"
Prince Randian, used to roll cigarettes with his lips.

Unzie the Albino
didn't look like an Australian aborigine,
but that's what he was.

"Darwin's Missing Link" they called **Krao,**
the hairy girl from Thailand.
She was a Ringling Brothers star for years.

Born without legs, **Harry Williams**
could walk on his hands as well as others can on their feet.

Midgets often grow somewhat with the years, and this had been the general's lot. He weighed fifty-two pounds now and he was ten inches taller. He wore a mustache and he had a mature look. A lofty star in the American theatrical firmament, he had fame and wealth, pedigreed horses, a yacht. Only one thing was lacking for him to be completely happy.

That thing was love.

17

Tom Thumb and Lavinia Warren

Whenever Tom Thumb came to New York he used to drop in to see his old friend P. T. Barnum. One day his interest was powerfully attracted by a new "wonder" at the American Museum. Her name was Lavinia Warren.

Lavinia was as pretty as she was petite. Born in Middleboro, Massachusetts, in 1841, she had stopped growing at age ten. She was thirty-two inches tall and weighed twenty-nine pounds when the general first laid eyes on her.

Both of Lavinia's parents were tall, and she had two sisters and four brothers whose height was normal. She did, however, have a younger sister, Minnie, who was a midget, too, even shorter than she was.

Lavinia had taught school in Middleboro. She must have had a strong personality, for even the shortest of her pupils was taller than she was. Then she succumbed to the lure of show business. For a while she traveled on a Mississippi River showboat.

The general, after talking to Lavinia, headed

directly for Barnum's private office. He asked to see the showman alone.

"Mr. Barnum," the little man said earnestly, "that is the most charming little lady I ever saw. I believe she was created on purpose to be my wife.

"Now, you have always been a friend of mine. I want you to say a good word for me to her. I have got plenty of money, and I want to marry and settle down in life. I really feel as if I must marry that young lady."

To Barnum, the general seemed unusually excited. He urged him to calm down and proceed cautiously, as he could hardly expect to win Lavinia's affection overnight.

Barnum revealed to him, too, that he had a rival for the young lady's heart. This was the volatile Commodore George Washington Morrison Nutt, another of Barnum's little people.

"The Thirty-Thousand-Dollar Nutt"

Nutt was the son of a New Hampshire farmer. An attractive, clever young man of eighteen in 1862, he stood twenty-nine inches high and weighed twenty-four pounds. Barnum paid him a top wage: two hundred dollars a week, plus expenses and the profits from the sale of autographs, pictures, and books about him. Because he had a three-year contract stipulating thirty thousand dollars, the midget was known as "the thirty-thousand-dollar Nutt."

Barnum had called his first successful midget a general, so he decided to make Nutt a commodore. He provided him with a naval uniform and, in deference to his name, a coach built along the lines of a walnut.

Commodore Nutt bore more than a little resemblance to the general before the latter had added to his height and weight. Many patrons of the American Museum noticed the resemblance and asserted that Commodore Nutt was none other than Tom Thumb, who had not been exhibited in the city for years. The fact that Barnum had been caught in hoaxes in the past helped to support this impression.

As usual, the showman found a way to turn the situation to his advantage. Getting in touch with Tom Thumb, who was then touring in the West, he asked him to accept an engagement in New York.

In August the general stepped out on Barnum's stage with the commodore. They were billed as "the Two Smallest Men and Greatest Curiosities Living." The joint appearance attracted large numbers of New Yorkers, who came to resolve the controversy for themselves. Many left absolutely convinced that Commodore Nutt was General Tom Thumb. The general himself was widely taken to be an impostor because he was so much heavier and taller than his admirers remembered. Adding piquancy to the exhibition was Anna Swan, the lovely seventeen-year-old Nova Scotia giantess, advertised as the tallest woman in the world. We shall get to know her better in a later chapter.

The Commodore and President Lincoln

That same year Barnum and Nutt called at the White House on the invitation of President Lincoln. The cabinet was in session, but the president had left word that Barnum and Nutt were to be admitted whenever they arrived. After a short stay the visitors prepared to depart. Lincoln took Nutt's hand.

"Commodore, permit me to give you a parting word of advice. When you are in command of your fleet, if you find yourself in danger of being taken prisoner, I advise you to wade ashore." (The implication was, of course, that the commodore's tiny ship would not be in very deep water.)

The little commodore was not to be upstaged. Placing himself at the president's side, he slowly raised his eyes up Lincoln's long legs. "I guess, Mr. President, you could do that better than I can," he replied.

Witty and sharp-tongued, with a temper as short as his height—such was the rival with whom General Tom Thumb would have to contend for Lavinia Warren's hand.

Jealous Rivals

During the weeks that followed the general's intimate conversation with Barnum, he became a constant caller at the American Museum. On each visit he never failed to pay his compliments to the young lady on whom he had set his heart.

As Barnum had foretold, Commodore Nutt was not indifferent to the general's presence. Whenever he saw Tom Thumb approaching, he strutted around like a bantam rooster. One day, somehow, the two got into a scuffle. The general was older and heavier, and he was a man of peace. The commodore, by contrast, was not only lithe and wiry, but took an interest in the art of self-defense. Before the general knew it, he had been thrown on his back. In all future meetings with the commodore he was careful to keep his distance.

Meanwhile, the general was making progress in the wooing of Lavinia. Fearful that his mother might not approve of his plans, he was eager to have her meet Lavinia under favorable circumstances.

Barnum, like Tom Thumb, had his home in Bridgeport. The general begged him to ask Lavinia to his house the following weekend and invite him and his mother as well. Barnum agreed.

The moment the showman chose to extend the invitation to the young lady was hardly a favorable one. Commmodore Nutt was seated nearby. Instantly interested, he told Barnum he wanted to come to Bridgeport, too. It was impossible to refuse him, especially since Lavinia liked the idea. It was agreed that Nutt would come out for the weekend after his Friday night performance.

When Barnum and Lavinia arrived at the Bridgeport railroad depot that Friday, they found the general waiting for them in his carriage. Dropping Barnum at his house, Tom Thumb took the young lady out for a ride. In the course of the afternoon he brought her to his mother's house and pointed out to her his considerable holdings in real estate. In the evening he dined with his mother and Lavinia at Barnum's. The general's mother returned home, but he stayed on; he had accepted a prearranged invitation to spend the night.

Tom Thumb Proposes

Mr. and Mrs. Barnum retired early, so the two midgets could be alone together. But a couple of young ladies who were guests in the house suspected what was afoot. They decided to stay in the darkened hallway outside the sitting room and eavesdrop. To them and Barnum we are indebted for the account that follows.

The little couple had been playing backgammon. Tom Thumb began to talk of his business interests and how secure he was financially. They chatted about the trip that Lavinia was to make to Europe with Barnum in a couple of months.

"I wish I was going over, for I know all about the different countries, and could explain them all to you," Tom Thumb said. "I should like it first rate if Mr. Barnum would engage me."

"I thought you remarked the other day that you had money enough and was tired of traveling."

"That depends upon my company while traveling."

"You might not find my company very agreeable."

"I would be glad to risk it. Would you really like to have me go?" The general quietly slipped an arm around her waist, but hardly touched her.

"Of course I would."

The little arm clasped the little waist closer. "Don't you think it would be pleasanter if we went as man and wife?"

That, Lavinia told him, was an odd way to joke.

The matter, he replied, was much too serious for joking. "The first moment I saw you I felt that you were created to be my wife."

"I think I love you well enough. . . . But I've always said I would never marry without my mother's consent."

"Oh! I'll ask your mother."

The listeners in the hall heard the sound of kissing. Minutes later a coach rattled into the driveway and the doorbell rang. It was the commodore.

"*You* here, General?" he said petulantly. Hardly pausing, he stamped up to Barnum's bedroom.

"Mr. Barnum, does Tom Thumb *board* here?" he asked, his words dripping sarcasm, and went out in a huff.

Ten minutes passed. Tom Thumb rushed in. He caught hold of Barnum's hand. "We're engaged, Mr. Barnum!" he whispered. "We're engaged! We're engaged!"

Tom Thumb was fearful about breaking the news to the commodore, whose temper he was only too well acquainted with. Barnum and Lavinia undertook the task. When Nutt heard their announcement he turned pale. His voice breaking, he wished the bride every happiness.

A Midget Wedding

News of the approaching wedding set New York by the ears. Barnum engaged the general to appear with Lavinia at the American Museum. Business boomed; the showplace took in three thousand dollars a day. In an effort to keep the golden stream flowing into his treasury, Barnum offered the midgets fifteen thousand dollars if they would postpone the wedding a month while continuing to appear on his stage.

"Not for fifty thousand dollars!" was the general's heated reply. The bride-to-be nodded vigorous approval.

The showman had promised the tiny couple a genteel wedding and he kept his word. On February 10, 1863, at Grace Church, in New York, Tom Thumb took Lavinia Warren to be his wife. (See photo insert). Commodore Nutt was the best man and Lavinia's sister, Minnie, the maid of honor. Two thousand guests were invited. Millionaires, senators, governors, generals, and society leaders attended. Gifts poured in from everywhere; President and Mrs. Lincoln sent a set of Chinese fire screens.

Afterward, a reception was held at the Metropolitan Hotel. Mr. and Mrs. Tom Thumb stood on a piano and greeted the long lines of guests. The wedding cake weighed eighty pounds. Interest in the wedding was so intense that it pushed the Civil War off the front pages of newspapers.

Tom Thumb at the White House

The couple headed southward on their honeymoon. In Philadelphia and Baltimore they were given impressive receptions. In Washington they were invited to the White House, where President and Mrs. Lincoln gave a reception in their honor. The hall was crowded with the dignitaries of wartime Washington and their families. The general wore an elegant wedding suit; the bride was dressed in a white satin gown with a two-yard train sweeping behind her. Tad, the president's son, personally served wine and ices to the couple. Lincoln was especially impressed by the marked resemblance Lavinia bore to Mrs. Lincoln.

The president bantered with the general. "You are now the great center of attraction. You have thrown me completely in the shade. . . . What is your opinion of the war, as a military man?"

"My friend Mr. Barnum," Tom Thumb replied, "would settle the whole affair in a month."

Standing next to the midget, the long, lanky president commented to Tad, "God likes to do funny things; here you have the long and the short of it."

Grace Greenwood, who was among the guests, wrote, "I noticed the president gazing after them with a smile of quaint humor; but in his sorrow-shaded eyes there was something more than amusement—a gentle sympathy in the apparent happiness and good-fellowship of this curious wedded pair—come to him out of fairyland."

Around the World

The happy couple retired to Bridgeport but soon wearied of the quiet life there. Under Barnum's management they toured the country with Minnie and Commodore Nutt. From 1864 to 1867 they exhibited in Europe. It was estimated they earned between ten and twenty thousand pounds a year.

In 1869 the little people were off again, this time on a world tour that was to take them to Australia, Japan, China, India, and Egypt, as well as back to Europe. They were received by the maharajah of Benares, who offered Tom Thumb a hunting elephant. The khedive of Egypt lent them his private train. Emperor Franz Joseph of Austria, King Victor Emmanuel of Italy, and Pope Pius IX were others who received them. When they finally came home in 1872 they had traveled 56,000 miles and given 1,471 performances.

Little Parents

Repeatedly the public heard that Commodore Nutt and Minnie Warren were married. They never were. "My fruit is plucked," the commodore told Barnum once, evidently alluding to Lavinia. Nutt died, reportedly unmarried, in 1881, aged thirty-seven.

Minnie, however, did get married. In 1874 an English fancy skater named Major Edward Newell, diminutive but not a midget, joined the Tom Thumb show, and three years later he and Minnie were married. They made their home with the Tom Thumbs, who had built a house in Middleboro, close to the home of the girls' mother. The following year Minnie gave birth to a child. The baby weighed five and a half pounds. Both mother and child died.

In 1881 Barnum and James A. Bailey formed the Barnum and London Circus and Mr. and Mrs. Tom Thumb accepted an engagement with it. Barnum decided that the little pair might draw bigger crowds if they had a baby. The Thumbs had never succeeded in having a child of their own, but the problem was an easy one for the old showman to solve. He simply announced that Lavinia had become a mother and he hired a baby, which Lavinia held during her appearances. Its real mother stood nearby, posing as a nurse.

The Thumbs were photographed with the baby and copies of the photograph, at twenty-five cents each, were sold in large quantities.

From this trick of Barnum's grew the erroneous belief that the midgets actually had a baby. Reputable reference works, including the *Dictionary of American Biography,* report the child's birth and its death at an early age.

Death of the General

When the circus closed its season, Mr. and Mrs. Tom Thumb continued to tour with their own manager. In 1883 they narrowly escaped death when the Milwaukee hotel in which they were staying caught fire. The general's manager carried the little couple to safety. But somehow Tom Thumb was never the same afterward. His health began to deteriorate.

On July 15, 1883, Tom Thumb was at his home in Middleboro. Early in the morning he suffered a stroke and died. He was only forty-five years old.

Ten thousand attended the funeral of General Tom Thumb in Bridgeport. Most were women and girls. The four-foot coffin was buried with Masonic honors in Mountain Grove Cemetery. A tall marble shaft had already been raised on the Stratton plot. On it stood a life-size statue of the little general, which he had posed for when he was nineteen years old.

Tom Thumb, at his death, was three feet four inches tall. He weighed seventy pounds. His last pictures show a portly little figure, with whiskers and a mustache. He had earned a few million dollars in his time, but little of it remained at his death. Lavinia inherited only sixteen thousand dollars, some securities, and a few lots in Brooklyn, New York. All the rest of his fortune had disappeared in poor investments and luxurious living.

Lavinia and Count Primo Magri

Tom Thumb had been in his grave only three months when Lavinia began touring again. Some say she was driven by financial necessity, others that she wanted to forget her grief. In her little company were two Italian dwarfs, Count Primo Magri (who had received his title from the Pope) and his brother. The count was eight years younger than Lavinia and three feet nine inches tall. Age differences are less significant in the world of the little people, where the choice of partners is limited. Two years after Tom Thumb's death, Lavinia and the count were married.

Count Magri was a skillful pugilist and fencer; he also played the piano and piccolo. However, he never achieved any marked distinction; he usually was referred to as Mrs. Tom Thumb's husband. For a while he and his wife had an opera company of midgets. They appeared at fairs, in sideshows, and in vaudeville. One of the high points of their career was a venture into the new medium of film. They played in four comedies.

An era was closing in American show business. Barnum was dead, and midgets had lost the fascination they held for the public in Tom Thumb's day. The aging count and countess often had a hard time of it, traveling from one whistle stop to another across America. For some years they had a home in Marion, Ohio, which they filled with midget furniture and kept open for tourists. Later they appeared in a sideshow at Coney Island. They also kept a general store and ice cream parlor for tourists in Middleboro, when they were not at Coney Island. They called it "Primo's Pastime."

A Midget's Lot

Lavinia became a Christian Scientist. She was active in the Daughters of the American Revolution and the Eastern Star. With the years she came to dwell more and more in the past. She wrote her autobiography, in which she reminisced about her first husband's triumphs and her own. She recalled that he had kissed millions of ladies and she wrote: "I can with equal assurance assert that I have *shaken hands* with more human beings . . . than any other woman in existence." She was a fat little old lady now, but she still remembered her days of glory, when she was photographed more than any other woman in America.

Her lot, Lavinia decided, had not been an easy one. "If nature endowed me with any superior personal attraction it was comparatively small compensation for the inconvenience, trouble and annoyance imposed upon me by my diminutive stature." In that restrained sentence throbs all the hurt and pathos of those who have been selected by fate to be among the Very Special People.

Lavinia died on November 25, 1919. She was seventy-eight years old. To the end she had worn a picture of Tom Thumb in a locket around her neck. At her request she was buried at his side. Her simple headstone bears a single word: "Wife." In the same cemetery, only a short distance away, her friend and Tom Thumb's, P. T. Barnum, had lain at rest since 1891.

Tom Thumb has been history for almost a hundred years. Many people believe he never really lived, but is a legend, like the Sir Tom Thumb of King Arthur's court. But he was a real person and his life was an exciting, rewarding one that brought joy to millions. He is the best-known midget of all time. If you ever find yourself in the vicinity of Bridgeport, Connecticut, and you want to learn more about him, stop in at the Barnum Museum at 804 Main Street. It is crowded with fascinating photographs, relics, and memories of little Tom Thumb and his big friend P. T. Barnum that will bring their wonderful, thrilling times back to life for you.

18

Why—and What—Is a Midget?

Why do some people fail to grow to a normal height? Not until 1915, many years after Tom Thumb's death, did science discover that much dwarfism is the result of a defect of the pituitary gland. And it wasn't until our own day that it became possible to do something about that defect.

The pituitary gland is one of the endocrine glands, which regulate our growth and development. Often called the master gland because of the significant role it plays, the pituitary is located at the base of the brain. One of the vital substances this gland pours into the blood stream is HGH, the growth hormone. If the gland produces an insufficient amount of the hormone a child will suffer from pituitary dwarfism—he will be a midget. If the gland produces an excessive amount, he will be a giant.

There are many other causes of dwarfism. The condition can be produced by disease, thyroid deficiency, diabetes, sex gland failure, or nutritional trouble.

Not all dwarfs are of the perfectly formed minia-ture type. Frequently they have a normal-sized torso but short arms and legs and a big head and face. These dwarfs were popular with the nobility of Europe in ear-lier times, and are often seen in the paintings of Velázquez. Nothing can be done to cure this condition, which is a skeletal disorder caused by a genetic muta-tion. However, achondroplastic dwarfs, as they are called, are vigorous people, have a normal sexual en-dowment, and enjoy a normal life span.

So far as doctors are concerned, anyone well be-low normal height is a dwarf. In popular usage, however, if a dwarf is perfectly proportioned, he is called a midget. By common acceptance a dwarf is an individual under four feet six inches tall. Pygmies are taller, averaging just under five feet. Dwarfism occurs about once in every ten thousand births. According to Dr. Thaddeus Kelly of Johns Hopkins University's Moore Clinic there are about one hundred thousand dwarfs of all types in the United States. Most are midg-ets.

Normal Parents, Midget Children

Tom Thumb, you will remember, was a normal baby at birth, even larger than average. But by the time he was five months old, his pituitary had stopped func-tioning normally and his growth ceased for some years. Lavinia Warren stopped growing when she was ten. Some midgets, however, are born tiny and do not grow at all.

Tom Thumb's parents were people of normal height. So are the parents of most other midgets. Any normal couple can produce a midget child. Some families, like those of Lavinia and Minnie Warren or Count Primo Magri, may have a number of midget children. Midgets themselves, however, with few excep-tions, have children of normal height and weight. By the time these children are seven or eight years old they are frequently taller than their parents.

Midgets like Tom Thumb and Commodore Nutt

have normal proportions. They may grow all through life, but seem especially likely to do so after the age of thirty. Usually, however, they do not reach normal height. In adulthood they are frequently taken for children. The males often have little hair on their faces and bodies. Their voices are pitched high. Although their physical strength is frequently not outstanding, it is greater than a child's. Some midgets, through constant practice, develop their bodies to such a degree that they become capable gymnasts or acrobats.

Sexual Potency of Midgets

Sex drive is variable in midgets. In a large number, potency is a long time in developing; it may not reveal itself before the individual is close to twenty. After that, he will be completely normal. Some midgets, however, lack sex hormones, and will develop sexually only if given hormone shots. In midget women, the onset of menstruation may occur much later than it does in their big sisters. Wrinkles often appear early.

Midget Marriages

Facts on midget marriages are scant. In the early 1930s Walter Bodin and Burnet Hershey made a survey that suggested most midgets do not marry, but the sampling was a small one. Of those who married, more than half had midget spouses. But a substantial percentage—44 percent in this study—married men and women of normal height and weight. Midgets, like others of the Very Special People, have the same aspirations and ideals as the rest of mankind, so it's natural that many should set their hearts on the same kinds of mates. The study revealed, however, that only 41 percent of the midgets who married became parents.

Childbearing

For the midget mother-to-be, childbearing may pose a problem. Midgets are born with different kinds

of growth-hormone deficiency. Depending on the type
of deficiency she and her mate have, the child may be
either of normal size or a midget. Since her own birth
tract is tiny, a caesarean delivery is required if the child
is of normal size. Women who are fearful of this type of
delivery will try to avoid having children. However,
some midget mothers have been the parents of large
broods.

Normal Life Span

Midgets are likely to have a normal life span. Although Tom Thumb died at forty-five, his wife lived to
seventy-eight and her second husband to seventy-one.
Count Boruwlaski, a celebrated Polish midget, was
ninety-eight when he died in 1837.

Midget heights vary. So do records as to who was
the smallest midget that ever lived. Adele Ber, of Yonk-
ers, New York, at age nine was reported to measure
eighteen inches. A Sicilian girl, Caroline Crachami, who
died at age nine, was somewhat taller; her skeleton,
preserved in the Museum of the Royal College of Surgeons in London, measures 19.8 inches. Lya Graf, the
attractive Ringling Brothers midget who won fame by
sitting on J. P. Morgan's lap, was said to be twenty-one
inches tall. Probably the record belongs to Lucia Zarate, who was under twenty inches as an adult.

Endocrine Therapy

Dwarfs are becoming scarcer because of the development of knowledge of endocrine and other
disorders and how to treat them. Women receive better
care in pregnancy, and this apparently reduces the
possibility of growth deficiency.

A prominent clinic for the treatment of dwarfism
is at Johns Hopkins University. Another is at Harbor
General Hospital, which is operated by the University
of California at Los Angeles. This clinic is under the
direction of Dr. David Rimoin, a geneticist. He says
that pituitary dwarfs, or midgets, can achieve a height

that is close to normal with the help of growth hormone. The hormone, obtained from the pituitaries of human cadavers, is not available in sufficient supply. According to Dr. Rimoin, twenty-five out of one hundred midgets could be helped with these injections. However, there is enough of the hormone for less than half of this number.

Had hormone therapy been available in Tom Thumb's day, it might have helped him to grow to a nearly normal height. However, the likelihood is that, if he had received it, he would not have become the celebrated Very Special Person that he did.

What Is It Like to Be a Midget?

What is it like to be a midget? You exist in a world that is too big for you. You have the needs of an adult but the body of a child. Everything around you—houses, stores, theaters, furniture, fixtures, automobiles, stairs, curbs—is made for people of normal size. For the little people it is an alien world, a world full of inconvenience.

Beds are a problem—climbing into and out of them requires care. Tables and chairs are just not the right size. When you go to a barber shop, you may have to sit in an auxiliary chair—the kind that is used for giving children haircuts. When you go to the theater, you'll have to raise your voice at the box office because you'll be below the ticket seller's level of vision. It may be necessary to bring along an inflatable pillow to sit on. Otherwise, you'll be unable to see over the shoulder of the person sitting in front.

Things are too big to handle comfortably. Knives, forks, and spoons aren't made for small hands to hold. Telephones are awkward to pick up and their weight may impose a strain. Combs, hairbrushes, and razors seem oversized. Getting into a bathtub and out of it requires special planning.

Midgets have trouble with their clothes. Some garments can of course be obtained in children's sizes. But suits and dresses usually have to be made to order. So must hats and coats and, frequently, shoes.

The routine actions that a man or woman of normal height performs without thinking can cause difficulty to a midget. If you want to open a window or turn on a light, you may have to reach your arm out to its full length or get up on a stool. Turning a doorknob or pressing a button to ring for an elevator may be close to impossible if you're very small. Tom Thumb, a man of wealth, was able to scale down the furnishings in his house to fit his size. He placed windowsills, doorknobs, cupboards, and lighting fixtures at a height convenient for himself. (Normal people might have gotten a crick in the back bending over to reach them.) Once the general was out of his own house, however, making his way in the world of the big people was a constant challenge.

Midgets in the Subway

A case in point turned up in a New York court some years ago. Two midgets were arrested for going into the subway without dropping coins into the turnstile slot.

"Why didn't you pay?" asked the magistrate.

"We couldn't pay," one of the midgets said. "We couldn't reach the slot."

The midgets explained that they never rode the subway because it was unsafe for them. Normal-sized people didn't see them and they were in danger of being stepped on. On the day in question they were late for work and couldn't get a taxi, their usual mode of travel. As they approached the turnstile they were swept along by the crowd and just lowered their heads a little to pass through.

The judge had to admit their defense was a valid one and he gave them suspended sentences. But he made them promise that if they used the subway in the future they would somehow arrange to pay.

Midgets of Today

Midgets were once a staple feature of sideshows and circuses, but they are seen less and less today. Aside from fact that fewer are born or have to go through life as midgets, many kinds of employment opportunities have opened up. In World War II the small people were extensively employed as aircraft mechanics, for they could get into parts of planes that people of normal size could not. Today you are likely to find them in every type of job—working as accountants, architects, brokers, salesmen, or physicians, or in any other kind of occupation. They even have an organization devoted to the advancement of their interests, Little People of America, Inc., which holds a convention every year. Still, among the little people as among the big there are divisions. Dwarfs prefer to associate with dwarfs, midgets with midgets.

19

Famous Little People of Past and Present

The little people—midgets, dwarfs, and others—have always fascinated their taller brothers and sisters. In every part of the world, myths have sprung up about them. Homer and Herodotus told of mythical small people dwelling far to the south—where, in relatively recent times, the Pygmies were discovered. To the people of northern Europe, dwarfs were creatures of mystery and magic, supposed to live in caves and to possess supernatural powers. Often, like the dwarf Alberich, around whom the Germans and Scandinavians wove dark legends, they were the masters of great treasures hidden in the bowels of the earth. In folklore they were called elves, goblins, and kobolds, and alternately viewed as capricious, friendly, or spiteful.

The dwarfs and midgets of today, as we have seen, are found in virtually every profession and trade, where they acquit themselves with skill and honor. They are not so likely to be entertainers, the role in which they made their greatest mark in the past.

Already in ancient Egypt, thousands of years before the birth of Christ, the pharaohs kept dwarfs to lighten heavy moments with their songs, dances, and humor. (We shall use the term "dwarf" here to describe the little people in general, since writers of the past did not differentiate reliably between dwarfs and midgets.) Pygmies from the Akka tribe of equatorial Africa were valued members of the courts of the early pharaohs.

Not only were dwarfs entertainers—they also gained distinction in other spheres of activity. The first dwarf whose name is known to us, Khnumhotou, who lived about 2500 B.C., was keeper of the wardrobe to the pharaoh, a post of some importance. He was probably of noble blood, and his tomb was an imposing one.

It's possible that the fondness displayed for the little people by the Egyptians was rooted in religion; one of Egypt's greatest gods, Ptah, creator of the universe, was occasionally portrayed as a dwarf.

Dwarfs in Ancient Rome

From Egypt an interest in the little people spread to Europe. Many of the Roman emperors had dwarfs in their courts. Augustus, who founded the Roman empire, set the style for his successors. He requested his agents to collect dwarfs all over his domain and send them to him. His basic requirements were that they should be attractive and well formed. One of his favorites was Lucius, a Roman knight, who was under two feet tall—and who reportedly had a powerful voice. The emperor Domitian made a particular hobby of collecting dwarfs, and even organized them into a school of gladiators for his amusement.

Dwarfs were high-priced merchandise in ancient Rome and producing them was a profitable trade. Children were put on special diets to stunt their growth; the unfortunate result was that they often developed bone diseases or died of malnutrition.

In later ages, dealers called *comprachicos* would buy children, dwarf them or deform them, and sell them. An old recipe for stunting growth has come down to us. It consists of the fat of various animals, including dormice, bats, and moles, which was smeared on a child's backbone. Its effectiveness seems doubtful.

Croesus and Attila

A number of important rulers have been dwarfs or exceedingly short persons. Croesus, king of Lydia in Asia Minor—his name is a synonym for wealth—was a dwarf. Attila the Hun, who led an army of half a million across Europe and earned the name of "the Scourge of God," may have been a dwarf. He is described by the historian Edward Gibbon as having "a large head, a swarthy complexion, small, deep-seated eyes, a flat nose, a few hairs in the place of a beard, broad shoulders, and a short square body, of nervous strength, though of a disproportioned form." Gregory, bishop of Tours, and Antoine Godeau, archbishop of Grasse and a distinguished poet, were both midgets, as were many other celebrated people of the past.

"Pages and Playmates of the Great"

In later ages the custom of keeping dwarfs in noble households gained increasing prominence. It probably reached its peak in the sixteenth and seventeenth centuries. Throughout Europe it was fashionable to have a dwarf or a midget to wait on the members of the household or divert them. Many paintings of the time portray these little servants or entertainers. If the dwarf was a hunchback and he possessed a sharp wit, so much the better; he might qualify for the role of court jester.

In some countries the custom persisted into the nineteenth century. In his book *Travels in Russia and Sweden,* Porter, who visited those countries in the early 1800s, observed that dwarfs "are here the pages and playmates of the great and at almost all entertainments stand for hours behind their lord's chair, holding his snuff box or awaiting his command. There is scarcely a nobleman in this country who is not possessed of one or more of these frisks of nature."

An Extraordinary Russian Wedding

No one carried an interest in dwarfs further than Peter the Great, the czar of Russia. Peter's favorite dwarf was named Valakoff. In 1710 he was married to a dwarf belonging to the Princess Prescovie Theodorovna, and the czar provided a wedding for the couple in royal Lilliputian style the like of which has never been seen since that day.

For the occasion the czar brought together a wedding party of seventy-two dwarfs of both sexes from all parts of the realm. Two tiny servants in a minuscule coach had delivered the invitations to the guests. A dwarf led the wedding procession, as master of ceremonies. Behind the towering czar walked the joyful little bride and groom, followed by ministers, boyars, and officials. After these came the seventy-two tiny celebrants, their little feet pattering on the pavement. Crowds of people of all stations closed the procession. During the ceremony the bridal wreath, which it was the Russian custom to hold over the bridal pair, was held by Peter the Great himself.

For the wedding meal, the table of honor was placed in the middle of the hall, and here the bride and groom supped with their seventy-two companions. The guests of normal stature were all seated along the walls, so they could enjoy an unobstructed view of the festivities. Every part of the banquet was proportioned to the size of the happy couple. The little guests were served by little waiters, they drank from miniature goblets, and ate from miniature dishes. The extraordinary celebration closed with a miniature ball. The artist Verestchagin commemorated the episode in his painting *The Wedding of the Dwarfs.*

Jeffery Hudson: King's Spy

One of the most colorful dwarfs in the history of England was Jeffery Hudson, soldier and spy. Born in Oakham, in Rutlandshire, in 1619, Jeffery was the son of a butcher. Although his parents were of normal height, Jeffery at age nine was only about eighteen inches tall, and "without deformity, wholly proportionable," according to a contemporary chronicler. His father brought him to the attention of the duchess of Buckingham, and she made him a member of her household.

When Charles I, king of England, and his queen, Henrietta Maria, dined with the duke of Buckingham, as a special treat a large pie was brought to the table—and out of it popped little Jeffery. The queen was so taken with him that she added him to her retinue. Jeffery became a royal favorite and was sent by the king and the queen on a number of missions.

Like many another little man, Jeffery was a favorite with the ladies, and tales are told of his escapades with them. According to one story, he was wooing a lady when her husband showed up unexpectedly. The lady quickly hid him away—not in the closet or under the bed, however, but under her skirts.

The king had a giant porter, William Evans, about eight feet tall. Just as giants and midgets in the circus often team up, so did these two. On one occasion the little man was almost blown into the Thames River by a strong wind, but held on to a shrub until Evans rescued him. They also performed together in a masque in which the huge porter "drew little Jeffery the dwarf out of his pocket, first to the wonder, then to the laughter of the beholders," says a contemporary account.

When civil war broke out in England, Jeffery reportedly served the king as a captain of horse in the struggle with Cromwell's forces. In 1644, the queen fled to Paris and Jeffery went with her. In 1649 he got into a quarrel with a gentleman named Crofts—some say over a girl—and challenged him to a duel. Crofts didn't take the midget seriously and showed up with a squirt gun. Insulted, Jeffery renewed the challenge. A second meeting took place, with Crofts on foot and Jeffery on horseback to make the match more equal. The midget shot his opponent dead. Obliged to leave the court, he embarked on a ship but it was captured by Turkish pirates and he was sold into slavery in Barbary. Here he underwent so many hardships before he was ransomed that, according to his own account, he grew to a height of three feet six inches or more.

After his release, Jeffery returned to England, where he lived on a pension provided by the duke of Buckingham. Jeffery was a Roman Catholic, and in 1679 he was arrested with others and charged with taking part in a "popish plot." He was imprisoned but released in a short while. Curiously enough, records of 1680 and 1681 show that he received substantial payments as "Captain Jeffery Hudson" from the king's secret service. He died in 1682.

Two portraits of Jeffery exist. One of them, at Petworth, England, is the work of the great Flemish artist Van Dyck, and shows the midget with the queen, Henrietta Maria. The other is at Hampton Court. At the Ashmolean Museum at Oxford, his blue satin waistcoat, stockings, and breeches are preserved.

Richard Gibson: Miniature Miniaturist

A good friend of Hudson's was the dwarf Richard Gibson. Appropriately enough, this little man gained fame as a painter of miniature pictures, which once had a great vogue.

Born in Cumberland in 1615, Gibson became the page of a lady at Mortlake. When she discovered he had artistic talent, she arranged for him to take lessons in drawing. Gibson, like Hudson, ended up in the court of Charles I and Queen Henrietta Maria. Here he received further training from one of the leading painters of the age, Sir Peter Lely; and went on, himself, to become a painter of royalty.

Gibson, at maturity, stood three feet ten inches tall. There was in the court a girl dwarf of about the same height, Anne Shepherd. It was the queen's whim that the two small people should marry, and Gibson does not appear to have objected. The wedding was performed at Hampton Court to provide a day's entertainment for the court. The king himself gave away the bride and the queen presented her with a diamond ring.

For the occasion Edmund Waller, the poet, wrote some verses which he called "Of the Marriage of the Dwarfs":

> *Design, or chance, makes others wive;*
> *But Nature did this match contrive;*
> *Eve might as well have Adam fled,*
> *As she deny'd her little bed*
> *To him, for whom heaven seemed to frame*
> *And measure out this only dame.*

The dwarf lived a long and happy life, watching rulers come and go and prospering under all of them. Charles I valued his work, especially a painting called *The Good Shepherd*. It was in the care of Van der Doort, keeper of the royal collections. The keeper put it in such a safe place that he could not find it again. Terrified that he might be charged with having stolen it, he took his life. A few days later the painting was recovered.

When Charles I fell and Oliver Cromwell became lord protector, he also was Gibson's patron. The little artist did several portraits of Cromwell. After the monarchy was restored he was made court miniature painter. He was also appointed drawing and painting instructor to James II's two daughters, Mary and Anne, both of whom were later to be queens of England. When Mary became the wife of the prince of Orange, Gibson went with her to Holland and stayed with her.

The dwarf lived to a ripe old age. At his death in 1690 he was seventy-four. His wife passed away in 1709, aged eighty-nine. Both are buried at Saint Paul's, Covent Garden, in London. Presumably they enjoyed a harmonious life together, for they had nine children, five of whom lived to adulthood. The children were of normal size and one daughter achieved a reputation as a painter.

Matthew Buchinger: Armless and Legless Dwarf

In the annals of the Very Special People, Matthew Buchinger occupies a very special place. For Buchinger was not only a dwarf—he was born without arms, legs, and thighs. Out of his shoulders grew two fleshy processes, like fins or fingers without nails; a later generation would have called him "a sealfin boy." Yet with this imperfect physical endowment Buchinger not only was self-supporting but did a multitude of things better than the average person with hands and feet.

Born in Anspach, Germany, in 1674, Buchinger was twenty-nine inches tall. Early in the 1700s he migrated to England. There both King George I and the earl of Oxford took a more than ordinary interest in him.

The collection of the British Museum includes an advertisement for a performance of Buchinger's elegantly penned by the dwarf himself. In the handbill he declares that "he makes a pen, and writes several hands as quick and as well as any writing master, and will write with any for a wager; he draws faces to the life, and coats of arms, pictures, flowers, with a pen, very curiously. He threads a fine needle very quick; shuffles a pack of cards, and deals them very swift. He plays upon a dulcimer as well as any musician; he does many surprising things with cups and balls ... he plays at skittles ... shaves himself very dexterously; and many other things too tedious to insert." The other things this thighless and legless man did, incidentally, included dancing a hornpipe.

One of the faces that Buchinger drew "to the life" was his own. In one famous self-portrait, beautifully executed on vellum, he ingeniously worked into the flowing curls of his wig the text of six of the Psalms as well as the Lord's Prayer.

James Paris described a performance by Buchinger that he attended. The actions that the dwarf performed with his flippers were astonishing. He played cards and ninepins. He combed, oiled, and powdered his wig. He also loaded and fired a pistol repeatedly— and never failed to hit his target. He darted a sword and hit a mark at a surprising distance. Paris commented on Buchinger's attractiveness, noting that he "was very well shaped and had a handsome face."

Buchinger, like many other Very Special People, possessed a deep fascination for women. He married four times and became the father of eleven children.

Only one of the dwarf's marriages was unhappy. His second wife spent his hard-earned money prodigally on clothing, luxuries, and drink for herself, but treated him in a niggardly way. She also beat him cruelly.

Buchinger was long suffering rather than helpless. One day his wife lost her temper and began to strike him in front of guests. When he could bear it no longer, he hurled himself at her with such force that she was thrown to the ground. Then he got on top of her and beat her with his flippers until she begged for mercy. Buchinger warned her that he would give her more of the same if she ever laid a hand on him again. She took the lesson to heart and thereafter played the role of a dutiful and loving wife.

Buchinger traveled and exhibited throughout Great Britain. He is reported to have died in Cork, Ireland, in 1732.

Count Josef Boruwlaski

One of the most famous midgets ever exhibited in Europe was a Pole, Josef Boruwlaski, who took the title of count. Boruwlaski was born in Halicz, Galicia, in 1739. He had five brothers and sisters, two of them remarkably short, like himself. The parents were of normal stature. At six he was seventeen inches tall, but later in life he grew to thirty-nine inches. He was attractive and perfectly proportioned.

After Josef's father died the family suffered hard times. An aristocratic lady offered to look after the boy and later she passed him to her friend, Countess Humiecka. With the countess he traveled throughout Europe. At the court of Vienna the Empress Maria Theresa took him up on her lap and inquired what was the most extraordinary thing in the city. "To see so small a man on the lap of so great a lady," he replied. The empress gave him a diamond ring, taken from the finger of her little daughter, Marie Antoinette, who was later, as queen of France, to perish under the guillotine.

The midget grew up to be a graceful, witty courtier. He could have passed his life in secure, easy circumstances as the protégé of the countess, but he was a man and he fell in love. At twenty-five he wooed a French actress in Warsaw. The actress pretended to be fond of him but in private she made fun of him. It was fortunate for Boruwlaski that she threw him over; the countess was angry with him and he was in danger of losing his protection.

When Boruwlaski was forty he fell in love again with a woman of normal size, Isalina Barboutan, who was in the employ of the countess. Isalina returned his affection. In a fit of fury the countess turned the two out of her house.

The midget was granted a small pension by the king of Poland and with his bride he began the life of a wanderer. He managed with the income from concerts that he gave, for he was something of a musician, and with the help of his aristocratic friends. Like Tom Thumb, he was a welcome guest at many European courts. Often, as in Munich, this polished little gentleman found the attentions of women embarrassing. He wrote: "Several charming ladies were eager to take me on their lap and clasp me in their arms. I could not help observing to them that, being forty-two and a child only in size, their fond caresses made me endure the most cruel torments."

In England Boruwlaski was received by the king, George III, who took a considerable interest in him. He also met the famous giant, O'Brien. "Our surprise," he wrote, "was, I think, equal; the giant remained a moment speechless, viewing me with looks of astonishment ... having come very near him ... it appeared that his knee was nearly upon a level with the top of my head."

In 1800 Boruwlaski settled near Durham, where he became a popular figure. He often had difficulty making ends meet, and was obliged to exhibit himself. But he pretended that he did not charge people to look at him; his valet simply collected a shilling from visitors for opening the door for them. Possessed of literary as well as musical gifts, he penned his memoirs. When a lady asked for his autograph, he wrote:

> *Poland was my cradle,*
> *England is my nest;*
> *Durham is my quiet place,*
> *Where my weary bones shall rest.*

Boruwlaski died in 1837, aged ninety-eight, and was laid to rest in Durham Cathedral. He had several children, all of normal height.

Richebourg: the Spy Who Posed As a Baby

One of the most extraordinary midgets in history was a Frenchman named Richebourg. He died in 1858 in Paris, reportedly at the age of ninety. It is said that he rarely left his house during the last quarter-century of his life.

In his youth Richebourg was in the service of the duchess of Orleans, whose son later became King Louis Philippe. During the terrible days of the French Revolution, when thousands of supporters of the royalist cause lost their heads under the guillotine, Richebourg played a strange and dramatic role. He was dressed as a baby and taken in and out of France and the French capital by a woman who pretended to be his nurse. Concealed in his clothing he carried secret dispatches to and from royalist sympathizers.

Little Richebourg had the size for his role as a baby—he was only twenty-three and a half inches tall. For his services to the house of Orleans he received a pension of three thousand francs.

Admiral Dot

In 1868 P. T. Barnum's museum in New York City burned to the ground a second time and he decided to retire from show business. Touring the United

States with friends, he stopped off in San Francisco. Here he had visitors: Mr. and Mrs. Gabriel Kahn, who brought their son, Leopold, to meet him. Although the parents were of normal stature—the father was actually a very large man—Leopold was only twenty-five inches high. Barnum could not help but be reminded of Tom Thumb and the successes the two had shared. The boy was, in Barnum's words, "so handsome, well-formed and captivating that I could not resist the temptation to engage him." Thus Barnum found himself back in show business—and little Leopold found himself launched on a career as a professional entertainer.

The boy's role called for a new name and Barnum quickly found it for him. He christened his little dot of a person Admiral Dot, or the Eldorado Elf, and dressed him in a British naval uniform. Then he invited the editors of San Francisco's newspapers to come to the Cosmopolitan Hotel and meet the newly elevated admiral. The next day the newspapers appeared with three-column announcements about the midget. "Immediately there was an immense furore," Barnum recalled, "and Woodward's Gardens, where Dot was exhibited for three weeks before going east, was daily thronged with crowds of his curious fellow citizens, under whose very eyes he had lived so long undiscovered."

In 1871 Barnum and W. C. Coup launched the Greatest Show on Earth, a huge traveling circus, and Admiral Dot became one of its featured artists. Besides singing and dancing, he played musical instruments. He was teamed up with Colonel Goshen, Barnum's "Palestine Giant," and sometimes the colossus held him in his great hand. He also appeared with Anna Swan and other giants. For a time he performed with a nephew of his, called Major Atom.

The admiral spent over twenty years in show business. He married Lottie Swartwood, whom he met in a midget show; she was taller than he by an inch. They had two children, both of normal size.

Eventually the admiral retired, buying a hostelry in White Plains, New York, which he named the Admiral Dot Hotel. John L. Sullivan was a notable figure at his bar. The admiral joined the Elks and was in time named honorary chief of the White Plains Fire Department. He took an active interest in the operation of the department and sang in the town choir. Gene Fowler, in his book *The Great Mouthpiece,* describes the little chief appearing on parade, "his helmet gleaming and his silver trumpet polished until it seemed it might have dazed a blind man." Fowler reports that the admiral's hotel was also called "The Hotel Peewee."

Lucia Zarate: the Smallest of Them All

Many circuses, carnivals, and sideshows have claimed that the midget they were featuring at the moment was the world's smallest man or woman. Experts generally agree, however, that the title of smallest midget rightfully belongs to Lucia Zarate, who is virtually unknown today. (See photo insert)

Born in San Carlos, Mexico, in 1864, Lucia made a very modest entrance into the world. Reportedly, she weighed only eight ounces and was seven inches long. At maturity she was under twenty inches tall. The length of her arms was eight inches; around the waist she measured fourteen inches; her weight at seventeen was no more than five pounds. Normal in every other respect, she was described as a bright and animated little lady.

Lucia first appeared in the United States when she was twelve years old. According to Frank Drew, who was associated with dime museums, she was one of the highest-paid midgets of all time, making twenty dollars an hour. Her exhibitor earned a fortune during the many years she appeared in this country.

Lucia's life came to a tragic end in 1890. The train she was traveling in stalled in the Rocky Mountains during a heavy snowstorm. Rescue was impossible and the tiny woman died of exposure.

Another little lady who achieved something of a record was Carrie Akers. Carrie, born in Virginia, was one of the fattest midgets that ever lived. Just an inch under three feet tall, she weighed 309 pounds—over one hundred pounds for each foot of her height!

Lya Graf: the Midget on Morgan's Lap

Early in 1933 a midget with the Ringling Brothers Circus made headlines around the world. Reputedly twenty-one inches tall (some say she was twenty-seven inches), she was, of course, billed as "the smallest woman in the world." Her name was Lya Graf—and she was photographed on the lap of J. P. Morgan, the richest man in America.

According to one account, a Ringling Brothers press agent wanted to publicize the circus, which was in Washington, D.C. J. P. Morgan was appearing before the Senate Banking Committee, then looking into the financier's banking methods. You will remember that those were the days of the Great Depression and financiers were not the most popular people in the world. The nation's attention was focused on the hearings. Reportedly, the press agent smuggled the midget into the room and she climbed into J. P. Morgan's lap while flashbulbs popped.

Some newspapermen, however, had another version. They said that the man who brought the midget in was not a press agent but a friend of a news photographer. The photographer had covered Morgan and his affairs on other occasions and been treated with frigid hauteur. On one occasion he had been pushed around. Morgan, in his appearances before the Senate committee, had been doing his best to create a friendly, democratic image of himself—one that was utterly false. The cameraman decided to get even. He was sure the icy financier would reveal his true nature as soon as he found Lya in his lap.

Actually, the millionaire came off very well. After a split second of shocked surprise he recovered his composure. As cameras clicked, he smiled at Lya, asked her questions about herself, and observed that he had a little grandson who was taller than she was.

When he found out her age—she told him she was twenty—he said the right thing: "You don't look it!"

The midget was delighted and so were the newsmen. J.P. Morgan wasn't disappointed either. In the world press the next day he appeared not as a cold-blooded Mr. Moneybags but as a genial, friendly grandfather type.

For Lya the story didn't end so happily. Her name, by the way, was actually Schwartz, and she had come from Germany only a year before. Her mother was a midget; her father, although quite short, was not. She had studied music, and then come to the United States to join the circus. Her tragedy began a few years later, when she returned to Germany.

In Germany the Nazis had come to power and Lya was to find there were three counts against her. She was Jewish. She was a midget—and the Nazis were embarking on a program of destroying everyone who was physically abnormal. And J. P. Morgan had smiled at her. Wall Street had refused the German Government a loan, throwing Hitler into a fury, in which he raved about a Wall Street conspiracy against the Nazis. Lya, obviously, was one of Morgan's tools!

In 1937 Lya was reported arrested by the Gestapo, who were conducting a drive against "vagrants." Her association with Morgan provided grounds for sending her to the concentration camp at Oranienburg. In 1941, with her parents she was shipped to Auschwitz. There they were gassed to death.

In circuses in Germany, midgets and dwarfs were reported to be in short supply after World War II. This was because there weren't any left. Under his "euthanasia" policy, Hitler had gassed approximately ten thousand of them and other exceptionally short people.

World's Largest Dwarf Family

A few of the little people somehow managed to escape execution at the hands of the Nazis. Among them, extraordinarily enough, were seven Jewish brothers and sisters who were dwarfs. Their name was Owitch and they were natives of Romania. Picked up by the Gestapo, they spent several years at Auschwitz, where Nazi doctors performed medical "experiments" on them. Miraculously, they were still alive at the end of the war.

In 1949 the Owitches migrated to Israel. At that time they were reported to be the world's largest dwarf family.

Midget Cities

If people find a single midget fascinating to watch, looking at a group of little people is even more fascinating. Over the years there have been many midget towns that have earned fame and, often enough, substantial income for their sponsors.

Peter the Great built a midget village on the ice-covered Neva River at Saint Petersburg as far back as 1710. Since the village was made of snow, it could not have lasted long. Peter, we saw earlier, was one of the big midget fanciers of all time.

Lilliputia

Inspired by Jonathan Swift's tales of the midget kingdom of Lilliput in *Gulliver's Travels,* almost two hundred years later a permanent midget community was erected in a more appropriate location, Coney Island. The island was enjoying its heyday in 1904 when Dreamland, a new amusement park, opened its doors and revealed to the public the little city of Lilliputia. Among Lilliputia's buildings were a fort, a firehouse, a theater, and private homes, all scaled down to midget size. The town was jammed with visitors from the day the park opened. It was the brain child of Samuel W. Gumpertz, who later headed the Ringling Brothers Circus and other leading amusement enterprises.

Lilliputia was built to hold some three hundred midgets. For the sake of contrast, it also included some giants. Many noted midgets spent various lengths of time in the city, among them Mrs. Tom Thumb and her second husband, Count Primo Magri, whom the Irish barkers used to call Count Magee. The glamorous little city came to a sudden end on May 27, 1911, when fire, spreading from a ride called Hell's Gate, burned down the entire amusement park.

Singer's Midgets

In 1913 Leo Singer, a Viennese producer of musical comedies, founded another midget town that became world famous. Singer said that he was inspired by Swift's book and a Russian painting of Peter the Great's snow village on the Neva, but we can suspect that word of Coney Island's Lilliputia had reached his ears.

Singer obtained the services of Joseph Urban, who later worked for Florenz Ziegfeld and Hollywood, to lay out and decorate the miniature community in Vienna. When the toy town was built, Singer hired 125 midgets to populate it. It was the right idea for the right time; his Lilliputian city became one of the showplaces of the old Austrian capital.

The fame of Singer's midgets spread beyond the country's borders and the impresario sent his little people on foreign tours. In 1924 he brought thirty-five of them to the United States. Their success was instantaneous, and for years they were part of the American theatrical scene. Numerous troupes were formed in imitation of the Singer midgets, but none matched them in popularity.

A curious sidelight of the story is that one of Singer's former midgets, Franz Ebert, made so much more appealing a child than normal children did that he was in constant demand as a model for child photographers. His image was widely used on cans of baby foods and talcum powder.

World's Fair Midget Towns

Midget towns have sometimes been a feature of big fairs in the United States and abroad. One notable town was Midget Village at the Century of Progress

Fair, held in Chicago in 1933. It was a depression year. Before the fair opened, American midgets, hearing there was a move afoot to import the population of the little town from Europe, agitated for the employment of Americans exclusively. So effective was their action that, reportedly, all seventy-two midgets hired were native or naturalized Americans or residents of long standing.

Some of the older midgets in the village actually went back to the era of Tom Thumb and had known the little general personally. Jennie Quigley, the oldest, had been born in 1850. The Adams sisters, born in the 1860s, had sung with Mrs. Tom Thumb's Lilliputian Opera Company.

The New York World's Fair of 1939 also boasted a midget city. Known as Morris Gest's Little Miracle Town, the miniature community covered thirty-six thousand square feet and even included a circus. Both the town and its population of 125 little people were brought over from Europe.

The Dancing Dolls

From the twenties through the forties not many midgets were as successful as the Dolls. There were four members of the family: Harry, forty-two inches tall; Tiny, two inches shorter than Harry; Grace, the oldest; and Daisy, tallest of the quartet, who was known as "the midget Mae West," and was midway between a midget and a short woman. Some or all of the Dolls were seen in big motion pictures of the time, including *That's My Baby, Good News, The Unholy Three, Freaks,* and *The Wizard of Oz* (in which they played the Munchkins). The midgets were also known professionally as the Earles.

Harry was featured with Lon Chaney and Victor McLaglen in *The Unholy Three* in 1925. Some famous anecdotes emerged from the making of that film. Once, a sweet old lady carried a baby into the wardrobe department of the studio. "Do you think I could borrow a clean dress for him?" she asked in a quavering voice.

"Of course, Mother," the wardrobe mistress replied sympathetically. "Why, I'll change the baby for you myself."

"Like hell you will, Madam!" the baby shouted. "Not this baby!" He twisted his way out of the old woman's arms. "You dirty double-crossing bum!" he cried at her. "That's the last time I'll ever fall for one of your jokes!"

The timid old woman was Lon Chaney, the screen's greatest master of disguise. The baby was Harry Doll. At the time he was twenty-three years old.

Victor McLaglen, who played a giant in the film, was also given to practical jokes. One of them was spiking the milk in Harry's nursing bottle with Scotch. After the initial surprise, Harry found he rather liked it. As a matter of fact, he became very annoyed when his co-stars began drinking his bottle themselves.

In the film, Harry played one of a gang of burglars. He was small enough to climb through transoms—yet when detectives came after him all they saw was a baby sucking on his bottle or playing with his rattle. The midget gave credit to Lon Chaney for teaching him everything he knew about acting.

Tod Browning, director of *The Unholy Three,* was so impressed by Harry Doll's performance that he looked for another script for him. That proved to be the scenario of the film *Freaks,* in which Harry and his sister Daisy both played starring roles.

Harry and his three sisters spent many years with Ringling Brothers, appearing with the circus from April to November. The rest of the year they passed in Sarasota, Florida, like many other circus folk. In their home—not very surprisingly named "the Doll House"—objects were arranged for the midgets' convenience. Light switches were a few feet from the floor; chairs and tables had short legs. The family used children's toothbrushes and table silver. Daisy, the tallest of the Dolls, drove the car, pressing down on special extension pedals. A sportsman, Harry often went hunting, using rifles with short stocks and barrels. He called his motorboat *The Little Skipper.*

The Dolls were born in Germany. Their name was originally Schneider, and they had four brothers and sisters whose height was normal. Harry (born in 1902 and given the name Kurt) grew at an average rate until he was about seven, when he stopped growing. Harry and Grace came to America in 1914. For a while they danced at a sideshow in Coney Island; the owner called them "the Dancing Dolls" and the name stuck. When the other sisters arrived in America they formed a song and dance team and performed in vaudeville. Later they signed up with Ringling Brothers.

For the Dolls, as for others of the Very Special People, life called for many adjustments and living by a special set of values. "When I was a teen-ager," Harry once told an interviewer, "I felt so strongly the difference between the other boys at school and myself. But, as time went by, I got used to that difference. Now we hardly notice it at all."

Johnny: a Living Trademark

Johnny Roventini's name was known to few but his voice was known to millions. It was the most famous living trademark in the world. Three times a week, for years, it was heard on major radio stations from coast to coast crying out the once-familiar slogan: "Call for Phil-ip Mor-ris!"

Johnny was about twenty years old and the year was about 1932 when an advertising man, Milton Biow, heard him paging guests in the Hotel New Yorker.

Biow was struck by the clarity of the young man's voice and asked him to page a Mr. Philip Morris (one of the agency's accounts was Philip Morris Cigarettes). Before the week was out Johnny had been signed to a $20,000-a-year contract—a steep step upward from the fifteen dollars a week he had been earning!

At the peak of his fame Johnny was forty-seven inches tall. He weighed fifty-nine pounds. His shoes were size two, his shirts size six. When he went to the theater he could lift the seat and sit on the edge. He had a collie but did not bother to walk it on a leash—

he could hold directly on to its harness. He drove a car that had extension pedals and occasionally people would call a policeman to stop the "little boy" who was stealing it.

Johnny's most precious asset, his voice, was insured for $50,000. For his own protection, his contract did not allow him to use the subway during rush hours. Although the record does not tell how many ladies kissed him, it does reveal that he shook hands with considerably more than a million people.

Michu of Ringling Brothers

Circuses, we have seen, like to bill their current midget star as the smallest man in the world—no matter how tall he is. Recently Ringling Brothers gave this title to Mihaly Meszaros, known as Michu. Without his boots, Michu was thirty-two and one-half inches tall, according to the circus.

Michu was brought to the United States from Hungary in 1973. He was then thirty-three years old. His parents were about eight inches taller than he, and were members of the Lilliputian Theater of Budapest. As a youngster he attended the circus school run by the state.

The midget's first job was with the Liebel Circus, which traveled from village to village in Hungary. Here Michu filled a variety of slots. He was a clown, a dancer, and a unicyclist. He also served as the Liebels' advance man, driving on to the next town they were going to play and making preparations for their coming. He had his own specially made small car he used for this purpose. At one time Michu also doubled as the circus chef.

A zealous fisherman, Mischu enjoys telling about the time he caught a carp in the Danube. He himself weighs only twenty-three pounds fully dressed; the carp weighed ten, and was eighteen inches long. In the tug-of-war that took place, the little man was pulled into the water. Fortunately one of the Liebels was standing by and intervened in time to save the fisherman and his catch.

Michu likes to smoke king-size Hungarian cigarettes, perhaps for the dramatic effect. His clothes are usually custom-made (his size is three), but like other midgets he obtains some of his garments in the children's department.

Children, incidentally, are often a problem to the tiny Hungarian. Most are a good deal bigger than he is, and occasionally they take out their aggressive drives on him. For this reason he seldom goes out without a normal-sized companion.

The midget has a girl who is three inches taller than he is. When he goes to see her, he pulls on a pair of high-heeled boots. His girl, who used to be his partner in a dance routine, is employed by the Liebel Circus as an acrobat and dancer. They have been keeping company for ten years. As Michu puts it, "She likes the free and easy life, too."

PART 5

THERE WERE GIANTS
IN THE EARTH

20

What—and Why—Is a Giant?

A giant, in common usage, is a person who is exceptionally tall. But how tall is tall? By general agreement if a man is over 6 feet 6.7 inches he's a giant. A woman doesn't have to be that tall to qualify—6 feet 1.6 inches will admit her to the giant class. Women don't run as tall as men, so giantesses are rarer than giants.

The tallest man on record was Robert Pershing Wadlow, whose story is told later in these pages. Wadlow grew to a height of 8 feet 11.1 inches, and was still growing when he died in 1940 at the age of twenty-two. His case, like so many, was a pathological one. The tallest "healthy" giant—that is, one whose height was not the result of a disease—was Angus MacAskill (1825-63), born in Scotland. MacAskill, at the time of his death in Nova Scotia, was 7 feet 9 inches tall.

Most giants tend to exaggerate their height. Either they're in show business, where every added inch means added dollars and their contract makes them promise not to reveal their actual height, or else they're in other lines but take a special pride in seeming to loom larger than anyone else around. Al Tomaini, a famous circus tall man who passed away in 1962, was billed as being 8 feet 4.5 inches tall; actually he was a mere 7 feet 6.5 inches. Eddie Carmel, a Ringling Brothers and Barnum & Bailey "Tallest Man on Earth," who gained great fame as a result of a memorable picture taken of him and his parents by Diane Arbus, the noted photographer, was said to be over 9 feet tall, and he looked it in Miss Arbus's picture. But a careful screening of other photographs of the giant convinced critics that he probably wasn't taller than about 7 feet 6 inches. Wherever possible we'll tell you the height that the giant alleged he was—and the height he was revealed to be as a result of actual measurement by qualified medical practitioners.

Fake Giants

Giants have often been faked, especially in the circus, Lord Sanger, the famous British owner, has told how this is done in his autobiography, *Seventy Years a Showman*. Sanger's father, who had a traveling show, featured "Mme. Gomez, the Tallest Woman in the World." As a giantess, she wasn't very gigantic—except with Mr. Sanger's help. "Madame was exhibited on a raised platform in the travelling booth," wrote the showman, "and when the company was assembled the curtains were pulled aside, and she stepped forward from a mass of draperies at the back. Her actual height, which might have been nearly six feet, was added to by her high heels and cork raisers in her shoes, and—note the point—her dresses were made very full and long."

To demonstrate her height, Sanger asked the tallest man in the audience to join Mme. Gomez on the platform. He was to put her to the "arm test"—that is, see if he could pass under her outstretched arm. "As he ascended the steps to the small platform Madame would pull her long dress aside, and draw backwards as if to make room. In making this movement she imperceptibly gained a little step or dais, cunningly concealed by the back draperies. This dais added at least seven inches to her height; while the long dress fell round her in seemingly perfect fit. The arm test was, of course, always easily passed under these conditions, and the spectators invariably went away satisfied that there was 'no deception.' "

Sometimes the giant was mounted on a higher platform. Barnum wrote of the "penny shows" that he visited in England. "While in the showmen's vans seeking for acquisitions for my Museum in America, I was struck with the tall appearance of a couple of females who exhibited as the 'Canadian giantesses, each seven feet in height.' Suspecting that a cheat was hidden under their unfashionably long dresses [who could have known better!], which reached to the floor and thus rendered their feet invisible, I attempted to solve the mystery by raising a foot or two of the superfluous covering. The strapping young lady, not relishing such liberties from a stranger, laid me flat upon the floor with a blow from her brawny hand. I was on my feet again in tolerably quick time, but not until I had discovered that she stood upon a pedestal at least eighteen inches high."

Normal Giants

We've suggested that there are both healthy and pathological kinds of giants. The healthy kind is born of a family or a race of big people and there's nothing abnormal about him. Many professional basketball players may be seven feet or more tall and are completely normal. The Watusi people of East Africa often grow to a height of seven feet and more. Sometimes tallness may be the result of a special grouping of chromosomes. Doctors call this type "genetic giantism."

The Pituitary Giant

Most other cases of giantism—true giantism in the medical sense—are abnormal. The primary kind is pituitary giantism. It's the exact reverse of being a midget.

The pituitary is a pea-sized gland located at the base of the brain. One of its secretions is the growth hormone. If this hormone is produced in inadequate quantities, the person is likely to be a midget. If the gland turns out an oversupply, the person may prove to be a giant. Sometimes the cause of the oversupply is a tumor on the gland.

Whether a person becomes a giant or not depends on how old he is when the pituitary starts to malfunction. If the trouble occurs in childhood or adolescence, the growing points or epiphyses of the long bones are still active, and they continue to grow long after growth has stopped in normal people. The result is that the person can grow to a great height, sometimes over eight feet. His lower jaw may become heavy and prominent, giving him a bulldog look. His hands, feet, and nose may increase in size.

On the other hand, if the person is older when the pituitary gland starts to malfunction, then he suffers from another condition. This is called acromegaly. The height of the person with acromegaly doesn't increase. But his hands, feet, and nose get larger and his teeth become spaced out.

Help for Giants

The outlook for the pituitary giant isn't particularly good. As a rule he's fairly weak and his sexual powers are not fully developed. He is susceptible to infections and foot trouble. Frequently he doesn't live beyond his twenties. Fortunately, today the pituitary giant can be treated, sometimes (but by no means always) with very good results. The treatment may include surgery on the pituitary or irradiation of the gland with X rays.

Other glandular troubles may turn people into giants. Failure of the testes to produce sex hormones can cause eunuchoid giantism. In girls the ovaries may fail the same way, with the same result. Both types are corrected by supplying the missing hormone.

The Psychological Side

On the mental side, too, the giant may face problems. People are always looking at him or pointing at him; he's made self-conscious about himself very early in life. He may feel like Robert Wadlow, that he has to apologize: "It's not my fault that I'm this way. . . . I didn't have anything to do with my getting this way." Wadlow, because of the good family life he had, felt less isolated than many. Others, like Jack Earle, seek solace in writing poetry, or in the arts. Often they become highly creative people.

Everything Is Too Small

Life for the giant is much like what it is for the midget, only in an inverse sense. Instead of being too big, everything is too small.

The minuteness, the fragility of things makes itself felt in childhood. The ordinary kiddy car or express wagon will buckle under your weight. In school, the chairs and desks made for a third-grader won't accommodate you if you're a nine-year-old giant over six feet tall. Your desk may have to be propped up on bricks; a bigger seat will be needed. Blackboards are too low to write on comfortably. Getting books out of a children's bookcase requires constant stooping. So does drinking from a fountain.

It's awkward writing with an ordinary pencil. Your hand will get cramped or you won't be able to keep up with the rest of the class in taking notes. Because you're more susceptible to infections and foot trouble (a lack of calcium in the bones is often associated with rapid growth) you may be absent from school more, and this interferes with your scholastic career.

Walking up and down steps is troublesome. The stairs aren't deep enough. Doorways aren't high enough.

Clothing Is Expensive

When you're ten years old, you've already outgrown ordinary sizes used by men. Everything has to be custom made. The frames for your glasses must be made to order. A normal wristwatch band won't fit. Suits have to be tailor-made and may require twice the yardage needed for the average man's suit.

One of Robert Wadlow's first specially made pairs of shoes cost his father thirty-five dollars. By the time he was twenty he was wearing size 37. It cost close to eighty dollars. But then the shoe was 18½ inches long, in contrast to the ordinary length of less than a foot. Not only does the giant have to pay a premium price for the things he wears, but he outgrows them rapidly.

Usually a child inherits the cast-off clothing of his older brothers and sisters. When the child's a giant, however, the situation is reversed. In Robert Wadlow's case, his father used to inherit his son's jackets and other garments he'd outgrown. Some had hardly been worn at all before they became too small for the boy giant.

When a Giant Travels

Riding on buses or trains has serious disadvantages. A giant of five may be the size of a youth sixteen or seventeen. Try convincing a conductor that your preschool giant is entitled to travel at half-fare!

And when the giant grows up? He'd better not fancy a sports car. He won't even be able to fit into the driver's seat of a big-sized station wagon. He'll need to have a special car built for his use, or have a standard car remodeled.

Feeding a Giant

It costs more to support a giant all the way around. Eating is a case in point. Patrick Cotter, the Irish giant, used to eat three big loaves of bread, twenty eggs, and three quarts of milk for breakfast—and complain that he was still hungry. When food was rationed in World War II, Ted Evans, an English giant, was granted a double ration.

Perhaps the chief advantage of being a giant is in

basketball. Even a moderate-sized giant of seven feet or so can stand by the basket, catch the ball tossed by his teammates, and deposit it in the basket with ease. On the other hand, since his feet aren't likely to be very good if he's a pituitary giant, he probably won't last long at the game.

Giants are especially useful in doing work around the house. They can clean the tops of closets and paint ceilings without a ladder. And cleaning the windows on the outside is a breeze.

No End of Disadvantages

On balance, the disadvantages outweigh the advantages. If you try to use a revolving door, you're likely to be too big. If you travel in an airplane—and Lord knows they're tight enough for normal-sized people—the seat in front of you will have to be removed. If you go to the movies, you'll have to sit in the last row or you'll block the view of the people in back of you.

When you come into an unfamiliar room, you must not only be careful not to bump your head in passing through the doorway—you have to keep an eye open for chandeliers or lamps suspended from the ceiling. You must be especially cautious about ceiling fans. You'd probably better stay out of subways for the same reason. Out of doors, your head is always banging into awnings and signs.

If you want to sit in comfort, you'll have to have your chairs made to order. Tables and bureaus will be too low. You'll need special ones. And beds? If you don't have your own giant one made to order, you'll have to place one at the end of another so you can stretch out in comfort.

Perhaps the worst disadvantage of all, as many giants have said, is that you'll have to listen to thousands of people who each think they're being incredibly original and funny when they ask you:

"How's the weather up there?"

21

Byrne and Cotter: the Two Irish Giants

John Hunter, the celebrated English surgeon and anatomist, was determined to have the Irish giant's skeleton for his collection.

The giant, Charlie Byrne, was just as determined not to let him have it. He had heard of Hunter's big kettle, which the doctor used to boil the flesh off his specimens. Sometimes Byrne had nightmares that his great body was turning and turning in Hunter's bubbling kettle.

Hunter offered the giant money for his body after death. Byrne turned him down cold. The scientist kept raising his offer. The giant kept refusing.

And always the nightmare kept coming back. He was being boiled in that huge kettle. Like a big chicken. Turning and turning. . . .

For Charlie Byrne, it was a short life but a merry one. He was born in 1761 in Ireland. In April, 1782, he was in London. An advertisement announcing his appearance declared: "To be seen this, and every day this week, in his large elegant room at the cane shop, next door to the late Cox's Museum, Spring Gardens. MR. BYRNE, the surprising IRISH GIANT, who is allowed to be the *Tallest man in the world;* his height is *eight foot two inches* and in full proportion accordingly; only 21 years of age. His stay will not be long in London, as he proposes shortly to visit the Continent."

Byrne, or O'Brien, as the Irish giant sometimes called himself, was evidently a well-known figure, for an impostor had already tried to trade on his name in London. "The nobility and gentry are requested to take notice," the advertisement warned, "there was a man showed himself for sometime past at the top of the Haymarket, and Piccadilly, who advertised and endeavoured to impose himself on the public for the Irish Giant. *Mr. Byrne* begs leave to assure them it was an imposition, as he is *the only* IRISH GIANT, and never was in this metropolis before. Thursday the 11th inst."

The Incredible John Hunter

People crowded in to see the tall youth. Among them were many of the nobility and gentry and members of the Royal Society. No doubt John Hunter, too, came to see him at this time.

Hunter, founder of the science of comparative anatomy, was the most important surgeon in England. Everything that happened in the natural world fascinated him. How a deer's antlers grow, how smallpox is communicated to unborn babies, the development of birds' eggs, the relation of health to sex, the nature of fossils were just a few of the countless subjects that this great scientist studied exhaustively. His contributions to medicine and surgery were enormous.

Hunter was indefatigable. When Leigh Thomas (who later examined Chang and Eng, the original Siamese twins) called on him for the first time—the hour was 5 A.M.—he found him busily engaged in dissecting insects. Hunter conducted thousands of experiments of every kind, including the poisoning of great numbers of animals to study the effect of poison on the body. (He loved animals, by the way.) To Edward Jenner, father of vaccination, who once gave him his thoughts or guesses on a subject, Hunter made a reply that has gone down in the history of science: "Why think? Why not try the experiment?"

The anatomist built a remarkable collection of scientific specimens of every kind. Cost was no object to him. He often borrowed himself into debt so he could add to his collection.

When Hunter saw Byrne, he felt that much could be learned from an autopsy performed on the giant's cadaver. He also felt that Byrne's skeleton would be a significant addition to his collection. The only difficulty was that Byrne was still alive. But Hunter took the long view.

Porter to King George III

Giants were favored by royalty as porters, and it's said that for a brief period Byrne served George III in that capacity at Saint James's Palace. But the giant soon wearied of the post and went back to exhibiting himself.

His Fortune Stolen

Byrne had a deep fear of thieves, and took all of his savings with him wherever he went. He must have been a very successful giant indeed, for by 1783 he had earned £770, which he carried around in his pocket in the form of two banknotes.

It was a mistake. "The Irish Giant, a few evenings since, taking a lunar ramble," said a newspaper account on April 23, 1783, "was tempted to visit the Black Horse, a little public-house facing the King's Mews, and before he returned to his own apartments, found himself a less man than he had been the beginning the evening, by the loss of upwards of £700 in banknotes which had been taken out of his pocket."

Drinking Himself to Death

Byrne was a drinker, and he drank more heavily than ever after his loss. It is said that he came home after a night's carousal with friends in a heavy downpour and contracted pneumonia.

As the giant lay ill, he was told that one of John Hunter's agents had been coming to the house and inquiring about his health. Feeling death drawing close, he asked some of his countrymen to promise that his body would be carried out on the Irish Sea, weighted, and dropped overboard. That way no anatomist would get him.

His friends agreed, and Byrne died peacefully.

The Surgeons Close In

Apparently Hunter wasn't the only physician interested in acquiring Byrne's remains. "The whole tribe of surgeons," said one periodical, "put in a claim for the poor departed Irishman and surrounded his house, just as harpooners would an enormous whale. One of them has gone so far as to have a niche made for himself in the giant's coffin, in order to be ready at hand on the 'witching time of night, when churchyards yawn.'"

The interest of medical circles in Byrne's cadaver must have been widespread, for another journal reported, "Since the death of the Irish Giant, there have been more physical consultations held than ever were conveyed to keep Harry the VIII in existence. The object of these Aesculapian deliberations is to get the poor departed giant into their possession; for which purpose they wander after his remains from place to place, and mutter more fee, faw, fums than ever were breathed by the whole gigantic race, when they attempted to scale heaven and dethrone Jupiter!"

The Body Snatchers

In the end the persistent Hunter won the prize. He is said to have paid £500 for it. As Francis Henry Butler told the story in his biography of the scientist. "His [Byrne's] undertaker, who had entered into a pecuniary compact with the great anatomist, managed that while the escort was drinking at a certain stage on the march seawards, the coffin should be locked in a barn. There some men he had concealed speedily substituted an equivalent weight of paving stones for the body, which was at night forwarded to Hunter, and by him taken in his carriage to Earl's Court, and, to avoid risk of a discovery, immediately after suitable division, boiled to obtain the bones."

Byrne's Skeleton Today

The "division," of course, included a dissection, performed by Hunter to satisfy his insatiable curiosity. And so, after a short stay in Hunter's kettle, Byrne's skeleton was displayed, white and shining, in the Hunterian Museum, which the great surgeon had erected to house his collection. After Hunter's death ten years later—his own bones came to rest in Westminster Abbey, which is, in effect, a museum of British history—his collection passed into the hands of the Royal College of Surgeons in London, where you can see Byrne's skeleton to this day. A little under seven feet nine inches high, it towers over the skeleton of a man of normal height, placed next to it for contrast.

Patrick Cotter: the Other O'Brien

About the same time that Byrne was appearing in London, another Irish giant came on the scene. Like Byrne, he called himself O'Brien and claimed to trace his descent from Brien Boreau, an ancient king of Ireland.

Cotter was born in 1760 in Kinsale, Ireland. For a while he worked as a bricklayer's apprentice. But his enormously rapid growth soon made it impractical for him to lay bricks and practical to go into show business, and his father hired him out to a traveling exhibitor. When Cotter asked for some money for himself, he was thrown into a debtors' prison. Finally, with the help of a sympathetic friend, he managed to obtain his freedom.

Lighting His Pipe at a Street Lamp

The young giant traveled through England, exhibiting himself in various towns. In Northampton a journalist wrote: "Mr. O'Brien enjoyed his early pipe and the lamps of the town afforded him an easy method of lighting it. When at the door of Mr. Dent in Bridge Street, he withdrew the cap of the lamp, whiffed his tobacco into a flame and stalked away as if no uncommon event had taken place." The story is probably not exaggerated. Cotter was actually almost seven feet eleven inches tall—although, as we'll see in a moment, he claimed to be taller.

In 1782 Cotter was appearing in London, where he was much admired. A few years later, in an advertisement he issued announcing that he was exhibiting himself, he said, "He acknowledges he is only eight feet three inches and a half high, though Brien Boreau, the puissant ancient king of Ireland, his ancestor, was nine feet high, which he hopes to attain before he is of age, being now between eighteen and nineteen years old."

In 1785 Cotter was acting in a play at the Sadler's Wells Theater. In one of the high spots of the evening, an actress had to walk up a flight of stairs to greet Cotter, who was standing on the stage. According to a statement given out by the management, "with great ease he shakes hands with the spectators in the upper boxes." Later that year he was appearing with trained dogs, acrobats, and dancers in the theater.

The Giant's Cave

The following year was a big one in even a giant's life: Cotter got married. Newspaper writers were as witty then as they are today. "O'Brien, who last winter exhibited his person in St. James's Street," declared a newspaper account, "was lately married at Pancras

Church, to a young woman of the name of Cave who lived in Bolton-row, Piccadilly. She may now for more reasons than one, without impropriety, be termed the *Giant's Cave*."

An old print in the possession of the Ringling Museum of the Circus in Sarasota, Florida, depicts Count Boruwlaski, the famous Polish midget, calling on O'Brien. In the picture the midget barely reaches the giant's knee. In an earlier chapter we gave Boruwlaski's version of the meeting. According to one account, the two attended a Masonic dinner in 1790 at which Cotter reached into his capacious pocket and took out—Boruwlaski!

A Surgeon's Visit

Although Cotter made a great impression on the public, he was less successful with a medical visitor. In 1804 a surgeon, W. Blair called on Cotter. He found that he displayed the typical signs of weakness that were later to be identified with an overactive pituitary gland.

"He was of very extraordinary stature but not well-formed," wrote the surgeon. "As he would not suffer a minute examination to be made of his person, it is impossible to give any other than a very slight description of him.

"He declined the proposal of walking across the room, and I believe was afraid of discovering his extreme imbecility [weakness]. He had the general aspect of a weak and unreflecting person with an uncommonly low forehead; for as near as I could ascertain, the space above his eyebrows in a perpendicular line to the top of his head, did not exceed two inches. He told me his age was thirty-eight years and that most of his ancestors by his mother's side were very large persons.

"A Huge, Overgrown, Sickly Boy"

"The disproportionate size of his hands struck me with surprise and in this he seemed to make his principal boast. He refused to allow a cast to be made of his and said, 'it had been made many years ago' . . .

"All his joints were large and perhaps rickety. His legs appeared swollen, misshapen and I thought dropsical. The feet were clumsy, and concealed as much as possible by high shoes. His limbs were not very stout, especially his arms, and I judge he had scarcely got the use of them . . . He certainly had a greater redundancy of bone than of muscle, and gave me the impression of a huge, overgrown, sickly boy, his voice being rather feeble as well as his bodily energies . . .

"The state of his pulse agreed with the general appearance of his person, viz. feeble, languid and slow in its motions."

His Actual Height

"With regard to his actual height, I felt anxious to detect the fallacy he held out of its being almost nine feet.

"Upon extending my arm to the utmost, I reached his eyebrow with my little finger. Allowing his height to have been two inches and a quarter above this, it could not be more in the whole than seven feet ten inches, so that I am persuaded the common opinion founded on the giant's own tale is greatly exaggerated." (Actually Cotter's height was 7 feet 10.86 inches.)

The giant had managed to save a substantial sum of money and he retired not long after his interview with Blair. He settled near Bristol, where he lived in comfort, but for only a few years. He died on September 8, 1806.

Precautions Against Ghouls

Like Charles Byrne, Cotter was afraid his body would end up on a dissecting table and he had no interest in advancing medical knowledge. Grave robbing to obtain cadavers for medical students was a common practice in that time; the robbers were known as ghouls. In accordance with Cotter's instructions, his grave was made twelve feet deep in rock. After the burial, it was carefully secured with iron bars and arched over with bricks.

Cotter was a local celebrity, and his funeral was a major event in Bristol. It had been scheduled for 6 A.M. to avoid a crowd, but a large throng—possibly as many as two thousand persons—attended, despite the early hour. Police officers had to be brought in to keep order. The coffin, made of lead, was nine feet two inches long. Fourteen men were needed to carry it to the grave.

22

Swan and Bates: Two Giants in Love

It was the biggest baby that had ever been born. From the soles of its feet to the crown of its head it measured thirty inches. The length of its feet was five and one-half inches. It weighed close to twenty-four pounds.

The baby was a giant, but then, so were its parents. As Anna Swan, "the Nova Scotia Giantess," and Captain Martin Bates, "the Kentucky Giant," they had toured the United States and Europe and been seen by millions. The combined height of the couple was fourteen feet eight inches. Anna, a beautiful young woman, stood seven feet five and one-half inches tall. Her husband was a few inches shorter. They were the tallest married couple in the whole world. (See photo insert)

Anna was P. T. Barnum's discovery. Born in 1846 in New Annan, Nova Scotia, she was the child of Scottish immigrants. There was nothing unusual about the height of her parents. Her father was six feet tall, her mother five feet two inches. People raised big families in those days: Anna was the third of thirteen children.

Anna, at birth, weighed eighteen pounds. At six, she was as tall as her mother. At fifteen she looked down on her from a height of seven feet. In school she sat on a high stool and worked at a table that were both raised by planks.

A girl that tall (and well proportioned, too) doesn't go unnoticed. New York City, where P. T. Barnum had his headquarters, is a long way from Nova Scotia but it didn't take him long to learn about Anna.

"I first heard of her through a Quaker," wrote Barnum in his autobiography, "who came into my office one day and told me of a wonderful girl, seventeen years of age, who resided near him at Pictou, Nova Scotia, and who was probably the tallest girl in the world.

"I asked him to obtain her exact height. He did and sent it to me, and I at once sent an agent who in due time came back with Anna Swan.

"She was an intelligent and by no means ill-looking girl, and during the long period she was in my employ she was visited by thousands of persons."

At the American Museum in New York, Anna was placed in the care of tutors and supervised by her parents. She was a prepossessing figure. Good natured as well as good looking, she had a liking for people, and people liked her. Barnum exhibited her along with Commodore Nutt, Tom Thumb, and other human oddities. Billed as "the Tallest Woman in the World," she became one of his leading attractions. She delivered lectures on giants and took part in tableaux.

A Confederate Attack on the American Museum

Periodically Barnum went through what might be called an ordeal by fire. At one time or another, all of his major possessions—his museums, his elaborate, pseudo-oriental palace called Iranistan, in Bridgeport, and his circus—were destroyed by fire. Anna Swan shared his misfortunes, at least in the museums.

In November, 1864, with the tide of battle in the

Civil War turning against the South, a band of Confederate agents slipped quietly into New York. General Sherman had ravaged the South, and the southerners were hoping to even things up. On the appointed day they set fire to nineteen hotels, the Winter Garden, Niblo's Garden, and several vessels in the North River. And, perhaps because Barnum had made substantial financial contributions to the Union cause and was a staunch supporter of Lincon, one of the Confederate agents, Captain Robert C. Kennedy of Louisiana, made his way into the American Museum and flung a glass bomb at its great main staircase. The building caught fire instantly.

Firemen rushed in to help those who were trapped by the flames. One they assisted was a giantess. Irving Wallace, Barnum's biographer, believes it was young Anna Swan. Groping her way through the dense smoke and gasping for breath, she became hysterical. A few firemen tried to help the big girl, but in her terror she bowled them over like ninepins. Finally a larger group of men succeeded in quieting her and giving her a sedative.

Saved by a Derrick

That fire was one of Barnum's smaller ones—he put the damage at a thousand dollars. On July 13, 1865, however, the museum suffered a holocaust. The fire started in the engine room, where Barnum had machinery that pumped water into his aquarium and supplied steam to turn fans in the building. In a matter of minutes giant tongues of flame were lapping hungrily at the five-story building. On the upper floors many of the human oddities were overcome by the smoke.

Anna was discovered almost unconscious on the third floor. Reportedly, she weighed almost four hundred pounds at the time.

"We believe that all the living curiosities were saved," said the *New York Tribune* the following day, "but the giant girl, Anna Swan, was only rescued with the utmost difficulty. There was not a door through which her bulky frame could obtain a passage. It was likewise feared that the stairs would break down, even if she could reach them.

"Her best friend, the living skeleton, stood by her as long as he dared, but then deserted her, while, as the heat grew in intensity, the perspiration rolled from her face in rivulets, which pattered musically upon the floor.

"At length, as a last resort, the employees of the place procured a loft derrick which fortunately happened to be standing near, and erected it alongside the museum. A portion of the wall was then broken off on each side of the window, the strong tackle was in readiness, the tall woman was made fast to one end, and swung over the heads of the people on the streets, with eighteen men grasping the other extremity of the line, and lowered down from the third floor, amid enthusiastic applause.

"A carriage of extraordinary capacity was in readiness and, entering this, the young lady was driven away to a hotel."

The account sounds exaggerated. Barnum himself said the reporter was "facetious." But the museum did burn right down to the ground. For Barnum it was a major catastrophe, costing him hundreds of thousands of dollars. Anna lost all her savings in the fire—twelve hundred dollars in gold and United States bonds—and her entire wardrobe.

Barnum Retires

Thirteen was an important number in Barnum's life. His museum had burned down on July 13, 1865. On November 13, 1865, the showman opened his New American Museum and resumed business. Anna rejoined him. Things went well for both. For almost three years.

On the morning of March 3, 1868, Barnum was at

home in Bridgeport. He was leisurely reading the morning paper when he said suddenly, "Hallo! Barnum's Museum is burned."

His family thought he was joking. He wasn't. During the night a fire had started at the new museum. When the flames finally sputtered out, only the front granite wall of the building was left standing.

Barnum had had it. He decided to retire. Anna Swan, who reportedly had again lost her savings, her personal property, and almost her life in the fire, looked for greener pastures. She went on a tour of the West. In 1869 she was in Europe. In England she appeared before Queen Victoria, who made quite a pet of her—if such a word can be used for such a large girl.

In 1871 Anna's manager, Judge Ingalls, took her on another European tour. One of her companions on this journey was the man she was going to marry.

A Real Captain

Captain Martin Van Buren Bates, unlike many people in show business whose names were preceded by military titles—General Tom Thumb and Admiral Dot are two who come to mind—had actually earned his rank in the military service. Entering the Fifth Kentucky Infantry in 1861 as a private, he was later transferred to the calvary, where he eventually was made a captain.

Bates, like his bride-to-be, was born into a large family: he had ten brothers and sisters. A native of Whitesburg, Kentucky, he was born on November 9, 1845. At fifteen he was six feet tall. The Civil War broke out while he was attending college in Virginia and he enlisted. All through the war he continued to grow, until he achieved the proportions of a giant. After his discharge, he found his way into show business. By his own account, his growth didn't stop until he reached the age of twenty-eight. He was then 7 feet 2½ inches tall and weighed 470 pounds.

A Handsome Couple

Anna Swan and Captain Bates made a handsome couple. Standing next to the captain, Anna looked (and was) taller by a few inches. But the difference wasn't very conspicuous, and you could attribute it to her hairdo. When the two were photographed together there was usually a third person in the picture—and he was so much shorter than either that that was the thing that caught your eye.

Soon after the giants made their appearance in London they gave a performance at Buckingham Palace at the command of Queen Victoria. The program included little plays, monologs, and readings. Anna stood out for her acting talent as well as her size; she had already appeared in New York in the role of Lady Macbeth. As was the queen's custom, she gave both Anna and her captain presents.

The couple was deeply in love—so deeply, they couldn't wait till they got back home to America. On June 17, 1871, they were married in one of London's exquisite old churches, St. Martin's-in-the-Fields. Many important people attended. The bride wore a gown of white satin with orange blossoms; it was said to have been made with one hundred yards of satin and trimmed with fifty yards of lace. The cluster diamond ring on Anna's finger was a wedding gift from the queen. The richly engraved watch and the chain worn by the groom were also a gift from the queen. An ancestor of today's alarm wristwatch, it sounded a chime on the hour. Judge Ingalls, who managed the couple, gave the bride in marriage. Outside the church the crowds were so dense the police had to work strenuously to clear a way for the wedding party.

Four days later Anna and her captain gave a private levee for the Prince of Wales, who was accompanied by Grand Duke Vladimir of Russia and Prince John of Luxembourg. The giants appeared twice before the queen. They were guests of the Princess of Wales at Marlborough House. They also exhibited at some big London theaters and in the grand concert hall of the

Crystal Palace, a historic iron-and-glass showplace out-side London. Then they made a tour of the provinces. In Edinburgh they called on Sir James Young Simpson at the university, and were examined by him just as Chang and Eng, the original Siamese twins, had been.

On May 19, 1872, after the giants completed their tour of Scotland, Anna gave birth to a daughter. The baby weighed eighteen pounds and was twenty-seven inches tall. She died at birth.

House of the Giants

After a long tour of the Continent and some years of travel in the United States the Bateses settled in Se-ville, Ohio. Farming was in the captain's blood and a farmer he would be. Outside the town he bought 130 acres of rich farmland. On it he built a house the like of which had not been seen since the days of Jack the Giant Killer.

Just as Tom Thumb scaled his house to the size of little people, the captain built his for giants. The man-sion had eighteen rooms. In the main wing, the ceilings were twelve to fourteen feet high. Doorways rose 8½ feet from the floor. The furnishings were in keeping with the height of the owners. Anna's piano was mount-ed on heavy stilts three feet high. The fireplaces were made of Italian marble and the sliding doors had panels of rare wood. At the back of the house the rooms were lower and smaller; they were intended for servants. Bates stocked the farm with Norman breed draft horses and shorthorn cattle.

Friends of the giants also settled in Seville. One had been a barker and ticket seller for the couple. An-other had been a Barnum employee. On his farm he bred doves, which he dyed in brilliant colors and sent to New York for Barnum to use in his spectacles.

Anna and her captain had not been on their farm very long when they were lured away by the Cole Brothers Circus. For three seasons, from 1878 to 1880, they traveled with Cole. Then they settled down for good.

The couple became popular members of the Baptist church. Four inches was added to the depth of their pew so they could sit in comfort. Anna took an active part in church groups. The captain busied himself on his farm, which gained a reputation for its excellent crops and handsome cattle.

Mrs. Tom Thumb and the Giants

Old friends from museum and circus days began to drop in. Millie-Christine, the black Siamese twins, were two. A third was the living skeleton—probably the same one who stayed at Anna's side when the flames were crackling in the American Museum.

Tom Thumb's widow, Lavinia Stratton, came to stay for a while after her husband died. After picking Lavinia up at the railroad station, the giants headed for home. They came abreast of the carriage of one of their neighbors. Captain Bates took great pride in the Clydesdales that pulled his custom-built carriage, and he enjoyed racing with friends he encountered on the road. Cracking his whip over his horses, he pulled ahead of his neighbor, who joined in the contest. The carriages rattled along wildly over the rough country road.

Tiny Lavinia was forgotten. For her it was a nightmare. Her black veil blowing off her face, she was thrown from side to side. She tried to hold on to her bag, her friend Anna, and the seat, to keep from being hurled from the carriage. It was some minutes before Anna could make her husband realize what he was doing to their minuscule guest. The rest of the ride was more comfortable.

The Giant Baby

In 1878 the giantess became pregnant. It was a happy time for her. But it was also a fearful one, for she remembered only too vividly the baby she had lost in England.

On January 15, 1879, she was feeling labor pains.

Joyfully, the captain called her physician, Dr. Beach. When he arrived, the doctor found the pains were still infrequent. He examined his patient and decided he might have a good long wait.

He was right. It was thirty-six hours before the pains reached the serious stage.

Late in the afternoon of January 18, the bag of waters burst. Six gallons of fluid poured out. Then the baby's head appeared. But it moved no further. Anna's abdominal muscles had stopped their action.

Dr. Beach took out his forceps. The head was enormous, with a circumference of nineteen inches. Although most of it emerged, the baby was caught by its great shoulders.

Realizing he needed help, Dr. Beach wired another physician, Dr. Robinson of Wooster. He arrived the next morning. After a vain attempt at using the forceps again, the two doctors slipped a bandage over the infant's neck. One of them pulled the baby to the side, and the other finally managed to draw out an arm. More careful manipulation and the shoulders came free. At last the baby had been delivered.

At 23¾ pounds (the weight differs from source to source, but this was what Dr. Beach reported), the infant was the size of a six-month-old child. It was thirty inches high, taller than Commodore Nutt and other midgets with whom Anna had appeared. It was the biggest new-born baby whose height and weight had been recorded to that date.

The child, a boy, was born on January 19. It was extraordinary that he had survived such a difficult birth, and he did not survive it for long. He lived less than a day. He was laid to rest in Mound Hill Cemetery in the family plot. The headstone on his grave bears a single word: "Babe." A photograph of the infant is preserved by the Medina County Historical Society. You can see a life-size plaster model of the baby in an exhibit at the Cleveland Health Museum, 8911 Euclid Avenue, Cleveland, Ohio.

Anna had resilience, for she was able to resume

her tour with the circus during 1880. But that was her final season.

The Floor That Collapsed

Over the years, the giants made many friends in Seville. They were especially fond of children. Mable Anna Mapledoram—the "Anna" is after the lady giant—was a frequent visitor at their home, with her parents. Although Captain Bates was considered a gruff, argumentative man, she remembered sitting next to him at church and when she became restless he would hold his huge watch to her ear until its loud ticking quieted her down. Other Seville residents recalled in their old age that they had been held in Anna's lap when they were children.

For a long time a floor was shown in the town that had collapsed under the weight of the giants during a lively dance.

Death of a Giantess

Anna died suddenly on August 5, 1888, just one day before her forty-second birthday, presumably of a heart ailment. A curious tale is told about her casket. Reportedly, the captain wired Cleveland for a coffin, giving his wife's measurements. The manufacturer apparently thought there was an error, for when the coffin arrived it was of standard size. The funeral had to be delayed until an adequate casket could be obtained.

Anna was a local celebrity, and a large crowd turned out for her funeral. According to her obituary in the *Seville Times,* "a large concourse attended, and the spacious house being too strait to hold them, the services, necessarily brief, were held on the veranda, the people sitting and standing in the yard.

"The procession of carriages which followed the remains to their last resting place extended over the whole distance lying between the house and the cemetery. . . ."

After the funeral the captain sent to England for a

monument to place on the grave. The monument, life size, depicts a woman in a Greek robe. It's not considered an actual likeness of Anna, but the robe is said to resemble some she wore in her performances. On the left side is an inscription from Psalm 17: "As for me, I will behold thy face in righteousness: I shall be satisfied when I awake, with thy likeness."

The Coffin in the Barn

Some years after Anna's death the captain remarried. His second wife was Lavonne Weatherby, daughter of the pastor of the Seville Baptist Church. She was just a little over five feet tall. Bates gave up the giant house he had built for Anna and moved to a smaller one.

Remembering the trouble with his wife's casket, Bates is said to have ordered one for himself while he was still living. He kept it in his barn. The coffin was made of brass and was so heavy it required four men to lift it. The captain also chose six of his friends to be his pallbearers when his time should come.

That time came in 1919. The funeral director, deciding that the men Bates had chosen were not strong enough for the task, made them honorary pallbearers. Eight men were selected to carry the coffin. Then it was found that the hearse was too small for the casket. The doors of the hearse had to be tied shut around the end of the box.

The graves of Captain Bates and his family can still be seen in Mound Hill Cemetery. The giants' house, with its fourteen-foot-high ceilings, was too big and drafty for normal-sized people; it was torn down in 1948, and much of the lumber used to build a new dwelling on the site. Only Bates's barn is left, with his name painted on the roof.

23

Jack Earle: the Lonely Giant

The fall was frightening, nasty. The teen-age giant—he was 7 feet 7½ inches tall—had been standing on a lofty scaffolding mounted on an automobile during the filming of a comedy. Suddenly the scaffolding had come apart under his feet. The giant reached out for something to hold on to. But there was nothing. As he fell, a flying timber banged him on the head.

When the giant youth came to, it was a while before he realized where he was. He was covered with bruises. His nose was broken. Everything was a blur.

Seventy-two hours later the blur darkened. He was completely blind.

The giant's parents brought him home to Texas. Specialists studied his case. Their diagnosis: He had a tumor on the pituitary gland at the base of his brain, and the fall had driven it up against his optic nerve. The prescription: Treatment with X ray, to reduce the tumor.

And so, for month after month, the tumor in the giant's head was massaged by the invisible but incredibly powerful fingers of the X-ray machine. Little by little the tumor shrank. Miraculously, he began to see again.

Simultaneously, something even more astonishing happened.

Ever since his seventh year the giant had been shooting upward at a dizzying rate. His growth had been the despair of his parents. Doctors were unable to tell when it would stop.

Now, suddenly, as a result of the X-ray treatment, his growth had come to a halt.

A Tiny Baby

It is a striking fact that Jacob Ehrlich, one of the tallest men of modern times, was so small when he was born—the place was Denver, the year 1906—that doctors were afraid he wouldn't live. He weighed only four pounds.

But, somehow, little Jacob pulled through. He began to put on weight. He was always a little smaller than other children his age, but otherwise he was normal.

Then, abruptly, his growth pattern changed. He began to add inches and feet to his height at a remarkable rate. His parents were pleased at first. The boy, they said, was making up for lost time. The family had moved to El Paso, Texas, where the father ran a jewelry business. Maybe it was something in the air that was stimulating Jacob's growth; everything was so big in Texas.

But Jacob didn't stop growing. At ten he was over six feet tall. His feet were so big that his shoes had to be made to order. He towered over school friends. They began to call him Pecos Bill, after the Paul Bunyanesque cowboy hero who was so big and powerful he could hug grizzly bears to death. The boy became intensely self-conscious. As soon as school was out he would run off by himself to escape the malicious gibes of his classmates.

The gigantic youngster's parents, deeply concerned, took him to see doctors. But at that early date the science of endocrinology was only finding its feet. It had not yet isolated the growth hormone. The physicians recognized that Jacob was a pituitary case, but they told the Ehrlichs nothing could be done for him.

A Giant of the Screen

Word about the youthful giant got around. He was still in his teens when he was offered a job acting in motion picture comedies. It was everybody's dream in the 1920s to make it in the movies. Jacob was a shy boy, but the thought of rubbing shoulders with Harold Lloyd and Douglas Fairbanks in Hollywood was irresistible. How envious those kids who had been mocking him home in El Paso would feel when they suddenly beheld his tall figure on the screen!

The boy giant must have had talent, for he acted in close to fifty comedies, with a youthful star known as Baby Peggy, whose name is legendary. In the course of Jacob Ehrlich's film career the producers changed his name to Jack Earle, and Jack Earle he remained forever after.

Bigger Than the Tallest Man on Earth

Jack's accident on the set ended any hopes he had of becoming a star of the silent screen. After his recovery he enrolled in college.

One day the youthful giant and some friends went to see the Ringling Brothers and Barnum & Bailey Circus, which was playing in El Paso. Jack found himself in the sideshow tent. There, on the platform in front of him stood Jim Tarver, also a Texan, billed by the circus as the tallest man in the world. Jack looked at him and scratched his head. As he stared at Tarver, people around began to stare at him—for he was taller than "the tallest man in the world" by quite a few inches!

It wasn't very long before the manager of the circus sideshow had tracked Jack to his home. A year's contract as a giant with the sideshow was spread out on the table before the youth and his father. Jack had his misgivings about a career in the circus. Whenever he felt his shyness had disappeared, it suddenly found its way back, like mildew in a rainy summer. But he certainly didn't feel well adjusted at home. He decided to give Ringling Brothers a try.

Fourteen Years in the Circus

The towering youngster found circus life a vast change from college. He could seldom enjoy a moment's peace. Always he was surrounded by noise and excitement—and he loved quiet and contemplation. Now he had to be a showman. He was tricked out in a tall hat, high-heeled shoes, and a gaudy red costume covered with gold braid. It made him appear so tall when he looked in the mirror that even he was surprised.

Jack made some good friends in the circus, especially among the midgets, with whom he was frequently paired. Most of all he liked the Dancing Dolls, the family of four little people whom we met in an earlier chapter. A familiar sight in the circus was the giant walking between the tents, his big voice booming in reply to a high-pitched remark from little Harry Doll or some other midget who was perched on his shoulder. In Jack's first season with the circus, Harry, in particular, was very helpful to him. When Jack felt ill at ease the midget pointed out to him that there were more "freaks" in the audience than there were on the sideshow platform.

The World's Tallest Traveling Salesman

In 1940 Jack had been with the circus fourteen years. That, he felt, was fourteen years too many. He decided that he was tired of standing in front of a curious crowd and trying to divert them. He was ready for something different. So, when the season came to a close, he resigned. A few months afterward he was working as a salesman with a wine company.

People in the wine trade found it a novelty to be called upon by a giant. They liked it. Sales boomed, and Jack was a success. He had a new billing now. He was the World's Tallest Traveling Salesman.

Jack had always had a creative side, which had been ripening when he was with the circus, and now it began to bear fruit. He painted. He sculptured. He wrote poetry—thoughtful poetry full of deep feeling and melancholy. Occasionally he recalled his experiences in show business in his verse. Eventually he published a book of his poems which he called *The Long Shadows*. He was also a prize-winning photographer.

The giant enjoyed making the rounds of his customers. He drove a special car, a remodeled five-passenger coupe. The front seat had been taken out and the steering wheel was lengthened about twenty inches. To drive the vehicle he sat on the back seat. He used to say that although it had cost him a lot, it had one advantage—he didn't need to buy any insurance against theft.

Jack was a carefree driver until he had an accident one winter in Colorado. The car overturned and he was trapped inside. His back was wrenched so severely that he had to go to the Mayo Clinic for treatment.

In 1952 the big man's life came to an end. He was forty-six years old.

That, for a pituitary giant, was an advanced age.

24

Robert Wadlow: the Alton Giant

The doctor weighed little Robert Pershing Wadlow the day he was born and showed him to his parents. "He's a beautiful, perfectly normal baby. Eight and one-half pounds. You can be proud of him."

Robert (See photo insert) was born in Alton, Illinois, on February 22, 1918, the first child of an engineer. His height and weight didn't stay normal for long. When he was a year old he weighed over forty-four pounds. That was almost twice what he should have weighed. But, then, every child has his own rate of growth, and the parents saw nothing to be ashamed about.

However, when he was five years old he weighed 105 pounds and was five feet four inches tall. He looked more like an adult than a child. The doctor assured the Wadlows that the boy was in excellent health.

That year he was examined for an insurance policy. The application was mailed in to the company. It came back with a query. Someone, the insurance company said, had made a mistake in the child's age or his weight and height. The doctor assured the company that the figures were right, and Robert got his policy.

At age 5½ he started in school. The biggest boys' suit size, seventeen, was already too little for him. In the classroom the tables and chairs were for much smaller children. He was a good pupil and scored high in his I.Q. test. His teachers found it hard to view this enormous youngster as an ordinary child. But in spirit at least that's what he was. He played and enjoyed exactly the same games as other children his age.

Nine Years Old: 6 feet 2½ inches

His growth was inexorable. He was over six feet tall when he entered the third grade. At nine, said *Time* magazine, he was taller than his father and could toss him around. The newspapers had discovered him and called on him for photographs whenever he had a birthday.

On his tenth birthday they found he was six feet five inches tall and weighed 210 pounds.

Eleven Years Old: 6 feet 7 inches

Doctors were interested in the boy—they had never seen a larger one. He became a regular visitor at the Barnes Hospital, in Saint Louis, where his case was studied and his measurements taken. After diagnosing his case as pituitary giantism the doctors said an operation could be made on the pituitary gland, but they didn't recommend it. Too dangerous. The boy giant was exhibited to medical students at Washington University Medical School.

For a child, the probing and questioning of doctors is disturbing. But the boy's great height brought him compensations. He was becoming a celebrity. In 1929 he was taken to meet Primo Carnera, the Italian prizefighter. Carnera, then a newcomer in the United States, was to win the world's heavyweight championship in 1933. He was six feet five inches tall and was often referred to as a giant. For the boy it was a thrill to shake hands with the Goliath of the ring—although he himself was tall enough to look down on the boxer's head. (Endocrinologists described Carnera as an acromegaly case.)

On his twelfth birthday the boy was 6 feet 10½ inches tall.

On his thirteenth birthday he was 7 feet 1¾ inches tall and weighed 255 pounds.

Fourteen: 7 feet 5 inches

In 1931 he joined the Boy Scouts. It was a big moment for him—and the Boy Scouts of America as well. He was the tallest scout in the whole world.

The boy was already earning money. Like other giants he had to have his shoes specially made. The firm that supplied them signed him to a contract to make personal appearances at their stores. In exchange he received his shoes free of charge as well as a fee. He also appeared in a film advertising children's shoes.

In 1932, when he turned fourteen, he was seven feet five inches tall. He weighed 301 pounds. Every year he had grown about three inches, and he was to go on doing so. He was far taller than his father and mother, and his brother and two sisters were of average height. Earlier, his mother had been able to touch his shoulder by standing on tiptoe, and the older of his sisters had held his hand as she walked beside him. But they couldn't reach high enough to do so any more.

Sixteen: 7 feet 10 inches

At sixteen the boy was seven feet ten inches tall. His weight was creeping up toward four hundred pounds. No person on the North American continent was as tall as he was.

From time to time he would injure his legs or feet or suffer an infection in them. They were always to be his vulnerable point.

Eighteen: 8 feet 3½ inches

The young giant was casting about for a career. The idea of becoming a lawyer appealed to him when he entered college in 1936. Then 8 feet 3½ inches high, he would surely have become the tallest lawyer in the world, a title later held by Clifford Thompson.

On the campus the boy began to run into problems because of his great size. He found it hard to keep up with the other students in taking notes; even the biggest fountain pen available was a toothpick in his massive hand. Working in the biology lab was a torment, for he had to handle tiny instruments and make delicate adjustments on the microscope. In the giant's world everything seemed to be made for children.

The winter brought special difficulties when the ground was covered with ice. The giant had to gingerly pick his way flanked by classmates, and hold on to their shoulders. His weight was enormous, his bones extremely fragile. If he fell, it could mean a long stay in the hospital—if not worse.

Nineteen: 8 feet 5½ inches

He'd been making a good sum of money each year promoting Peters Shoes and now the idea struck him that having a shoe store of his own or a string of them might be better than being a lawyer. He needed money to start, however.

In 1937 Ringling Brothers asked him to make appearances with the circus in Boston and New York and he accepted. One of his conditions was that the circus should provide a hotel suite for his father and himself and pay all their expenses. Another was that he wouldn't be part of the sideshow. His appearances, twice a day, were just a few minutes long. The three rings were cleared out and then he stepped into one of them. The circus had wanted to dress him up in a costume that would exaggerate his height, as it did with all its big men, but he refused. He wore an ordinary business suit.

The giant began to make more and more public appearances, always accompanied by his father. He operated concessions at fairs. Great crowds turned out to see him. When he appeared at shoe stores a platform was often put up outside, where he could sit in comfort.

He developed an entertaining routine. Frederick Fadner, in his biography of Wadlow, *Gentle Giant* tells this joke, which the giant and his father used very effectively in public appearances. " 'The greatest trouble I ever have with Robert,' Mr. Wadlow would say, 'is trying to keep him from walking down the hallways in hotels and peeking over the transoms above the doors.'

" 'Yeah, maybe I did,' Robert would admit with a twinkle in his eye, 'but the only thing wrong with Dad was he got mad when I quit lifting him up for a peek.' "

Twenty-one: 8 feet 8¼ inches

He had reached the age of twenty-one. He stood 8 feet 8¼ inches tall. He was eager to exercise his privilege as a citizen. His secret ballot, however, wasn't very secret. Once he pulled the polling booth curtain shut behind him he towered head and shoulders above it. His hat touched the ceiling. He filled in his ballot, resting it high up on the wall.

In Minnesota a group of Indians made him a member of their tribe. They gave him an Indian name.

"What does it mean in English?" he asked.

"Tall Pine," they replied.

Twenty-two: 8 feet 11.1 inches

By 1940 he had grown again. He measured 8 feet 11.1 inches now. His weight was a ponderous 439 pounds. He walked with a cane.

As usual, he was traveling and making personal appearances. On July 4, he was in Michigan, at a lumbermen's festival. He and his father were scheduled to ride in a parade. At lunch his father noticed that he wasn't eating. Later he complained he didn't feel well—and he looked it. His father wanted to get medical attention for him but their car was trapped in the parade. Hours passed before they were able to get out of it.

Robert was rushed to a hotel and his father called a doctor.

The New Brace

The young giant was running a fever and he had an infected ankle. One consequence of his enormous growth was that sensation in his legs was defective. "He is unaware," a physician once said, "of a wrinkle in his sock or a foreign body in his shoe until a blister, followed by an ulcer, is formed." He was wearing a new brace on his ankle and it had scraped the flesh, setting up an infection. But he hadn't noticed it.

The doctor wanted to put him in the hospital but he refused. A nurse was stationed at his bedside around the clock.

His condition grew worse. He was in great pain. His mother was called.

His parents were with him night and day. Day after day.

Sometimes his pain eased a little and his mother and father felt hope. But always the pain came back and wrapped itself around him, pulling its coils tighter and tighter, like some great snake.

On July 14, the giant was disconsolate. A family reunion, at which his grandparents were to be present, was scheduled for the end of the month. The doctor had told him he wouldn't be able to attend.

That day he was in extreme pain.

In the small hours of the morning of July 15 his parents opened their bedroom door in answer to a peremptory knocking. They saw his nurse's sagging white face.

The joy that their giant son had brought into their lives for twenty-two years was at an end. So was the terror.

A Special Casket

Robert's remains were taken back home to Alton. Great crowds came to view him in the funeral home. A special casket had been made for him: it was ten feet long and thirty-two inches wide. When the undertaker found the casket was too big to pass through the door of the church, services were held at the funeral home. Like Tom Thumb, his tiny opposite, Robert Wadlow was a Mason and he was buried with Masonic honors.

An unusual measure was taken to protect the coffin. It was enclosed in a thick shell of reinforced concrete.

Robert Wadlow had read the story of Charles Byrne and John Hunter, the anatomist who coveted his bones and had his body stolen to get them.

He wasn't taking any chances.

≡⊃◻═══⊐◻═══⊐◻══════⊐◻══════⊐◻═══⊐◻═══⊐◻⊏

25

Giants Yesterday and Today

≡⊃◻═══⊐◻═══⊐◻═══════⊐◻═══════⊐◻═══⊐◻⊏

Giants have been scaring people out of their wits ever since time began. From Goliath, the massive Philistine who was laid low by a well-placed stone from young David's slingshot, to the giant who went around roaring, "Fee, fi, fo, fum" in the tale of Jack the Giant Killer, they have been represented as fearsome, brutish creatures who somehow or other were always outwitted and undone by their normal-size opponents.

Around the world, in older times, it was believed that the first race that inhabited the earth was one of giants. We find such traditions among the peoples as diverse as the American Indians and the ancient Greeks. In part these widespread beliefs may have resulted from the discovery of very big fossil bones in earlier times. In 1712, for example, a thigh-bone seventeen feet in length and a tooth that tipped the scales at 4¾ pounds were uncovered in New England. Increase Mather, president of Harvard College, promptly wrote to the Royal Society of London that this proved a race of giants had lived on the earth before Noah's flood. The

254

bones doubtless belonged to a mammoth or a mastodon.

The Book of Genesis tells us "There were giants in the earth in those days; and also after that, when the sons of God came unto the daughters of men which were of old, men of renown." In other parts of the Bible we read of a number of giant races. "And there we saw the giants," says the Book of Numbers, "the sons of Anak which come of the giants; and we were in our own sight as grasshoppers, and so we were in their sight." These may have been normal human beings but of greater stature than the Hebrews, who, with the natural tendency that all people have to exaggerate, called them giants.

When Magellan and his men visited Patagonia in South America in 1520, they reported seeing Indians who were formidable figures "five cubits high." (A cubit is about eighteen inches—the distance from your elbow to the end of your middle finger.) The Tehuelche Indians of Patagonia, whom the explorers saw, actually averaged six feet in height.

Giant Rulers

Big people there have always been, and those who are bigger than others are likely to be called giants. Perhaps the first giant known to history was Sesokhris, a pharaoh, who lived in the Third Dynasty, and was reputedly some eight feet tall. Pliny, the historian, mentions two giants in the reign of Augustus. Supposedly they were over ten feet tall (doubtless an exaggeration). Their bodies were preserved in the Sallustian Gardens.

"A young barbarian of gigantic stature," Edward Gibbon tells us, became the emperor Maximin of Rome in 235 A.D. He is said to have been eight feet tall and of tremendous strength, so that he could pull a wagon that two oxen weren't able to. According to the ancients, Maximin drank six gallons of wine a day and ate forty pounds of meat. A bloodthirsty ruler, he lasted only three years on the throne. As Gibbon pointed out, if

Maximin had lived in an earlier age, "tradition and poetry might well have described him as one of those
monstrous giants whose supernatural power was constantly excited for the destruction of mankind."

Royal Porters and Others

During the Renaissance, kings wanted to have
their giants, just as they did their dwarfs. Francis I of
France enlisted a giant as an archer in his guards.
Queen Elizabeth I had a giant porter at the door of her
palace. So did her successor, James I. James's man was
named William Parsons, and many tales were told of his
strength. According to one, "sometimes by way of merriment he would take two of the tallest Yeomen of the
Guard under his arms and carry them as he pleased (in
spite of all resistance) about the guard-chamber." Parsons was succeeded as porter by William Evans, friend
of Jeffery Hudson, the dwarf favorite of Charles I.
Evans was even taller than Parsons.

When King Charles was dethroned and the Com-
monwealth established, Oliver Cromwell continued the
royal tradition by employing a giant porter. This man,
named Daniel, was a fanatical Puritan and a preacher
in his spare time. He was reputedly seven feet six inches
high. On the back of the terrace of Windsor Castle
there is a big O that is said to mark his height.

A Regiment of Giants

Frederick William I, king of Prussia, collected
giants just as Peter the Great of Russia collected little
people. Frederick had the largest collection of tall soldiers in history. His palace at Potsdam was guarded by
twenty-four hundred huge grenadiers.

For the king, his regiment of giants was a special
delight. He reviewed their lofty ranks every day, armed
with a sergeant's stout cane. "The first rank," Voltaire
tells us, "was made up of men the smallest of whom
stood seven feet high. His agents purchased these men
in various parts of Europe and Asia."

The Giant of Jülich

To enlist great grenadiers for Frederick, his agents went to great lengths—sometimes excessive ones. History records the case of a carpenter named Zimmermann, of the town of Jülich, whom they wanted to recruit. A sergeant dressed in plain clothes called on the carpenter, measured his six feet six inches with his eye, and asked him to make a box a little over six feet six inches long. When Zimmermann finished the box the sergeant rejected it. He said it wasn't the required length.

"But I made it to your exact specifications," the carpenter protested. "I'm six feet six myself, and I know I'll fit inside it."

To prove his point, Zimmermann lifted the lid, climbed into the box, and extended himself to his full length.

Instantly the sergeant banged the lid shut and locked it. He called in a group of his men who were waiting outside and ordered them to convey the box to headquarters. Unfortunately, the carpenter suffocated en route.

The Giant Women of Potsdam

To enlist an Irish giant named Kirkman, Frederick spent six thousand dollars, according to Thomas Carlyle. The king's men had less success when they kidnapped a huge man who was on his way to England. He turned out to be the Austrian ambassador.

Frederick's regiment of giants was stationed at Potsdam for fifty years. By the end of that period an observer noted that the people dwelling in the area were exceptionally tall; he was especially struck by "the numerous gigantic figures of the women." Frederick had filled his garrison with giants, and the giants had done as much for the town.

Chang: the Chinese Giant

In 1865 a nineteen-year-old Chinese giant named Chang appeared in London and made a considerable impression on the public. His levees at the Egyptian Hall were always crowded.

A pamphlet Chang sold declared he was nine feet tall and weighed over 360 pounds. Since he wore the thick-soled slippers of a Chinese gentleman and a long silken robe, and was never without his Chinese hat—and Chung, a tiny dwarf, always sat at his feet—people thought him considerably taller than he actually was. Reliable medical measurements cut him down to a mere 7 feet 8½ inches!

Chang Wu-gow was born in 1846 in Foochow. His parents, according to his pamphlet, were of ordinary height. After a short illness he began to grow rapidly, reaching adult height by the age of twelve.

Francis T. Buckland, the natural history writer, rarely missed an opportunity to see natural oddities displayed in London. His picture of Chang at the Egyptian Hall is interesting. "On entering the room one is immediately, as it were, transferred to a private house in China. Chang is seen at the end of the room sitting like a stone joss upon a kind of throne, dressed in the most lovely white satin garments, highly ornamented with beautiful devices wrought in needlework. At his right hand, on a sort of minor throne, is seated his wife, and at his feet is seated the dwarf, also from China. The steps to the throne are guarded on each side by two Chinamen in their native costume."

Chang was a pleasant-looking man with an attractive smile. He was well educated and spoke a number of foreign languages. He said that he had a brother almost seven feet tall and a sister six feet tall; one sister who had died was ten inches taller than Chang was.

During his reception by the Prince and Princess of Wales, the giant was asked to write his name in Chinese ideographs on the wall. His writing was measured and found to be close to ten feet from the floor.

Chang went home to China after his successful European appearances but was back again in 1878. After touring Europe he settled in southern England and retired. He died in November, 1893.

Ella Ewing: the Saintly Giantess

Wilkie Collins, author of *The Moonstone*, once remarked that by a merciful dispensation of providence giants are, for the most part, created gentle. Most of the giants in our book live up to that description, but none more so than Ella Ewing.

Born in Lewis County, Missouri, on March 9, 1872, Ella started to grow very tall between the ages of nine and twelve. At ten her height was six feet nine inches. Most of her length was in her legs and arms; from her hips to her shoulders she was of normal proportions. Her hands and feet were exceptionally big.

All her life Ella was devoted to the church. As a young person she taught in Sunday school. Attendance in her classes was very good. Was it because she was living proof of the truth of the scriptural phrase "There were giants in the earth in those days"—or because the children enjoyed an opportunity to see a real giantess without paying admission?

In her upper teens Ella was seven feet tall. Her extraordinary height caught the attention of a fair manager at Memphis, Missouri, and he proposed that she exhibit herself. Ella seems to have resisted the idea, but when her father ran into financial difficulties she began to make public appearances. For years she traveled with Barnum and Bailey. The girl kept growing, until at twenty-five she was seven feet six inches. (The circus claimed she was eight feet four inches tall.) She weighed about 250 pounds.

Circus advertisements portrayed Ella as a handsome giantess. She didn't come up to Anna Swan in looks, but she did have good features and a strong, pleasant face. As a young person she stooped somewhat in order to minimize her great height. Ella built a home that a giantess could feel at ease in. Ceilings were 15 feet high. Doors were fully 10 feet high, and doorknobs were placed about a foot above their usual position. Her bureau was 6 feet high, her tables 4½ feet. Her bed was a long one—9½ feet. Her bathtub was 6 feet long, so she could sit in it comfortably. Her closets were said to be the size of ordinary bedrooms.

The Saintly Giantess passed away on January 10, 1912. Her death was attributed to consumption (tuberculosis). She was, at the time, reportedly the tallest woman in the United States, and her coffin the biggest made up to that date in this country. Twenty-five yards of material were used in her burial gown.

Tallest Woman That Ever Lived

The tallest woman on record was an English giantess named Jane Bunford. She was born on July 26, 1895. In 1906 she suffered a head injury and began to grow rapidly. Two years later her height was six feet six inches. At the time of her death in 1922 she measured seven feet seven inches tall, and might have been five inches taller but for a curvature of the spine. The medical museum of Birmingham University, England, has her skeleton on display.

Clifford Thompson: Tallest Lawyer on Earth

When Clifford Thompson was in the circus, claims were made that he was the tallest man on earth. Eight feet seven inches tall—that's what they said he was. Sober critics, studying photographs of the giant, insisted he couldn't be more than seven feet five inches.

Thompson was born in 1904 on his parents' farm in Wisconsin. His rate of growth seemed normal, with one difference—he didn't stop growing when most children did. His upward ascent continued until he was twenty-seven years old.

After attending a teachers' college, Thompson gave up the idea of becoming an educator and went to work for a circus as a giant. He stayed in show business for twelve years. In 1939 he married Mary Bars, who was five feet five inches. She persuaded him that a giant didn't have to limit himself to being a giant. So he went to work as a salesman for a Milwaukee brewery.

Later Thompson set his sights higher. He entered

Marquette University Law School, graduating in 1944. In the 1950s he was practicing law in Portland, Oregon. We might well disagree with his claim that he was the tallest man on earth—but he certainly was the tallest lawyer!

PART 6

FAT AND SKINNY

26

They Don't Come Any Heavier

Robert Earl Hughes: Half a Ton of Man

It was one of the oddest cases in the history of American medicine. The 1,041-pound man had lain for days in a trailer in the parking lot outside the Bremen Community Hospital, in Bremen, Indiana. He was gravely ill. But the hospital staff wouldn't take him into the hospital . . .

Robert Earl Hughes was born in 1926 in Illinois. He was a large baby, but not exceptionally so. He weighed 11½ pounds.

When he was three months old he had a severe attack of whooping cough. His parents believed that upset his endocrine balance.

For the rest of his short life he put on poundage as it had never been put on before in recorded history. At the age of six he weighed 203 pounds. Four years later, when he stepped on the scale, it registered 378 pounds. At eighteen he weighed 693 pounds. And at twenty-five? An incredible 896 pounds.

And still he kept putting it on.

In February, 1958, Hughes weighed 1,069 pounds. It was the heaviest medically authenticated weight that had been achieved by a human being. Proudly he declared that he measured 122 inches around the waist, 124 inches around the chest, 40 inches around the upper arm.

Hughes went to work as a farm boy, but he was soon too big for the job. For a person of his dimensions there seemed to be only one place—the sideshow. And that was where he spent the rest of his life. He wore enormous baggy overalls most of the time. He often went without shoes—not because he had been a farm boy but because it was too hard for him to bend over and tie the shoelaces. He had an easygoing, engaging manner.

In 1958, the big, genial young fellow was touring Indiana with the carnival of the Gooding Amusement Company. It was almost impossible for him to get around under his own power and he spent a great deal of his time in his mobile home, which was a heavily reinforced semitrailer truck.

In July, Hughes came down with the three-day measles. Even simple ailments can be serious in a person of his dimensions, and he was rushed to the nearby Bremen Community Hospital. One look at him and the nurses ran to inspect their beds and doorways. Unquestionably, he was too big to fit on a normal hospital bed. And there wasn't a chance that he could be squeezed through the doorway of one of the rooms.

Hughes was compelled to stay on the special bed he had in his trailer. But a regular procession of nurses, technicians, and physicians kept moving back and forth between the trailer and the hospital.

The measles seemed to be clearing up. Then the patient developed another illness—uremia. In this grave ailment the kidneys stop functioning normally and poisons accumulate in the blood.

By the evening of July 10 Robert Earl Hughes was dead.

A Casket As Big As a Piano Case

Hughes's funeral, on July 13, at Mount Sterling, Illinois, was, as the *Quincy Herald Whig* described it, to some extent a "production." His photograph was on sale, and permission was given for pictures to be taken. A huge casket had been made. Said to be as large as a piano case, it was eighty-five inches long, fifty-two inches wide, and thirty-four inches deep. It was placed on a flatbed truck with the help of a loading machine.

A circus-type tent had been erected over the open grave in Benville Cemetery. With twelve men helping, the heavy coffin was moved on rollers and heavy planks to the grave. The casket was opened and visitors were allowed to view the body. Hughes was dressed as he had been in life, in his baggy overalls and a blue shirt. Two long lines of people filed by the casket. After the services, the huge casket was lowered into the grave by a loading machine.

"Thus ended the funeral of a big man," the *Quincy Herald Whig* reported, "big in size and big in heart."

Johnny Alee

If reports about him are accurate, Johnny Alee may have been the greatest heavyweight of all time. He reputedly achieved the spectacular weight of 1,132 pounds. Thus he seemed to have weighed sixty-three pounds more than Robert Earl Hughes at his peak.

Alee was born in Carbon (now Carbonton), North Carolina, in 1853. Although he was a heavy child, his weight was not abnormal. In his tenth year, however, he started to eat at an exceptional rate and his weight zoomed. In five years he had grown so huge that he was unable to pass through the front door of his house. Reportedly his upper thigh was so huge that an adult had difficulty getting his two arms around it.

The fat man sat in a special chair he'd had built to support his great weight. He was so heavy he couldn't rise to his feet without help. It was hard for him to move around at all. To reach a table about fifteen feet away required a quarter of an hour. Afterward it took him quite a while to recover from the exertion.

Alee's house stood on a hillside. Part of the structure rested on logs some eight feet from the ground. He kept getting heavier—but the floor of his house didn't get stronger. One day in 1887 he was walking over the log-supported floor when he crashed through. He didn't fall all the way—he was caught at his armpits. Friends rushed to help. Before they could lift him back up he stopped breathing.

It was the opinion of physicians who examined Alee that his death was caused by heart failure, probably brought on by fright. To ascertain his weight at death, reportedly the coal company's scales had to be used.

Happy Jack Eckert

He weighed 739 pounds and he had a waist measurement of eighty-seven inches, he said. "Happy Jack Eckert" they called him in the circus and carnival. But how happy could he have been, with his great sagging breasts, his belly an enormous paunch hanging down below his knees when he was seated—a mountain of human flesh?

Still, Happy Jack managed to look happy. He smiled at his public. That's what's expected of professional fat people, and Jack managed to live up to expectations. No matter how he felt inside.

Eckert, a native of Lafayette, Indiana, started life in a big way. He weighed nineteen pounds at birth. At ten he weighed 265 pounds. And at ten he started in show business.

The fat man became a familiar figure in leading circuses and carnivals. He traveled across the Atlantic Ocean with Barnum and Bailey. He appeared at the World's Fair held in Chicago and at the Panama Pacific Exposition in San Francisco. For ten years he traveled with carnivals.

Eckert found great difficulty in walking. He made his home in a truck, which also served as his showplace.

In February, 1939, he was traveling to Mobile, Alabama, to appear in the Mardi Gras carnival there when his vehicle collided with a freight truck. He was injured.

Lifting Eckert into the ambulance was a major undertaking. Ten men were needed for the task. At the hospital, nurses pushed two extra-strong beds together for him. He was found to have sustained internal injuries and some ribs were broken.

A few weeks later Happy Jack was dead. He was sixty-two years old, and had been a trouper for over half a century.

Attendance at the funeral services at Mobile, Alabama, was one of the biggest the city had ever seen. Seven hundred and fifty people traveled out into the country to be present at the interment. The coffin was an enormous one, made especially for Happy Jack.

Ironically enough, there would have been no need for a coffin if the old circus man's last wish had been respected. Happy Jack had always wanted to give his remains to medical science, so doctors could discover what had caused his condition and perhaps find a way to keep others from repeating his experience. But since he hadn't set down this wish in writing, medical schools were unwilling to accept his body, fearing they might be sued.

Baby Ruth Pontico

Baby Ruth's weight—at its peak said to be 815 pounds—made her fortune. Thousands of people used to pass through her tent when she was with Royal American Shows or look at her open-mouthed in the Ringling Brothers Circus.

But Baby Ruth's weight also limited her activities. Eventually it contributed to the development of two large tumors on the inside of her knees. Her doctor recommended surgery, saying the operation was a simple one.

So it turned out to be. Simple—and final.

Ruth was born Ruth Smith in Kempton, Indiana, in about 1904. Her mother had been a circus fat lady before her with Ringling Brothers, reputedly weighing six hundred pounds. Ruth inherited her mother's predisposition to obesity; she believed it was glandular.

The big girl had no ambition to follow in her mother's capacious footsteps as a circus fat lady. She went to secretarial school and then took a job with a telegraph company. But she was just too large for the equipment in the office, and she didn't stay long.

Her second position was in a lawyer's office. The attorney valued her speed as a stenographer and she had a specially made chair in the office. But she already weighed four hundred pounds, and people were always barging in to get a look at her. It became impossible to work in a businesslike way.

Ruth fled to the big top. There, at least, she belonged. With Ringling Brothers she traveled from one end of the country to another. She even found love in the circus. She weighed a reported 697 pounds when Joe Pontico, who used to sell colored balloons in Madison Square Garden, saw her. It was love at first sight. As he used to tell it, he was almost a hundred feet away when his eyes fell on her majestic form. At once he exclaimed, "That's my woman!" Ruth found him equally appealing, and after a short while they were married. In the winter Joe used to run a restaurant near Sarasota, Florida.

Fat ladies have a reputation for being cheerful and friendly. Of no one was that truer than Ruth Pontico. Circus employees used to call her the "fairy godmother"—they could always count on her for assistance when they needed it most.

One of the best paid of sideshow employees—she is said to have earned three hundred dollars a day— Baby Ruth wasn't one of the happiest. Her weight kept her from living like a normal human being. Almost everything she used or owned had to be specially made. Her house had reinforced floors. Her porch had special supports. Chairs had to be extra large and strengthened to bear her weight. A bed of normal height would have given her problems; hers was a special one, low and exceptionally wide, with reinforcements.

When Ruth wasn't exhibiting, you would usually find her sitting in a chair. She couldn't get around very easily. Just a walk across the room was a trial to her. She couldn't fit into an ordinary automobile. Places of entertainment, such as theaters, were closed to her because their seats were too small. So were restaurants and churches. Special equipment was needed in the railroad car in which she traveled with the circus. Once she fell through the steps of a railroad coach.

Baby Ruth continued to gain at the rate of forty pounds a year. Finally she developed tumors on the inside of her knees. She planned to have them removed so she would be ready for the 1942 circus season.

When Baby Ruth checked into the hospital in Tampa, Florida, for her operation, something unforeseen happened. The bed she was put in collapsed under her weight. The hospital simply didn't have a bed that would hold her and she had to go home.

For her next visit to the hospital, Ruth wasn't taking any chances. She brought her own special bed along.

The operation took less than thirty minutes. It was a success. But as Ruth came out of the anesthesia she started to disgorge. The nurses tried to turn her over to free her throat. But her weight, over eight hundred pounds, was too much for them. The gigantic woman was immovable. As they heaved desperately, she choked to death.

Ruth's weight was so great that she had to be transported to the funeral parlor in her own special bed. A steel casket more than six feet long and three feet wide, weighing over two hundred pounds, was constructed for her. To push it into the hearse, sixteen brawny pallbearers were required. Among the mourners was her daughter of nineteen, who weighed under one hundred pounds.

Baby Flo: Heaviest Woman on Record

Although Baby Ruth was reported to weigh 815 pounds, she wasn't the heaviest woman on record. That is said to have been Flora Mae Jackson, known as "Baby Flo" to carnival people. She was five feet nine inches tall and weighed 840 pounds. Mrs. Jackson died in 1965 in Florida at the age of thirty-five.

Jolly Irene

"The bigger they come the harder they fall," runs an old saying. It certainly holds true for fat ladies.

"Amanda Siebert, Coney Island sideshow fat lady," declared *The New York Times* on December 2, 1937, "fell out of bed last night at her furnished room at 2854 Stillwell Avenue, Coney Island. It required the combined efforts of five heaving policemen to put her back again. She weighs 650 pounds."

It was unquestionably a hard fall for Jolly Irene, as Amanda Siebert was professionally known—but she doubtless took it with the unfailing good humor with which she greeted life's slaps and knocks. In the sideshow she was famous for her broad, friendly smile. The countless thousands who gazed at her on the platform remembered her gay, cheery personality as much as her extraordinary avoirdupois.

Jolly Irene was born in about 1880. Her weight was completely normal when she was growing up. In 1901, she was a pretty young woman of twenty-one weighing 120 pounds, and had been married one year. Then she had her first child. The birth reportedly disturbed her endocrine balance. She began to put on weight at a rapid rate.

Upset, Irene went on a diet. She ate barely enough to maintain a living skeleton (as a thin man in the circus is traditionally known). But still her poundage continued to mount.

Since Irene couldn't fight her glands she decided to take advantage of what they were doing to her. She joined the Ringling Brothers Circus.

During the years Irene traveled with the circus, her weight kept increasing. This was all to the good, financially. A fat lady used to be paid in proportion to her weight; if she added pounds to her girth, the management added dollars to her salary. But after a while Irene became too heavy to travel and she decided to seek a more sedentary life. The story went around that she had gotten too fat to fit into ordinary railroad cars and the circus had suggested that she travel in a baggage car; insulted, she quit. It seemed like a press agent's story.

Jolly Irene settled in Coney Island, where she worked in the sideshow. At Coney she married for a second time. Her groom was George Siebert. In the winter Siebert worked as a clerk at the hotel where they lived. In the summer he worked as talker for his wife at the sideshow.

On one occasion Jolly Irene had to go to court, where her testimony was required. When her turn came to be heard, she was asked to step forward and sit in the witness chair. Jolly Irene took one look at the Lilliputian seat and stood glowering. The spectators burst out in laughter. Banging his gavel vigorously to restore order, the judge gave her permission to remain on her feet while she presented her evidence.

As Jolly Irene approached her sixtieth birthday, sickness began to take away some of her great weight, which had reportedly gone as high as seven hundred pounds. She weighed only about five hundred pounds when she died in November, 1940.

A requiem mass was held for Jolly Irene in the Church of Our Lady of Solace, attended by many Very Special People who had known and loved her. Jolly Irene herself couldn't be present. Her coffin was at least twice the size of a normal one and the undertaker found he couldn't get it into the church.

27

Celesta Geyer and William J. Cobb: from Heavyweight to Lightweight

"Diet or die," her physician told her.

The fat lady listened to him incredulously. For fifty years she had been satisfying her appetite without stint. If she didn't have her five pounds of meat a day, four loaves of bread, heaps of potatoes, gallon of milk, and innumerable helpings of cake, pastry, ice cream, and candy she would go to bed hungry.

But now she was gasping for breath. Her blood pressure was 240 over 132. Five heart specialists had looked at her electrocardiograms and shaken their heads. She weighed 555 pounds—over a quarter of a ton. That enormous poundage was a burden on her heart, and her heart was ready to give up.

"Diet or die," the doctor said. "There are no two ways about it."

For Celesta Geyer, born in Cincinnati, Ohio, on July 18, 1901, nothing was more natural than to put on weight. She was completely normal at birth, weighing in at 7½ pounds. She had no glandular problem. But she did have a German mother who loved to cook and bake. To her Old World parents, a fat child was a healthy child. Celesta developed a passion for food. It became the most important thing in her life.

By the time the girl was in the fifth grade she weighed 150 pounds. Earlier, when her playmates called her "Fatty," her mother could console her by telling her it was only baby fat and it would go away. But at eleven or twelve years of age there was nothing babyish about it. When a teacher suggested to her that she could take some of her pounds off by swimming at the YWCA, she jumped at the idea. She went religiously to the Y and swam and swam. But the exercise only stretched her appetite. She went home and ate more than usual.

At school she no longer could fit into her seat. It had to be unscrewed from the floor and moved further away from the desk.

At fifteen Celesta weighed 191 pounds.

At twenty-one she weighed 261 pounds.

A Cure for Depression

She had been out of school for a long time. She'd tried various jobs—soap wrapper, eyelet-machine operator, manicurist—in all of which her steadily increasing weight created curiosity or amusement. Worst of all was the ridicule she had to face.

Often Celesta come home depressed. But mother knew exactly how to console her little girl. She covered the table with a richer, more elaborate dinner than usual, full of Celesta's favorite delicacies. And Celesta would rise from the table a happier girl—and a heavier one.

At 275 pounds, when she went into a theater, she couldn't fit into a seat. The theater manager had to put two ordinary chairs together to accommodate her. She didn't go into a theater for a long time after that.

A Suitor for the Fat Lady

Surprisingly enough she had beaus. By any standards, Celesta was strikingly pretty. For many men, a fat girl has a special appeal. She's often gentler and more feminine than thinner, more active girls. There's something motherly and reassuring about her large form that seems to strike a chord in the male subconscious.

Celesta found a serious suitor in young Frank Geyer, a neighbor's son. They were married in 1925. The bride wore blue: that color emphasized her three hundreds pounds less than the traditional white wedding gown would have.

Sorrow had always given Celesta a reason to overeat. Happiness did, too, and she continued to gain. Everything was grist to her mill. When an insurance company turned down her application for a policy because she was such a poor prospect, she ate even more.

By now she was seriously worried. With her husband's sister, also a heavyweight, she decided to try diet pills. There are pills and pills. The one that the two girls took had unforeseen consequences. Celesta's sister-in-law died. And she herself came down with uremic poisoning and kidney disease. She was an invalid for months.

Jolly Pearl: 700 Pounds

In the spring of 1927, after her recovery, Celesta and her husband went to a carnival. She was attracted to the fat lady's tent. Celesta, at 338 pounds, was certain she would be considerably bigger than the woman on display inside.

She turned out to be very mistaken. The fat lady, Jolly Pearl Stanley, weighed seven hundred pounds. Jolly Pearl took at once to her pretty young visitor. She proposed to Celesta that she join the show and even offered to employ her husband as a ticket seller. After hesitating a few days Celesta and Frank accepted. It was an important decision. During the next twenty-three years she was to become one of the outstanding fat ladies of the American circus and carnival.

The "It" Girl of the Fat Ladies

Celesta chose as her professional name Jolly Dolly Geyer. Her career took her throughout the United States and into Canada. She played the Palace Theater in New York, then the dream of everyone in show business. She traveled with a whole string of carnivals, including the Johnny Jones show. She went to Hawaii with a company of entertainers. She worked for the World Circus Side Show at Coney Island. There, Clara Bow, the screen star who was known as the "It" girl, told Celesta that she was the "It" girl of the fat ladies. She took a new name that was to stay with her in all her years in show business—Dolly Dimples.

On a visit home to Cincinnati in 1930 Celesta met another fat lady, Baby Ruth Pontico, who was with Ringling Brothers Circus. A few weeks later Baby Ruth took sick, and Celesta opened in her place in Madison Square Garden.

Madame Celeste

By 1939 Celesta weighed a little over five hundred pounds. She was being billed as "the World's Most Beautiful Fat Lady." Winters she and her husband spent in Orlando, Florida. She hit on the idea of taking up palmistry to supplement her income during the off-season. In the carnival season she was Dolly Dimples. During the winter she was Madame Celeste, Palmist—and, later, Psychic Reader.

In Florida Celesta built herself a home that would be comfortable for a lady of her proportions—555 pounds in 1950. It had a floor of concrete, so there'd be no chance of falling through—one of the fears of very heavy people. She had a special toilet and a shower that would take a lady of her girth. Chairs and sofas were capacious and reinforced. Doorways were extra wide.

Crisis

But with Celesta's great size and success came great problems. She was finding it more and more diffi-

cult to move about. On a visit to her family her ankles
became abnormally swollen. Then, suddenly, she
couldn't breathe. The family doctor examined her. He
spoke to her family. In their frightened faces she could
read the diagnosis.

Celesta was rushed back to Florida. When she was
brought into the Orange Memorial Hospital she was
gasping for breath and semiconscious. It was there that
a doctor delivered the fateful decision to her: "Diet or
die!"

Eight Hundred Calories a Day

Instead of eating everything she wanted, as she'd
done since childhood, Celesta was put on a severely
limited diet in the hospital. Her heart improved. She
seemed to be losing weight, but it was impossible to tell
how much—she was too heavy for the scales in the
hospital. After several weeks she was allowed to go
home.

On the way home, Celesta and Frank stopped at
an official station for weighing trucks. She got on the
scale. Her weight was 524 pounds. She was down
thirty-one pounds. She was definitely on her way.

For the World's Most Beautiful Fat Lady it was a
long hard pull, eating only eight hundred calories a day.
At last she was under five hundred pounds. As time
went by it became harder and harder to take weight off.
After five months she weighed 405 pounds.

In her moving book, *Diet or Die* (which she wrote
with Samuel Roen), Celesta told of the anguish of dieting. One day she just had to stop. Strangely her doctor
gave her permission. He said she could have a pie covered with whipped cream. But he insisted she had to eat
the whole pie. What she began with relish she finished
with revulsion. Her stomach had shrunk.

Slowly but steadily Celesta's weight sank. She
went down to three hundred pounds. Finally her weight
sank below two hundred pounds. Dieting had become a
way of life to her.

A Fantastic Weight Loss

In July Celesta celebrated her fiftieth birthday at her sister's home at Fort Thomas, Kentucky. Her weight was 154 pounds and she was still losing. Her bust, which had once been seventy-two inches, had gone down to a neat thirty-eight. Her sixty-eight-inch waist had more than halved—it was a slender thirty-two. Her hips, once reported to be a massive seven feet around, measured no more than forty-two inches.

Celesta's fantastic loss of weight was news. The press wanted to know all about it.

"It's really very simple," she said. "All anyone has to do is diet properly—and have will power to stick strictly to the diet." She told them that she ate vegetables, meats, and fruits. She stayed away from sugars and starches of all types, including bread and sweets.

Glands and Overweight

Celesta Geyer's story of how she took off over four hundred pounds is a highly dramatic one. Fundamentally, it's a tale of mind over matter . . . and habit. For most of the first fifty years of her life Dolly Dimples had been digging her grave with her teeth. Her family ate well, and she went them one—or many—better. She never blamed her overweight on heredity or glands. Hers was simply a case of unremitting overeating.

On the other hand, many overweight persons believe they have a hereditary tendency or malfunctioning glands that make them put on excessive weight. It's not their fault—it's fate.

In the vast majority of cases, that is absolutely not true. Listen to what a respected medical text, *The Merck Manual,* consulted by physicians throughout the United States, has to say on the subject:

"Although heredity may play a contributory role, there is only one immediate cause of obesity: a caloric intake persistently exceeding caloric output. . . . Endocrine disorders do not primarily cause obesity, but they may favor its development by encouraging either an increased food intake or a decreased energy output."

In simple language, your glands may increase your appetite or they may make you too sluggish to burn up unneeded calories—but they don't make you fat. Overeating does that. Except in rare cases—and some of the fat people discussed earlier were such cases— most instances of obesity are within the control of the individual, provided he has proper medical supervision.

William J. Cobb: 802 Pounds

There is on record a case of weight loss even more striking than Celesta Geyer's. It's the case of William J. Cobb. Cobb, born in Georgia in 1926, was a professional wrestler known as "Happy Humphrey." Wrestling takes beef—or fat—and Cobb had both. In 1962 his weight reached 802 pounds.

Cobb was a gigantic eater. He used to put away three or four loaves of bread with a meal. On one occasion he is said to have eaten nineteen pounds of catfish in under sixty minutes. In a wrestling match, all he had to do to overcome his opponent was get him down and sit on top of him.

At 802 pounds Cobb weighed too much for his own good. Whenever he took a few steps he had to stop and rest. He had only the heart of a normal-sized man (he was six feet tall). It couldn't pump fast enough to deliver sufficient oxygen to keep his vast bulk going. That is the lot of everyone who carries excessive weight around with him.

Lost—570 Pounds!

Cobb, like Celesta Geyer, decided it was a matter of diet or die. By strict control of his eating he brought his weight down to 644 pounds. Then he entered the Eugene Talmadge Memorial Hospital Obesity Clinic in Augusta, Georgia, as a volunteer for obesity research. Doctors put him on a 1,000-calorie-a-day diet, without exercise. Every eight weeks his fare was changed— from high protein to high fat to high carbohydrate.

It was eighty-three weeks before Cobb was discharged from the hospital. Like Dolly Dimples, he couldn't go back to his former occupation. He was a mere featherweight of 232 pounds.

Still, if he missed the money he didn't miss the knocks. And every time he looked down at his waistline he could see it was a svelte 44 inches—a far cry from his former measurement of 101 inches!

28

Living Skeletons

For generations the fat lady's partner in the sideshow has been the living skeleton, a person so thin he's little more than skin and bones. Many tales are told about romances between fat ladies and living skeletons, and occasionally a wedding has taken place. They aren't always long-lived or happy affairs. Like fat ladies, living skeletons often aren't the healthiest of people.

Of course, a living skeleton can be in perfect health. He can be a person who just happens to be unusually tall and thin by nature. By accustoming his body to short rations, he makes it thinner still—and acquires a fat contract.

More commonly, however, he's likely to be the victim of some special medical condition. His extreme thinness may be the result of a case of tuberculosis that's been arrested; his body is emaciated but continues to function fairly normally. Sometimes the living skeleton's condition is caused by malfunctioning glands or some other medical problem that makes the normal fatty and muscular tissues waste away.

Claude Seurat: a Roll and a Little Wine

A famous living skeleton was exhibited in England in the 1820s. He was a Frenchman named Claude Seurat, born in 1798. His skin was stretched very tight over his bones, so that his skeleton stood out. It was possible to watch his heart beating. His voice was remarkably shrill and weak. Seurat's health was said to be good. He kept himself thin by eating a minimum of food—just a little wine and a roll all day, according to reports.

Calvin Edson: an Early American Living Skeleton

Calvin Edson, another living skeleton, exhibited himself at Tammany Hall in New York City in May, 1829. He was the earliest living skeleton to win fame in the United States. A native of Stafford, Connecticut, he was then forty-four years old and weighed sixty pounds.

An old handbill gives us some interesting details about Edson. He was, it said, five feet three inches tall. "He can ride on horseback, and lift 100 lbs. Eats, drinks and sleeps as well as any man. He attributes the cause of his wasting to his having slept on the damp ground the night after the battle of Plattsburgh [during the War of 1812] at which time he was serving in the American Army . . . From that moment he began to waste away, until he became the extraordinary memento he is at present. There is nothing in his dress or appearance to alarm the most delicate."

Isaac Sprague: "the Original Thin Man"

Can you picture an adult man so thin that his arms look like walking sticks—and his knee bones are the largest diameter of his leg?

Such a person was Isaac Sprague, often referred to as "the Original Thin Man." Although Calvin Edson has a better claim to that title, Sprague was a more widely known figure.

Sprague, born in East Bridgewater, Massachusetts,

on May 21, 1841, was a vigorous, healthy child. He enjoyed swimming greatly, and used to spend a good deal of his time in the summer in a large pond near his house. When, at about the age of twelve, he began to lose weight at an alarming rate, it was blamed at first on excessive swimming. However, leading physicians who examined the boy declared that the cause of his condition was a mystery to them.

"They unanimously concurred in the opinion that I would continue to lose my flesh until I had lost the use of my limbs, but still might eventually live to be an old man," Sprague said in a pamphlet he used to sell in the circus.

For a while Sprague worked as a shoemaker, then as a grocer. In 1864 his condition was still worsening and he had to give up his grocery store. "I had then begun to lose not only my flesh, but my muscles likewise."

The following year Sprague went to see a circus with his brother. "My brother spoke to the doorkeeper and asked him if he had anyone as fat as I was, or had an arm as fat as mine. This interested him." The man felt Sprague's arms. Their leanness won Sprague a free admission to the circus. When he came out, the proprietor was waiting for him with a proposition that he join the circus. The thin man had just given up his occupation and he was at a loose end. He accepted.

For a while Sprague toured with the circus, then exhibited himself at fair grounds. Being a living skeleton didn't place much strain on him; he decided to make it his permanent profession. The name Barnum was a golden one to Sprague as to so many of the Very Special People of that era. He wrote to the showman, describing himself and his case. When he didn't get an answer, he decided to go to see Barnum or his agent in person.

In New York City Sprague had an interview with Ferguson, Barnum's assistant.

"I was shown to a room and, arranging my costume, was put upon the stage at an entertainment where Mr. Barnum himself was to be present. When my turn came to be lectured upon, Mr. Barnum stood very near me, and I overheard him say to his agent, 'Pretty lean man . . . where did you scare him up?' 'Down in Massachusetts,' said he; 'he is a live Yankee.' "

The thin man had passed the test; he now had a secure place with Barnum.

Sprague was at the New American Museum when the great fire of 1868 destroyed it. Asleep in the building, he escaped just in time to avoid being burned to death.

While Barnum's agents were collecting material for another museum Sprague was collecting a wife. She was a Massachusetts girl, who bore him three healthy sons. Meanwhile Sprague traveled with the Great Golden Menagerie. In 1868, at the Zoological Institute in Boston, he was visited by many physicians, among them Dr. Oliver Wendell Holmes, medical pioneer and poet, who studied him and delivered lectures about him to medical students. His case was declared to be one of "excessive progressive muscular atrophy." Sprague's condition, said Holmes, would continue until all the muscular tissues of his body had disappeared.

Other doctors, over the years, confirmed the diagnosis. They declared that "the joints of my frame will knit and join together as broken bones do until the entire body becomes one solid mass of bones."

Sprague traveled with many different amusement enterprises, including the North American Circus and the Greatest Show on Earth. An interesting backstage view of him is provided by an old circus fan.

"I have gazed upon many of these extra-thin people," wrote the fan, "and for years wondered if they were on a diet, until one day I saw Sprague, the living skeleton, that traveled with Barnum's circus many years, eating his breakfast off a tray that had been brought over to the sideshow tent from the cook house.

"There was enough on that tray to feed a giant, and it returned empty to the cook house. I saw him devour every crumb of it, except a half a slice of bread that he fed to Jumbo, the giant elephant, who was being kept in the sideshow out of sight, until the menagerie tent was up. [Jumbo, the biggest elephant exhibited up to that time, gave the word "jumbo" to the English language. He was killed in a railroad accident in 1885.]

"Sprague was then about forty-eight years of age, weighed fifty-two pounds, and was five foot four inches tall. He was married and then had two sons.

"He used to lecture on himself and said he had never had a sick day in his life. He would stand up during this lecture to show he was strong and would close his talk putting up his fists in fighting position and offering one thousand dollars to any man of his size and weight that he could not whip. This always caused a laugh."

James W. Coffey: "the Skeleton Dude"

Another living skeleton was James W. Coffey. (Seephoto insert) Coffey developed an interesting wrinkle for his exhibition: he dressed up with great elegance, which earned him billing as "the Skeleton Dude." He wore a high hat, morning coat, wing collar, and bow tie, and carried a cane. A favorite costume of his was a striped suit; it fitted his body almost skin tight, emphasizing his remarkable thinness.

The Skeleton Dude was born in Ohio on March 11, 1852. His weight was normal at birth. At nineteen (according to *The Wonder Book of Freaks and Animals*, published by Barnum and Bailey in 1898) he came down with a disease which "impaired the muscular and nervous powers of his limbs." He was about five feet six inches tall and weighed seventy pounds.

Coffey exhibited himself for many years in circuses and carnivals in the United States and Europe. He used to deliver a lecture on himself. "I want to get married," he would declare on the platform, "but I've never found a lady who liked her Coffey so thin."

Harry V. Lewis: "Shadow Harry"

Unlike the Skeleton Dude, Harry V. Lewis didn't bother to have his clothes tailored to bring out his extraordinary thinness. But when he appeared in the sideshow, wearing a pair of boxer's shorts, his emaciation was so extreme that feelings of pity welled up in his audience.

Lewis, born in Leon, Iowa, on August 15, 1895, was 5 feet 7½ inches tall and weighed 75 pounds. He looked like a sick man, and he was a sick man. But let him tell you about it himself.

"At the age of twelve, I noticed a weakness in my hips and shoulders, caused by a wasting away of the muscles, slowly spreading to nearly all parts of my body.

"Local physicians could advance no theory as to the cause of my trouble, so I consulted the Mayo Clinic of Rochester, Minnesota, also the McLain Orthopedic Sanitarium of Saint Louis, and just a short time ago was released from the Battle Creek Sanitarium at Battle Creek, Michigan . . .

"I was informed by both Dr. Foucar and Dr. Nielson that I was suffering from the juvenile form of generalized muscular dystrophy, a disease of the muscles, and no one knew the cause, therefore, could advance no treatment, other than for me to give attention to my diet . . . and to keep on my feet as much as possible, to avoid losing the strength in the groups of muscles used in standing."

Obedient to his doctors' orders, Lewis stayed on his feet from the time he got up in the morning until he went to bed at night. He spent about eleven or twelve hours of that time on the sideshow platform, standing, it seemed, in one spot. He ate standing up and read standing up.

Pete Robinson

Carnival publicity men have always tried to arrange marriages between extremes, like the giantess and the midget or the living skeleton and the fat lady. Often, when such marriages are staged, they're not actual marriages or else they're cancelled soon afterward.

In 1924 an authentic and lasting marriage took place between extremes. It united in wedlock Pete

Robinson (See photo insert), who weighed fifty-eight pounds, and Bunny Smith, an attractive lady whose official weight was 467 pounds. Robinson was Ringling's living skeleton at the time (later he acted in the film *Freaks*) and the marriage was celebrated with great ceremony at Madison Square Garden.

After the wedding, the press was invited to the couple's apartment at a rooming house at Coney Island to watch Pete help Bunny prepare their first breakfast. They revealed that they had been keeping company for eight years, and the courtship had been carried on in circuses, on the stage, and at Coney Island (where the couple did a dancing act that was a great hit for many seasons). During World War I, Bunny had tried to fatten Pete up so his weight would be acceptable to recruiting officers and he could serve his country. But Pete was simply unable to keep enough pounds on his bony frame—although he pushed his weight up so far that he almost lost his job with the sideshow!

PART 7

AN ODD LOT

29

Zip and Other Pinheads

One of the most famed of Very Special People was Zip, often described as Barnum's original "What-Is-It?" Zip's career as a professional human oddity spanned a vast era of circus and carnival life. He was already a star at Barnum's museum when the first shot was fired at Fort Sumter. After World War I, reporters were still clustering around him when the Ringling Brothers Circus opened at Madison Square Garden every spring. He was popularly known as "the dean of freaks."

An old handbill of Barnum's museum shows one of the first representations of Zip. He stands against a jungle background, a scary-looking creature with a head and face like a humanoid ape. He has incredibly long hands, fingers, and nails. His body is covered with fur. He was simply indescribable, a new species—so, in the language of the day, he was called a "nondescript."

"This nondescript," said the handbill, "was captured by a party of adventurers who were in search of the Gorilla. While exploring the River Gambia, near the mouth, they fell in with a race of beings never before discovered. They were six in number. They were in a PERFECTLY NUDE STATE, roving among the trees and branches, in the manner common to the Monkey and Orang Outang. After considerable exertion the hunters succeeded in capturing three of these oddities—two males and a female ... The present one is the only survivor. When first received here his natural position was ON ALL FOURS ... When he first came his only food was raw meat, sweet apples, oranges, nuts, etc., of all of which he was very fond; but he will now eat bread, cake, and similar things."

It was, of course, something of an exaggeration—one of the many that earned Barnum the title he wore so proudly, "Prince of Humbugs."

In reality, Zip was an American black. He had an odd, somewhat cone-shaped head. According to Fred Bradna of Ringling, "Zip accentuated this grotesqueness by shaving his head every day except for the topknot, which he left impudently erect like the scalp of a Sioux Indian. The peculiar shape gave his face a drawn look which resembled an aboriginal carving on a coconut husk—as did its color."

An individual with a receding forehead and a small skull, like Zip, is medically known as a microcephalus. In the language of the people, such a person is a "pinhead," which is an unkind but vividly accurate translation of the scientific term. The condition is usually associated with feeblemindedness. How defective Zip's intelligence was is still debated. Certainly he knew the value of a dollar. Everyone agrees that he was a warm, affectionate person.

Silenced by Barnum

According to one source, Zip was born in New Jersey. Another source says he was an illiterate whom Barnum found working in Bridgeport; still another says he came from Brooklyn. It was of critical importance that his origin should be shrouded in darkness; Barnum is said to have silenced the poor man by telling him that his pay of a dollar a day would be cut off on any day the showman caught him uttering a word while he was on exhibition. Reportedly Zip never talked. But he grinned frequently and uttered nonsense words.

"The What-Is-It?"

Barnum, seeing his comical face, is said to have named him Zip. An old legend declares that Zip received his nickname of "What-Is-It?" from Charles Dickens. As Irving Wallace tells the story in his book *The Fabulous Showman,* Barnum was guiding Charles Dickens through his museum during the author's first trip to America. The year was 1842. They came to Zip's platform.

"Dickens blinked up at him, and turned to Barnum. 'What is it?' asked the English author. Barnum clapped his hands with delight. 'That's what it is—a What-is-it!' And forever after, Zip, christened by the creator of Scrooge and Fagin, remained the 'What-is-it?' "

It's a good yarn, but there's one basic difficulty to it. When Zip died in 1926 the newspapers said he was eighty-four years old. That means he was born in 1842, which makes him a little young for the tale. Whoever created the nickname (Zip said it was his wife), he had it very early. He was first placed on exhibition in 1859. He was already well known in 1860, when the Prince of Wales (the same one who as a boy of three had greeted Tom Thumb) called at the American Museum and saw him. The *Herald* (October 14, 1860), in its report on the visit, said that "the first object of interest pointed out was the 'What Is It?' in which His Royal Highness manifested a great deal of curiosity. In compliance with his wish, the keeper went through the regular account of the animal."

How Feebleminded Was Zip?

Zip, according to old stories, used to believe he owned Barnum's museum, and would order the showman and others about. Most who knew Zip described him as possessing a subnormal intelligence. One of these was Robert Sherwood, who in the 1930s was Barnum's oldest living clown. Although Sherwood said Zip was "a pinhead and an imbecile," he added that "he could play the fiddle pretty well and played solitaire, etc. He had a very well-developed sense of the ridiculous and found in the crowds who gazed on him a never-failing source of interest."

According to Sherwood, Zip carried around a toy popgun and threatened to use it on rival pinheads. Presumably this was a publicity stunt; Sherwood was certain Zip knew the difference between a toy gun and a real one.

In 1918, Zip was taken down from the central dais in Madison Square Garden and put in a corner spot. Clikko, who was the circus's latest find, a "wild African bushman," was given Zip's former position of glory. Zip was reported to be furious. That again was probably a publicity gambit. Zip was always good for some free newspaper space when the circus came to town.

"The Man Monkey"

Zip appeared in different costumes. At the American Museum, he may at first have been clad in fur. An old Currier and Ives lithograph made for Barnum shows Zip in a curious cloth costume with bare legs and describes him as "the Man Monkey." Later he wore a reddish-brown wooly hairy-looking costume. Sometimes he appeared in a loincloth.

At Coney Island Zip was often exhibited in a cage. For a period he wore a white nightshirt, which he swirled around with mock savagery, making threatening gestures. When he stopped he was gentle and full of smiles. In 1922 he appeared in Madison Square Garden in a full-dress suit. The Man Monkey had at last worked his way up the evolutionary ladder into a monkey suit.

According to reports Zip didn't upset sideshow visitors the way some Very Special People do. "Zip didn't affect feelers [people likely to faint], and that's why he was more successfully exhibited than any other freak outside Tom Thumb," recalled a newspaper article in 1936.

Imitating John Ringling

One of Zip's popular routines with the Ringling Brothers Circus was to imitate John Ringling smoking a cigar. However, for this performance Zip insisted on having cigars equal in quality to those Ringling smoked.

The Broadway producer David Belasco, according to one famous tale, threw Zip a half-dollar once. Zip, instead of holding on to it, threw it right back. This convinced Belasco Zip was an idiot. However, the story, repeated thousands of times, brought Zip a great deal of useful publicity.

"Well, We Fooled 'em a Long Time"

Zip owned a chicken farm near Nutley, New Jersey, as well as other property. His long life came to an end on April 30, 1926, in Bellevue Hospital in New York City. A little while before his death he is reported to have turned to his sister and said, "Well, we fooled 'em a long time."

Zip was buried at Bound Brook, New Jersey, in a full-dress suit. Among the Very Special People who came to pay him homage were a fat lady, a living skeleton, a giant, a tattooed lady, and a rubber-skinned man, according to his obituary. He had been on the stage for sixty-seven years—one of the longest show-business careers on record.

Zip's Imitators

P. T. Barnum and those who followed him made a great deal of money by exhibiting Zip. "The Monkey Man" was a great drawing card for many years. He was imitated widely; there was even one pinhead who went under the name of Zup and was represented as being Zip's brother. According to Alva Johnston, "Other showmen decoyed scores of inmates from homes for the feebleminded, but were always disappointed in their quest for a rival for Zip. Three generations of circus and sideshow lovers refused to accept an imitation What-Is-It."

Schlitzie and the Snows

Several pinheads played supporting roles in the film *Freaks,* which MGM released in 1932. One of them, named Schlitzie, was forty years old at the time. Her head was tiny, her body of average proportions. Her I.Q. was that of a child of three. In the sideshows she had been exhibited as "Maggie, the Last of the Aztecs." She could dance and sing a little, and count up to ten, though not always perfectly. Elvira and Jenny Lee Snow, two other pinheads, sisters from Georgia, also played in the film. They were quiet girls who always had a smile on their faces, and were well liked by other members of the company.

Pipo and Zipo

In the 1920s and later two of the best-known pinheads were Pipo and Zipo. The pair, natives of Georgia, were brother and sister. The brother, Pipo, reportedly had the intelligence of a 1½-year-old child and Zipo that of a five-year-old. Sam Wagner of the World Sideshow Circus exhibited them at Coney Island. In order to prevail upon them to leave the South, Wagner induced Jimmy Walker, the mayor of New York, to write a letter to the mayor of their hometown. It worked.

When Pipo and Zipo were first exhibited, they were enormously self-conscious and covered their strangely shaped heads with their arms. After Wagner convinced them their heads were nothing to be ashamed of, they displayed them proudly. Earning seventy-five dollars a week during the Depression of the thirties, they could consider themselves well off, and they had a car of their own. Their winters were spent at home in Georgia.

"They have nothing to worry about," said Wagner in the bluff, wisecracking way of the professional showman, "and, I suppose you could say, nothing to worry with."

30

Half-Man, Half-Woman

The hermaphrodite—an individual born with the sex organs of both the male and the female—has always fascinated men and women whom nature has treated less lavishly.

Actually, every human being has the germ of *both* a male and a female within his body. But a special chromosome in the father's sex cell—not the mother's—makes almost everyone develop in one direction or the other.

But not everyone. Because of some abnormality of the chromosomes or some peculiarity of glandular development, occasionally an "intersex" is born. This is an individual with sex organs, glands, or physical characteristics belonging to both sexes.

Intersexes aren't rare. At the European Athletics Championships in Budapest in 1966 female athletes were told they had to take a physical examination to prove they were really women. Some chose to drop out of the meet rather than submit to the examination.

The hermaphrodite (or pseudohermaphrodite or

intersex) may be a male with small testes who develops breasts. It may be either a male or a female with a penis overgrowing a vulva. It may produce semen and menstruate scantily. It may be an individual of one sex with an extraordinary secretion of hormones belonging to the opposite sex which brings out the characteristics of that sex. One type grades into the next. The range of variations is enormous.

In the hermaphrodite the organs of one sex are usually much better developed than those of the other, and this development determines the individual's sex. According to Professor R. G. Hoskins of Harvard Medical School, only in three cases out of many studied were there both a distinct individual testis and an ovary. In the other cases these basic sex glands were mixed. Hermaphrodites are frequently sterile. They are found among animals as well as humans.

The First Hermaphrodite

The word "hermaphrodite" comes from Greek mythology. According to the poets, Hermaphroditus was a beautiful youth, son of Hermes and Aphrodite. A nymph fell in love with him, but he gave her the cold shoulder. She prayed to the gods to unite her with him. The gods just happened to be listening. The next time Hermaphroditus went for a swim in the nymph's spring, her body combined with his, and they were one forever.

Old-Time Hermaphrodites

In ancient times the birth of a hermaphrodite was considered unlucky; the Greeks and Romans usually drowned them. Accounts of hermaphrodites in the Middle Ages are frequent and exaggerated.

At fairs and carnivals, the hermaphrodite—often referred to popularly as a "morphodite" or "half-and-half"—has always been a great attraction. Hundreds of years ago, James Paris, servant to Samuel Pepys, the English Admiralty official and diarist, was an inveterate visitor of exhibitions of human oddities. (We've mentioned him earlier.) Among his papers is a drawing he made of a hermaphrodite which shows us how they used to be exhibited. In front of the costume there was a "trap," which lifted up.

How Hermaphrodites Are Faked

Most hermaphrodites exhibited to the public are likely to be faked to some extent. The typical individual appears as a male on one half of the body, a female on the other. On the male side the individual is hairy and muscular, and the breast is flat and manly. The hair of the head is clipped close. On the female side the hair of the head is long and the hair on the face, arm, and chest is not apparent.

Nature, however, doesn't divide people down the middle. When you see such a neat division in a person, you can be sure it owes more to art than to nature.

As a rule the sideshow half-and-half is a man who can speak in a high-pitched voice as well as a deep one. He keeps the body hair on his pretended female side well shaved and bleached to present a feminine appearance. He also uses makeup on that side. To fake a female breast he may inject paraffin, silicone, or some other substance under the skin. On the male side, the limbs get a lot of exercise, so they look manly and muscular. An actual hermaphrodite may do all of these things to his body because the half-and-half appearance is expected.

Occasionally a half-and-half has some abnormal physical condition that helps his presentation. For example, he could have a breast tumor that would give the breast female proportions.

Billie Christina: "For a Small Extra Charge"

George W. Lewis, who traveled with carnivals for years, has given us an interesting picture of a "morphodite" billed as Billie Christina. On the platform this half-and-half wore a low-necked gown that revealed a flat breast covered with hair on one side (that was

Billie) and a well-developed breast on the other (that was Christina). Christina had hair that fell in long sparkling tresses; Billie naturally had a crew cut. On the platform, while Christina ran a comb through her silky locks, Billie shaved his face. Meanwhile Gabbie, the talker, was delivering his spiel:

"Folks, you are now looking at one of the few single persons in the world who never gets lonesome for the companionship of the opposite sex. Billie Christina here could be shipwrecked on a desert island and, if they had food and shelter, could live very happily alone for the rest of time. If Christina gets tired of the monotony of being a woman all she has to do is move over to the other side of the bed and be Billie for a few days, weeks, or as long as he is happy being a man . . . I assure you this is no fake seated in this chair before you. If any of the gentlemen in the audience care to do so, for a small extra charge of fifty cents they may step behind this curtain and examine Christina more thoroughly. In this private booth Christina will strip for you and, if you so desire, you can examine her with your hands."

Since Christina stripped, she could have been an authentic hermaphrodite. Lewis didn't say what the gentlemen found when they entered the private booth with her or whether it was worth the additional fifty cents. This, in carnival lingo, was the "blowoff"—an extra little show for an extra charge at the end of the regular performance.

Bobby Kork: He Packed a Wallop

Bobby Kork (See photo insert) was a half-and-half who played the carnivals for years. He was said to be a true hermaphrodite by Edward Malone, who knew him. His body, however, showed the typical show-business rigging of male on one side, female on the other.

The masculine side presumably dominated in Bobby. He was said to be very strong and on at least one occasion gave a sound beating to a spectator who showed too much interest in the half-and-half's female half.

Mona Harris: Female Hermaphrodite

Mona Harris—that wasn't her real name—was a different kind of hermaphrodite. According to Harry Lewiston, who featured her in his show, she was a woman but had characteristics belonging to the opposite sex.

Mona, who had red hair, wasn't especially pretty. She possessed enormous breasts, remarkable because they had no nipples. According to Lewiston, at the side of her vagina she had a penis about five inches in length. She was sexually interested in women as well as men, though whether her penis was functional is uncertain.

Mondu: Too Sensitive

In the 1920s a half-and-half was exhibited in England and the United States under the name of Mondu. "Brother and Sister in One Body—the Ninth Wonder of the World," a pamphlet that he (or she) distributed declared.

Mondu was born in 1905 in Blackpool, England. According to this "human enigma," he was a girl until the age of twelve, when he had an operation that caused the other side of his body to take on male characteristics. "There is real drama and also a touch of genuine comedy in this mysterious process of evolution which forces a girl to shoulder the responsibilities of a man without having been prepared by a masculine training and a boy's background," Mondu's pamphlet declared.

In his pamphlet Mondu provided a list of questions he was frequently asked, with his answers. Here are a few of them:

"Are you man or woman?"

"I am half of each, one side male, the other female."

"What sex do you lean to the strongest, man or woman?"

"To the male."

"Are you married?"

"Yes."

"Are both sexes developed?"

"Yes."

"Do you show your body in private?"

"No, I have been offered as high as $100 to $500, but sorry to say I do not submit to this for I am so sensitive at this time of life."

31

Unzie the Albino and Other Oddities

What Is an Albino?

An albino is a person who has skin that's white or nearly translucent—no matter what race he belongs to. His eyes have a pink or blue iris and a dark red pupil. His hair ranges from nearly colorless to white. Sunlight is painful to his eyes, and his skin doesn't tan. Doctors classify albinism as a birth defect. The condition, caused by a lack of pigment in the skin, eyes, and hair, often runs in families.

You're not very conspicuous if you're an albino and live among people of northern European descent. But the situation is very different if you're a black, an Indian, or a Chinese—you'll look as though you belong to a different race.

Curiously enough, albinism is common among the darker-skinned races. In Nigeria, one in three thousand people is an albino. In the United States the number's just one in nine thousand.

Albinos of black descent were once common in

sideshows. Albinos enjoyed a great vogue in the 1840s and '50s, often appearing in groups or families. They were described as a separate race and were called "Night People." Reportedly, they lived deep in the earth, and came out only at night, when the light wouldn't hurt their eyes. They were said to be particularly abundant in Panama. It is an odd fact that among the San Blas Indians of that country one in 132 individuals is an albino.

Unzie: Australian Aborigine Albino

Unzie was probably the most celebrated of all albinos in show business. An Australian aborigine, he was born in 1869 in New South Wales. Like his parents he should have had a dark skin, but his was as white as paper and so was his hair.

The aborigines were a primitive people in Unzie's time and they're said to have regarded him with a mixture of dread and awe. Some wanted to put the child to death, but fortunately for him his father was a chief. Eventually an Englishman discovered him and took him to Melbourne, where he was reared. From there he came to the West.

Unzie had unusual eyes, even more so than the usual albino. Not only were they remarkably bright and expressive—they were said to change with the light that shone on them. In ordinary light they were pale red, but in subdued light a bluish gray. After sunset they were purplish red. Bright light hurt his eyes and made it hard for him to see, but in a dim light he did better. He was said to be able to see in total darkness.

Most remarkable of all was his hair. Snow white, luxuriant, and curly, it grew to an exceptional length. Unzie did it up in curling papers when he went to bed at night. After he removed the papers and brushed his hair out in the morning, it mushroomed out around his head and shoulders to a circumference of about six feet. He had a large, handsome mustache and white eyebrows, which often caused him to be compared to Jay Gould, one of the robber barons of that day.

Unzie first visited the United States in 1890. He was a person of some elegance, always appearing on the stage in a high hat and a dress suit. He enjoyed lecturing the public, and was a lively, interesting speaker.

"I never tip my hat to the ladies," Unzie used to say on the platform. "If I should, they'd think a bombshell had exploded." To prove his point he'd take off his hat—and his incredible white hair would puff out and surround him like an enormous white cloud.

Samuel D. Parks: "Hopp the Frog Boy"

Older sideshow fans will remember the banner outside the tent where Samuel D. Parks was featured. It showed a huge frog with a human head. That was something of an exaggeration, but Parks did present a most unusual spectacle.

No one knows a man better than his wife. We are fortunate in having a letter which Mrs. Parks wrote to *Billboard*, for many years one of the major voices of show business, asking the editor to insert it as an announcement of her husband's death. It tells his story honestly and directly.

"Samuel David Parks, known to all troupers as Hopp the Frog Boy, died at his home on October 26, 1923.

"Hopp was born in Boston, Massachusetts, October 20, 1874. His first appearance before the public as a freak was at the World's Fair in Chicago in 1893 before the Rush Medical students. He exhibited before the students of all the leading universities in the United States and Europe. Later he joined Barnum & Bailey Circus and was with that circus during their European tour. From then on he exhibited all over the United States and Europe in the leading circuses and largest carnival companies.

"Hopp was the only attraction of his kind in the World. His face, hands, and feet were human but the rest of his body was deformed similar to that of a frog. When he got down on all fours he looked exactly like a huge bullfrog . . .

"In 1906 Hopp married Miss Ida Granville of Baltimore, Maryland, and had two children by her. She died giving birth to their second baby. His first baby, a boy, is still alive and is about 17 years old . . .

"In 1910, while with the Great Patterson Shows, he met Helen Himmel, a Connecticut midget, whom he married at Lyons, Iowa. Hopp lived happily with his midget wife till his death here on October 26. Hopp was 49 years old on October 20, 1923."

James W. Coffey: "the Skeleton Dude"

Some people have skin that can be pulled out a foot or more, only to snap back like a rubber band when it's released. Doctors call the condition *cutis hyperelastica*—which really means nothing but extremely elastic skin.

Elastic skin is usually due to some failing of the skin fibers, and it's often hereditary. The medical profession can't do anything to correct the condition, but that hardly matters, since elastic skin doesn't give its possessor any problem—only the ability to frighten or entertain the people around him. Many a person with this kind of skin has been exhibited in sideshows, frequently under the name of "the India Rubber Man" or "the Elastic Skin Man."

An outstanding elastic skin man was James Morris, who traveled with the Barnum and Bailey Circus for many years. According to an old circus booklet, Morris was born in Copenhagen, New York, in July, 1859. "His entire body," the booklet declared, "presents the peculiarity of the dog's neck." Morris prepared for a career as a barber. He used to stretch his skin for the diversion of his friends and later for Elks' benefits and church socials in Rhode Island. Such a talent was worth money, and eventually he was earning it at a dime museum run by J. E. Sackett in Providence.

Starting in 1882, Morris was with Barnum, earning, it's reported, $150 a week. He appeared throughout the United States and later toured Europe. He was a person of some culture. According to one old sideshow authority, however, Morris was addicted to gambling and drinking, so that by the turn of the century, instead of being able to retire and live comfortably on the fortune he had earned, he still had to continue exhibiting himself.

There were many other elastic skin men, but Morris was considered one of the best. He was able to pull the skin of his chest up to the top of his head. He could pull out the skin of one leg and cover the other with it. He was able to pull his cheek skin out a good eight inches.

PART 8

VERY, VERY SPECIAL PEOPLE

32

The Strange Fate of Julia Pastrana

Some people become so famous for a special talent or a unique personal quality or achievement that in time their names are indissolubly linked with it. In this way, the name of Socrates stands for wisdom, Einstein for scientific brilliance, Marilyn Monroe for breath-taking female loveliness. In her day—well over a hundred years ago—the name of Julia Pastrana became, throughout the Western world, a synonym for ugliness.

"Poor woman!" people exclaimed with a shudder when Julia Pastrana made her first appearances in the dime museums and show halls of the 1850s. Few could remember having seen a human being as repulsive to look at as this unfortunate but talented young woman.

Julia was born in 1832. She stood only four and a half feet high. Most of her face, including her forehead, was covered with a shocking growth of shining black hair. Her tinselly red gown, which left a good part of her arms and bosom bare, revealed large expanses of hairy skin. Her ears were big and the loop earrings she wore made them look even bigger. Her nose was wide and squat, her nostrils enormous. Her lips, large and deformed, were surmounted by a heavy mustache. Her chin was prognathous, giving her an apelike appearance. Her teeth were irregular and abnormal; according to one account, she had a double row in each jaw.

The delicate flower that Julia held in her hand and the frilly ribboned little cap on the back of her head only accentuated the vast gulf that separated her from the rest of her sex. "Poor woman!" they said of her with justice—although she made Lent, the American showman who managed her, a wealthy man.

In order to add interest to Julia's appearances on the stage, for her as well as her audience, Lent had seen to it that she was taught to do some Spanish dances in the style of Lola Montez, who was then very popular. She also would sing the songs of her native Mexico in a small, gentle, nostalgic voice. As she sang or danced, she gazed out high over the heads of the curious, open-mouthed throng before her, trying to avoid their eyes. The look in her own was glazed, remote. Her face was expressionless.

Strange stories were told about Julia. The avid novelty seekers who clustered in front of her platform often whispered to each other that she could not be completely human. And Julia, who, try as she would, could not fail to see the shocked, incredulous look on their faces, must almost have agreed with them.

The Real Pastrana

Not many people ever succeeded in getting to know Julia Pastrana intimately. Yet those few who did found her a warm, sensitive person, with a heart full of feeling. They discovered she was intensely curious about the world around her, and she loved to read. She was not only a thoughtful human being, but a spiritual one. One of those who made friends with Julia was a singer, Countess Prokesch-Osten, who left a moving testimonial to her character and personality.

It was a curious thing to hear Julia talking about life and the world. She seemed to know these only out of books and from childhood experiences. Her adult years were passed in the almost cloistered seclusion to which so many of the Very Special People are condemned. Her manager did not allow her to spend much time with outsiders or to show herself in public; if people were allowed to see her coming and going, her novelty value could wear off and they might be less willing to pay to see her on the stage.

And yet when Julia finally found herself with someone who she felt did not look at her purely as a curiosity but as another human being—a woman like any other one, with the same feelings, hopes, and dreams—the icy wall of reserve that surrounded her would begin to melt. She would become warm and friendly, and show a touching, almost childlike trust. Sometimes she might be gay and high spirited, and chatter away with momentary abandon. Yet somehow, even in her most joyful moods, a look of melancholy often crept over her face.

"Her Features Were Simply Hideous"

Francis T. Buckland, the English author of *Curiosities of Natural History,* saw and spoke with Julia in 1857, when she was being exhibited in Regent Street, London.

"Her eyes," Buckland wrote, "were deep black, and somewhat prominent, and their lids had long, thick eyelashes; her features were simply hideous on account of the profusion of hair growing on her forehead, and her black beard; but her figure was exceedingly good and graceful, and her tiny foot and well-turned ankle, *bien chaussé,* perfection itself. She had a sweet voice, great taste in music and dancing, and could speak three languages. She was very charitable, and gave largely to local institutions from her earnings. I believe that her true history was that she was simply a deformed Mexican Indian woman."

In London a dentist named Purland made a cast of Julia's teeth, which he described as set in double rows in each jaw. Alfred Russel Wallace, codiscoveror of the theory of evolution, passed this information along in a letter to Charles Darwin. Darwin mentions it in his book *The Variations of Animals and Plants under Domestication* (1868) and points out parallels in the animal world between abnormal teeth and an abnormal skin covering.

"He Loves Me for My Own Sake"

Julia traveled not only in England but throughout Europe, making public appearances under the watchful eye of her manager. She depended on Lent, and showed great fondness for him.

One day Lent asked Julia to marry him. Malicious people said that he held a considerable amount of her earnings in trust for her and was afraid that she might become dissatisfied and ask for her money. According to some accounts, other showmen were maneuvering to win her away from him, and marriage offered a sure way for him to hold on to her. In any event, he didn't have to ask her a second time. "He loves me for my own sake," she is reported to have said on the morning of her marriage.

Julia's Baby

After a while Julia became pregnant. She was appearing in Moscow when she felt the first pangs of the approaching birth. To her delight, she was successfully delivered of a son.

Julia could hardly wait to get her first look at the boy. She was hoping for a normal, average baby—a baby who would take after his father, not his ill-favored mother.

Nature played Julia Pastrana false right up to the end. When the midwife held out the baby to her, she saw in the swaddling clothes a dark little miniature of herself. His tiny body was covered with hair and deformed. In thirty-six hours he was dead.

The blow was too much for Julia to take. She died

soon afterward—of a broken heart, it was said. The year was 1860. She was twenty-eight years old.

The Two Mummies

Lent had suffered a serious loss. Whether it was emotional—or just financial, as his enemies alleged—no one can say. But in the midst of his tragedy a strange, macabre idea was born in his mind—an idea for turning his misfortune into an asset. He knew that there was in Moscow a Professor Sokoloff who was an expert in mummifying—he could embalm a corpse so it would preserve a natural, lifelike appearance for a long time. It was said that the bodies he prepared looked more like the wax figures at Madame Tussaud's in London than they did like corpses. Lent engaged the professor's services.

Sokoloff's work lived up to his reputation and Lent resumed his interrupted tour. Julia was exhibited as before. Now, however, she did not sing or dance anymore. Instead, her strange hairy face stared out impassively from a glass case. Still, she was as strong a drawing card as ever. Perhaps even a stronger one, since the dead child was exhibited with her.

The word "nondescript" means a species not described before. In February, 1862, Buckland accepted an invitation to examine a great natural curiosity billed as "The Embalmed Female Nondescript," then being exhibited in London. When he set eyes on it he immediately exclaimed, "Julia Pastrana!"

"Yes, sir," said the proprietor of the exhibition—probably Lent himself—"it *is* Julia Pastrana."

Buckland was much surprised at what he saw. "The figure," he wrote, "was dressed in the ordinary exhibition costume used in life, and placed erect upon the table. The limbs were by no means shrunken or contracted, the arms, chest, &c. retaining their former roundness and well-formed appearance. The face was marvellous; exactly like an exceedingly good portrait in wax, but it was *not* formed of wax. The closest examination convinced me that it was the true skin, prepared in some wonderful way; the huge deformed lips and the squat nose remained exactly as in life; and the beard and luxuriant growth of soft black hair on and about the face were in no respect changed from their former appearance.

"There was no unpleasantness, or disagreeable concomitant, about the figure; and it was almost difficult to imagine that the mummy was really that of a human being, and not an artificial model."

The Restless Corpse

Buckland did not mention the baby. But another writer, Hermann Waldemar Otto, a German authority on circus and sideshow personalities, did. He saw Julia's mummy at the Prater, a large amusement area in Vienna.

"It was with very peculiar feelings that I stepped up to the glass 'coffin' in which the restless corpse was displayed," Otto wrote. "Strange thoughts went through my mind as I looked at the mummy. She stood there in a tawdry gown of red silk with the ghastly grin of the dead on her face. Next to her was her baby in an equally tawdry garment, on a bar, like a parrot. Outside, the rain was streaming down between the show booths of the Prater. The wind whined and raged around the tent. I felt a deep, deep compassion for the dead woman. She, however, could no longer hear nor see; she felt neither joy nor sorrow, neither lack of love nor my compassion. And I recalled that once she had said with a clear laugh, "He loves me for my own sake. . . ."

Enter Zenora

Countess Prokesch-Osten also saw the mummies in Vienna. That was in 1880, twenty years after Julia's death. In 1889 they were on display in Munich, at the "anthropological exhibition" of one J. B. Gassner. Appearing in the same show was another Pastrana—a living one. This was Miss Zenora, who was billed as Julia's sister.

Zenora had a full beard. Reportedly, an exceptional growth of hair covered her whole body, except her breasts. Her face was remarkably masculine. She was then in her upper twenties.

Zenora had a fine figure. Like Julia, she knew how to dance and revealed exceptional grace in her movements. She had a background in music, spoke several foreign languages, and was skilled in the domestic arts.

Julia's sister, it was said, was married to an American. She had had one child, a blond son. The boy, who died young, did not inherit his mother's hairiness.

An unusual footnote to the Pastrana story came to light a few decades later. People interested in human oddities have always wondered what the ultimate fate of Julia Pastrana's mummy was: whether she ever came to rest in a quiet cemetery somewhere or is perhaps still being exhibited in a corner in some small-town museum. In 1926 Alfred Lehmann told her story over the radio in Germany and ended by repeating the question: "What ever became of the remains of Julia Pastrana?" Surprisingly enough, although he did not receive an answer to his question, his talk elicited some information about Zenora.

The True Story of Zenora

Lehmann heard from a person who turned out to be a relative of Zenora Pastrana. According to this informant, Zenora was not the bearded woman's real name, nor was she related to Julia. Actually, her name was Marie Bartels, and she was the daughter of a Karlsbad businessman.

It was a family legend that Marie Bartels' mother had been frightened by her shaggy dog, and that as a result of this maternal impression the child was born covered with hair. Marie first shaved on her confirmation day.

Marie's father was cold and indifferent toward his hairy daughter. One day, when she was eighteen years old, she was in the garden, which was surrounded by a wall. Suddenly a paper bag came flying over it. She opened the bag and found it was full of sugar plums. Clambering up on the wall, she looked over. A strange gentleman waved to her from below. He informed Marie that his name was Lent and he asked if she would like to travel and see the world. Her answer is not hard to imagine.

Next, Lent presented himself to Herr Bartels, and after a short while he asked for Marie's hand in marriage. He swore that he had no intention of exhibiting her to the public. Bartels was more than happy to give his daughter to the showman. After the wedding Lent forbade his wife ever to put a razor to her face again, and he took her on tour. He christened her Zenora Pastrana to trade on the name of the dead celebrity, who was the most famous bearded lady of the age.

The couple went to England and France, where Lent exhibited his bearded wife. He made her learn to ride a horse bareback, to make her performance more interesting.

Lent Goes Mad

The pair continued their travels, earning a good deal of money. They were also received in royal courts. In Russia Lent set up a museum where he had a waxworks and other exhibits. Later, he began to behave strangely. One day, crossing the bridge over the Neva in Saint Petersburg, he tore up banknotes and threw them away, and he did other irrational things. In 1884 he died of brain disease.

Perhaps because she was now a wealthy woman, Marie's father insisted that the young widow come home and stay with him. But life with the overbearing Herr Bartels soon became insufferable, so she left and settled in Dresden. When she went out in the street she would wear men's clothing or cover her face with a heavy veil. At age forty-six she was married again to a man twenty years her junior. She died in about 1900.

Such is the remarkable story of Lent and his two

bearded wives, so far as the author has been able to work it out. Just as remarkable is the fact that the remains of Julia Pastrana and her son are reported to be extant today, and were recently exhibited in the United States. According to the Swedish press, the mummies of the pair were inherited by the owner of a Norwegian tivoli or carnival. In 1972 they were brought to the United States and shown by Gooding's Million Dollar Midways for Lund's Tivoli of Norway. Lorri Harmon, a correspondent of the author's, wrote that she saw the mummies in Pensacola, Florida, at a fair. "The remains of her son were placed close to hers," Miss Harmon related, "but in a glass case separate from Miss Pastrana. As well as I can remember, Miss Pastraña was dressed in the costume she is shown in in your book. Her son was, indeed, perched on a bar, and was dressed, I believe, in what appeared to be a red velvet suit." A photograph of the alleged Julia Pastrana appeared in the October 16, 1972, issue of *Amusement Business*, organ of the outdoor amusement trade.

In 1973 or so, the mummies were back in Norway. The carnival director now took the "apewoman," as she was called, and her son on tour in Sweden. In a town called Hudiksvall a health organization put a stop to the exhibition, and the embalmed corpses, with their impresario, were returned to Norway. The Swedish press reported that the bishop of Oslo was expected to arrange a funeral for them.

But as late as 1975 the mummies of Julia Pastrana and her infant son, which had moved the hearts of millions to pity and awe, had still not found peace.

33

Grace McDaniels:
The Mule-Faced Woman

Grace McDaniels (See photo insert) was the kind of person about whom legends are woven. She was billed as "the Mule-Faced Woman." Some thought she had a face more like a hippopotamus. Still, she attracted men. . . .

Many anecdotes were related of Grace in the circus. Dick Best, an entrepreneur of human oddities, told of the time she came to him complaining that an enthusiastic barker had called her the ugliest woman in the world.

"Look here," said Best to her, "those girls in the girl show are beautiful, and their bodies go in and out in the right places, and what do they get?—$25 a week. And what do you get?—$175 a week."

The lady with the mule face thought about this for a while and withdrew her complaint.

Harry Lewiston employed Grace McDaniels in his sideshow long ago. In his memoirs, *Freak Show Man* (written by Jerry Holtman), he gives a vivid picture of how she appeared. The talker or barker is speaking:

" 'In a minute . . . I'm going to ask Grace to take her veil off so you can see for yourself what she looks like. You won't want to look for long. Instead, you will want to think of yourself, think how lucky you are that you are not like her. Whether you are handsome or homely, beautiful or plain, you can thank your lucky stars you are not Grace McDaniels, "the Mule-Faced Woman" ' . . .

"As Grace lifted her veil, there rose from the audience a tremendous 'Ohhhhhhhhhh!' for she was truly a sight to bring on such reactions. It is impossible to describe her accurately. I can only try. Her flesh was like red, raw meat; her huge chin was twisted at such a distorted angle, she could hardly move her jaws. Her teeth were jagged and sharp, her nose was large and crooked. The objects which made her look most like a mule were her huge, mule-like lips. Her eyes stared grotesquely in their deep-set sockets. All in all, she was a sickening, horrible sight."

According to Lewiston, members of the audience, including men, sometimes fainted when they looked at Grace.

Despite Grace's weird appearance—William Gresham, the author, said her "nose, lips, and chin are a mass of bulbous tissue the color of a wine birthmark" and Slim Kelley, a carnival impresario, described her as "the most hideous female I ever saw"—everyone who knew her agreed she had a delightful personality. Gresham found her "a homespun, motherly soul, generous to a fault. After five minutes' conversation with Grace you forget all about the strange contours of her face and are aware only of the warm, courageous heart of the woman herself." Edward Malone, an old circus hand, said Grace "was always one of the most pleasant women I ever knew. She was attractive to a lot of men, too, believe it or not. I can't tell you how many proposals of marriage she received . . ."

Grace finally accepted one of these proposals from an attractive young man. They had a son, who, when he grew up, managed his mother's affairs and traveled with her until her death in 1958.

34

The Elephant Man
by Sir Frederick Treves

Here, good reader, as your reward for having read this book to the end, is one of the most extraordinary true stories ever told about a human oddity—"The Elephant Man," by Sir Frederick Treves.

The Elephant Man, John Merrick, lived a short life. For most of his twenty-seven years he was an object of horror to those who saw him. His affliction, neurofibromatosis, caused tumors to grow around the nerves under his skin and in his bones. His body was so grotesque that he did not dare to show himself on the streets. When he went out, he wore a hat with a hood that covered his face, and a loose cloak that hid his strange form.

Merrick's disease was the result of a spontaneous genetic change. It could not be treated. He was taken from town to town by itinerant showmen, who exploited him cruelly. In 1884, to Merrick's great good fortune, he made the acquaintance of Frederick Treves. Treves, one of the most gifted medical men of that day, included among his clients the British royal family; he

*was Surgeon Extraordinary to Queen Victoria. He was
also a talented man of letters. The doctor became the
Elephant Man's guardian angel, making the last five
years of his life the happiest he ever lived. Long after
Merrick's death, Treves told his story in his book* The
Elephant Man and Other Reminiscences. (*The head-
ings are mine.*)—*F.D.*

In the Mile End Road, opposite to the London
Hospital, there was (and possibly still is) a line of small
shops. Among them was a vacant greengrocer's which
was to let. The whole of the front of the shop, with the
exception of the door, was hidden by a hanging sheet of
canvas on which was the announcement that the Elephant Man was to be seen within and that the price of
admission was twopence. Painted on the canvas in
primitive colors was a life-size portrait of the Elephant
Man. This very crude production depicted a frightful
creature that could only have been possible in a nightmare. It was the figure of a man with the characteristics
of an elephant. The transfiguration was not far advanced. There was still more of the man than of the
beast. This fact—that it was still human—was the most
repellent attribute of the creature. There was nothing
about it of the pitiableness of the misshapen or the deformed, nothing of the grotesqueness of the freak, but
merely the loathing insinuation of a man being changed
into an animal. Some palm trees in the background of
the picture suggested a jungle and might have led the
imaginative to assume that it was in this wild that the
perverted object had roamed.

When I first became aware of this phenomenon
the exhibition was closed, but a well-informed boy
sought the proprietor in a public house and I was
granted a private view on payment of a shilling. The
shop was empty and grey with dust. Some old tins and
a few shrivelled potatoes occupied a shelf and some
vague vegetable refuse the window. The light in the
place was dim, being obscured by the painted placard
outside. The far end of the shop—where I expect the
late proprietor sat at a desk—was cut off by a curtain or

rather by a red tablecloth suspended from a cord by a few rings. The room was cold and dank, for it was the month of November. The year, I might say, was 1884.

The showman pulled back the curtain and revealed a bent figure crouching on a stool and covered by a brown blanket. In front of it, on a tripod, was a large brick heated by a Bunsen burner. Over this the creature was huddled to warm itself. It never moved when the curtain was drawn back. Locked up in an empty shop and lit by the faint blue light of the gas jet, this hunched-up figure was the embodiment of loneliness. It might have been a captive in a cavern or a wizard watching for unholy manifestations in the ghostly flame. Outside the sun was shining and one could hear the footsteps of the passers-by, a tune whistled by a boy and the companionable hum of traffic in the road.

The showman—speaking as if to a dog—called out harshly: "Stand up!" The thing arose slowly and let the blanket that covered its head and back fall to the ground. There stood revealed the most disgusting specimen of humanity that I have ever seen. In the course of my profession I had come upon lamentable deformities of the face due to injury or disease, as well as mutilations and contortions of the body depending upon like causes; but at no time had I met with such a degraded or perverted version of a human being as this lone figure displayed. He was naked to the waist, his feet were bare, he wore a pair of threadbare trousers that had once belonged to some fat gentleman's dress suit.

His Misshapen Head

From the intensified painting in the street I had imagined the Elephant Man to be of gigantic size. This, however, was a little man below the average height and made to look shorter by the bowing of his back. The most striking feature about him was his enormous and misshapen head. From the brow there projected a huge bony mass like a loaf, while from the back of the head hung a bag of spongy, fungous-looking skin, the surface of which was comparable to brown cauliflower. On the top of the skull were a few long lank hairs. The osseous growth on the forehead almost occluded one eye. The circumference of the head was no less than that of the man's waist. From the upper jaw there projected another mass of bone. It protruded from the mouth like a pink stump, turning the upper lip inside out and making of the mouth a mere slobbering aperture. This growth from the jaw had been so exaggerated in the painting as to appear to be a rudimentary trunk or tusk. The nose was merely a lump of flesh, only recognizable as a nose from its position. The face was no more capable of expression than a block of gnarled wood. The back was horrible, because from it hung, as far down as the middle of the thigh, huge, sack-like masses of flesh covered by the same loathsome cauliflower skin.

A Fin Rather Than a Hand

The right arm was of enormous size and shapeless. It suggested the limb of the subject of elephantiasis. It was overgrown also with pendent masses of the same cauliflower-like skin. The hand was large and clumsy—a fin or paddle rather than a hand. There was no distinction between the palm and the back. The thumb had the appearance of a radish, while the fingers might have been thick, tuberous roots. As a limb it was almost useless. The other arm was remarkable by contrast. It was not only normal but was, moreover, a delicately shaped limb covered with fine skin and provided with a beautiful hand which any woman might have envied. From the chest hung a bag of the same repulsive flesh. It was like a dewlap suspended from the neck of a lizard. The lower limbs had the characters of the deformed arm. They were unwieldy, dropsical looking and grossly misshapen.

To add a further burden to his trouble the wretched man, when a boy, developed hip disease, which had left him permanently lame, so that he could only walk with a stick. He was thus denied all means of escape from his tormentors. As he told me later, he could never run away. One other feature must be mentioned to emphasize his isolation from his kind. Although he was already repellent enough, there arose from the fungous skin-growth with which he was almost covered a very sickening stench which was hard to tolerate. From the showman I learnt nothing about the Elephant Man, except that he was English, that his name was John Merrick and that he was twenty-one years of age.

His Disguise

As at the time of my discovery of the Elephant Man I was the Lecturer on Anatomy at the Medical College opposite, I was anxious to examine him in detail and to prepare an account of his abnormalities. I therefore arranged with the showman that I should interview his strange exhibit in my room at the college. I became at once conscious of a difficulty. The Elephant Man could not show himself in the streets. He would have been mobbed by the crowd and seized by the police. He was, in fact, as secluded from the world as the Man with the Iron Mask. He had, however, a disguise, although it was almost as startling as he was himself. It consisted of a long black cloak which reached to the ground. Whence the cloak had been obtained I cannot imagine. I had only seen such a garment on the stage wrapped about the figure of a Venetian bravo. The recluse was provided with a pair of bag-like slippers in which to hide his deformed feet. On his head was a cap of a kind that never before was seen. It was black like the cloak, had a wide peak, and the general outline of a yachting cap. As the circumference of Merrick's head was that of a man's waist, the size of this headgear may be imagined. From the attachment of the peak a grey flannel curtain hung in front of the face. In this mask was cut a wide horizontal slit through which the wearer could look out. This costume, worn by a bent man hobbling along with a stick, is probably the most remarkable and the most uncanny that has as yet been designed. I arranged that Merrick should cross the road in a cab, and to insure his immediate admission to the college I gave him my card. This card was destined to play a critical part in Merrick's life.

I made a careful examination of my visitor the result of which I embodied in a paper. I made little of the man himself. He was shy, confused, not a little frightened and evidently much cowed. Moreover, his speech was almost unintelligible. The great bony mass that projected from his mouth blurred his utterance and made the articulation of certain words impossible. He returned in a cab to the place of exhibition, and I assumed that I had seen the last of him, especially as I found next day that the show had been forbidden by the police and that the shop was empty.

Shunned like a Leper

I supposed that Merrick was imbecile and had been imbecile from birth. The fact that his face was incapable of expression, that his speech was a mere spluttering and his attitude that of one whose mind was void of all emotions and concerns gave grounds for this belief. The conviction was no doubt encouraged by the hope that his intellect was the blank I imagined it to be. That he could appreciate his position was unthinkable. Here was a man in the heyday of youth who was so vilely deformed that everyone he met confronted him with a look of horror and disgust. He was taken about the country to be exhibited as a monstrosity and an object of loathing. He was shunned like a leper, housed like a wild beast, and got his only view of the world from a peephole in a showman's cart. He was, moreover, lame, had but one available arm, and could hardly make his utterances understood. It was not until I came to know that Merrick was highly intelligent, that he possessed an acute sensibility and—worse than all—a romantic imagination that I realized the overwhelming tragedy of his life.

The episode of the Elephant Man was, I imagined, closed; but I was fated to meet him again—two years later—under more dramatic conditions. In England the showman and Merrick had been moved on from place to place by the police, who considered the exhibition degrading and among the things that could not be allowed. It was hoped that in the uncritical retreats of Mile End a more abiding peace would be found. But it was not to be. The official mind there, as elsewhere, very properly decreed that the public exposure of Merrick and his deformities transgressed the limits of decency. The show must close.

Merrick Is Robbed

The showman, in despair, fled with his charge to the Continent. Whither he roamed at first I do not know, but he came finally to Brussels. His reception was discouraging. Brussels was firm; the exhibition was banned; it was brutal, indecent and immoral, and could not be permitted within the confines of Belgium. Merrick was thus no longer of value. He was no longer a source of profitable entertainment. He was a burden. He must be got rid of. The elimination of Merrick was a simple matter. He could offer no resistance. He was as docile as a sick sheep. The impresario, having robbed Merrick of his paltry savings, gave him a ticket to London, saw him into the train and no doubt in parting condemned him to perdition.

His destination was Liverpool Street. The journey may be imagined. Merrick was in his alarming outdoor garb. He would be harried by an eager mob as he hobbled along the quay. They would run ahead to get a look at him. They would lift the hem of his cloak to peep at his body. He would try to hide in the train or in some dark corner of the boat, but never could he be free from that ring of curious eyes or from those whispers of fright and aversion. He had but a few shillings in his pocket and nothing either to eat or drink on the way. A panic-dazed dog with a label on his collar would have received some sympathy and possibly some kindness. Merrick received none.

What was he to do when he reached London? He

had not a friend in the world. He knew no more of London than he knew of Peking. How could he find a lodging, or what lodging-house keeper would dream of taking him in? All he wanted was to hide. What most he dreaded were the open street and the gaze of his fellow-men. If even he crept into a cellar the horrid eyes and the still more dreaded whispers would follow him to its depths. Was there ever such a homecoming!

Rescued by the Police

At Liverpool Street he was rescued from the crowd by the police and taken into the third-class waiting-room. Here he sank on the floor in the darkest corner. The police were at a loss what to do with him. They had dealt with strange and mouldy tramps, but never with such an object as this. He could not explain himself. His speech was so maimed that he might as well have spoken in Arabic. He had, however, something with him which he produced with a ray of hope. It was my card.

The card simplified matters. It made it evident that this curious creature had an acquaintance and that the individual must be sent for. A messenger was dispatched to the London Hospital which is comparatively near at hand. Fortunately I was in the building and returned at once with the messenger to the station. In the waiting-room I had some difficulty in making a way through the crowd, but there, on the floor in the corner, was Merrick. He looked a mere heap. It seemed as if he had been thrown there like a bundle. He was so huddled up and so helpless looking that he might have had both his arms and his legs broken. He seemed pleased to see me, but he was nearly done. The journey and want of food had reduced him to the last stage of exhaustion. The police kindly helped him into a cab, and I drove him at once to the hospital. He appeared to be content, for he fell asleep almost as soon as he was seated and slept to the journey's end. He never said a word, but seemed to be satisfied that all was well.

In the Hospital

In the attics of the hospital was an isolation ward with a single bed. It was used for emergency purposes—for a case of delirium tremens, for a man who had become suddenly insane or for a patient with an undetermined fever. Here the Elephant Man was deposited on a bed, was made comfortable and was supplied with food. I had been guilty of an irregularity in admitting such a case, for the hospital was neither a refuge nor a home for incurables. Chronic cases were not accepted, but only those requiring active treatment, and Merrick was not in need of such treatment. I applied to the sympathetic chairman of the committee, Mr. Carr Gomm, who not only was good enough to approve my action but who agreed with me that Merrick must not again be turned out into the world.

Mr. Carr Gomm wrote a letter to *The Times* detailing the circumstances of the refugee and asking for money for his support. So generous is the English public that in a few days—I think in a week—enough money was forthcoming to maintain Merrick for life without any charge upon the hospital funds. There chanced to be two empty rooms at the back of the hospital which were little used. They were on the ground floor, were out of the way, and opened upon a large courtyard called Bedstead Square, because here the iron beds were marshalled for cleaning and painting. The front room was converted into a bed-sitting room and the smaller chamber into a bathroom. The condition of Merrick's skin rendered a bath at least once a day a necessity, and I might here mention that with the use of the bath the unpleasant odor to which I have referred ceased to be noticeable. Merrick took up his abode in the hospital in December 1886.

Merrick had now something he had never dreamed of, never supposed to be possible—a home of his own for life. I at once began to make myself acquainted with him and to endeavor to understand his mentality. It was a study of much interest. I very soon learned his speech so that I could talk freely with him. This afforded him great satisfaction, for, curiously enough, he had a passion for conversation, yet all his life had had no one to talk to. I—having then much leisure—saw him almost every day, and made a point of spending some two hours with him every Sunday morning when he would chatter almost without ceasing. It was unreasonable to expect one nurse to attend to him continuously, but there was no lack of temporary volunteers. As they did not all acquire his speech it came about that I had occasionally to act as an interpreter.

Both a Child and a Man

I found Merrick, as I have said, remarkably intelligent. He had learned to read and had become a most voracious reader. I think he had been taught when he was in hospital with his diseased hip. His range of books was limited. The Bible and Prayer Book he knew intimately, but he had subsisted for the most part upon newspapers, or rather upon such fragments of old journals as he had chanced to pick up. He had read a few stories and some elementary lesson books, but the delight of his life was a romance, especially a love romance. These tales were very real to him, as real as any narrative in the Bible, so that he would tell them to me as incidents in the lives of people who had lived. In his outlook upon the world he was a child, yet a child with some of the tempestuous feelings of a man. He was an elemental being, so primitive that he might have spent the twenty-three years of his life immured in a cave.

The Elephant Man's Mother

Of his early days I could learn but little. He was very loath to talk about the past. It was a nightmare, the shudder of which was still upon him. He was born, he believed, in or about Leicester. Of his father he knew absolutely nothing. Of his mother he had some memory. It was very faint and had, I think, been elaborated in his mind into something definite. Mothers figured in the tales he had read, and he wanted his mother to be one of those comfortable lullaby-singing persons who are so lovable. In his subconscious mind there was apparently a germ of recollection in which someone figured who had been kind to him. He clung to this conception and made it more real by invention, for since the day when he could toddle no one had been kind to him. As an infant he must have been repellent, although his deformities did not become gross until he had attained his full stature.

It was a favorite belief of his that his mother was beautiful. The fiction was, I am aware, one of his own making, but it was a great joy to him. His mother, lovely as she may have been, basely deserted him when he was very small, so small that his earliest clear memories were of the workhouse to which he had been taken. Worthless and inhuman as this mother was, he spoke of her with pride and even with reverence. Once, when referring to his own experience, he said: "It is very strange, for, you see, mother was so beautiful."

Mocked by the Mob

The rest of Merrick's life up to the time that I met him at Liverpool Street Station was one dull record of degradation and squalor. He was dragged from town to town and from fair to fair as if he were a strange beast in a cage. A dozen times a day he would have to expose his nakedness and his piteous deformities before a gaping crowd who greeted him with such mutterings as "Oh! what a horror! What a beast!" He had had no childhood. He had had no boyhood. He had never experienced pleasure. He knew nothing of the joy of living nor of the fun of things. His sole idea of happiness was to creep into the dark and hide. Shut up alone in a booth, awaiting the next exhibition, how mocking must have sounded the laughter and merriment of the boys and girls outside who were enjoying the "fun of the fair"! He had no past to look back upon and no future to look forward to. At the age of twenty he was a creature without hope. There was nothing in front of him but a vista of caravans creeping along a road, of rows of glaring show tents and of circles of staring eyes with, at the end, the spectacle of a broken man in a poor law infirmary.

Those who are interested in the evolution of character might speculate as to the effect of this brutish life upon a sensitive and intelligent man. It would be reasonable to surmise that he would become a spiteful and malignant misanthrope, swollen with venom and filled with hatred of his fellow-men, or, on the other hand, that he would degenerate into a despairing melancholic on the verge of idiocy. Merrick, however, was no such being. He had passed through the fire and had come out unscathed. His troubles had ennobled him. He showed himself to be a gentle, affectionate and lovable creature, as amiable as a happy woman, free from any trace of cynicism or resentment, without a grievance and without an unkind word for anyone. I have never heard him complain. I have never heard him deplore his ruined life or resent the treatment he had received at the hands of callous keepers. His journey through life had been indeed along a *via dolorosa,* the road had been uphill all the way, and now, when the night was at its blackest and the way most steep, he had suddenly found himself, as it were, in a friendly inn, bright with light and warm with welcome. His gratitude to those about him was pathetic in its sincerity and eloquent in the childlike simplicity with which it was expressed.

A Pariah and an Outcast

As I learned more of this primitive creature I found that there were two anxieties which were prominent in his mind and which he revealed to me with diffidence. He was in the occupation of the rooms assigned to him and had been assured that he would be cared for to the end of his days. This, however, he found hard to realize, for he often asked me timidly to what place he would next be moved. To understand his attitude it is necessary to remember that he had been moving on and moving on all his life. He knew no other state of existence. To him it was normal. He had passed from the workhouse to the hospital, from the hospital back to the workhouse, then from this town to that town or from one showman's caravan to another. He had never known a home nor any semblance of one. He had no possessions. His sole belongings, besides his clothes and some books, were the monstrous cap and the cloak. He was a wanderer, a pariah and an outcast. That his quarters at the hospital were his for life he could not understand. He could not rid his mind of the anxiety which had pursued him for so many years—where am I to be taken next?

Another trouble was his dread of his fellow-men, his fear of people's eyes, the dread of being always stared at, the lash of the cruel mutterings of the crowd. In his home in Bedstead Square he was secluded; but now and then a thoughtless porter or a wardmaid would open his door to let curious friends have a peep at the Elephant Man. It therefore seemed to him as if the gaze of the world followed him still.

Influenced by these two obsessions he became, during his first few weeks at the hospital, curiously uneasy. At last, with much hesitation, he said to me one day: "When I am next moved can I go to a blind asylum or to a lighthouse?" He had read about blind asylums in the newspapers and was attracted by the thought of being among people who could not see. The lighthouse had another charm. It meant seclusion from the curious. There at least no one could open a door and peep in at him. There he would forget that he had once been the Elephant Man. There he would escape the vampire showman. He had never seen a lighthouse, but he had come upon a picture of the Eddystone, and it appeared to him that this lonely column of stone in the waste of the sea was such a home as he had longed for.

He Could Only Go Out After Dark

I had no great difficulty in ridding Merrick's mind of these ideas. I wanted him to get accustomed to his fellow-men, to become a human being himself and to be admitted to the communion of his kind. He appeared day by day less frightened, less haunted looking, less anxious to hide, less alarmed when he saw his door being opened. He got to know most of the people about the place, to be accustomed to their comings and goings, and to realize that they took no more than a friendly notice of him. He could only go out after dark, and on fine nights ventured to take a walk in Bedstead Square clad in his black cloak and his cap. His greatest adventure was on one moonless evening when he walked alone as far as the hospital garden and back again.

To secure Merrick's recovery and to bring him, as it were, to life once more, it was necessary that he should make the acquaintance of men and women who would treat him as a normal and intelligent young man and not as a monster of deformity. Women I felt to be more important than men in bringing about his transformation. Women were the more frightened of him, the more disgusted at his appearance and the more apt to give way to irrepressible expressions of aversion when they came into his presence. Moreover, Merrick had an admiration of women of such a kind that it attained almost to adoration. This was not the outcome of his personal experience. They were not real women but the products of his imagination. Among them was the beautiful mother surrounded, at a respectful distance, by heroines from the many romances he had read.

His Nurses

His first entry to the hospital was attended by a regrettable incident. He had been placed on the bed in the little attic, and a nurse had been instructed to bring him some food. Unfortunately she had not been fully informed of Merrick's unusual appearance. As she entered the room she saw on the bed, propped up by white pillows, a monstrous figure as hideous as an Indian idol. She at once dropped the tray she was carrying and fled, with a shriek, through the door. Merrick was too weak to notice much, but the experience, I am afraid, was not new to him.

He was looked after by volunteer nurses whose ministrations were somewhat formal and constrained. Merrick, no doubt, was conscious that their service was purely official, that they were merely doing what they were told to do and that they were acting rather as automata than as women. They did not help him to feel that he was of their kind. On the contrary, they, without knowing it, made him aware that the gulf of separation was immeasurable.

Feeling this, I asked a friend of mine, a young and pretty widow, if she thought she could enter Merrick's room with a smile, wish him good morning and shake him by the hand. She said she could and she did. As he let go her hand he bent his head on his knees and sobbed until I thought he would never cease. The interview was over. He told me afterwards that this was the first woman who had ever smiled at him, and the first woman, in the whole of his life, who had shaken hands with him. From this day the transformation of Merrick commenced and he began to change, little by little, from a hunted thing into a man. It was a wonderful change to witness and one that never ceased to fascinate me.

Meeting the Nobility

Merrick's case attracted much attention in the papers, with the result that he had a constant succession of visitors. Everybody wanted to see him. He must have been visited by almost every lady of note in the social world. They were all good enough to welcome him with a smile and to shake hands with him. The Merrick whom I had found shivering behind a rag of a curtain in an empty shop was now conversant with duchesses and countesses and other ladies of high degree. They brought him presents, made his room bright with ornaments and pictures, and, what pleased him more than all, supplied him with books. He soon had a large library and most of his day was spent in reading. He was not the least spoiled; not the least puffed up; he never asked for anything; never presumed upon the kindness meted out to him and was always humbly and profoundly grateful. Above all he lost his shyness. He liked to see his door pushed open and people to look in. He became acquainted with most of the frequenters of Bedstead Square, would chat with him at his window and show them some of his choicest presents. He improved in his speech, although to the end his utterances were not easy for strangers to understand. He was beginning, moreover, to be less conscious of his unsightliness, a little disposed to think it was, after all, not so very extreme. Possibly this was aided by the circumstance that I would not allow a mirror of any kind in his room.

The height of his social development was reached on an eventful day when Queen Alexandra—then Princess of Wales—came to the hospital to pay him a special visit. With that kindness which marked every act of her life, the Queen entered Merrick's room smiling and shook him warmly by the hand. Merrick was transported with delight. This was beyond even his most extravagant dream. The Queen made many people happy, but I think no gracious act of hers ever caused such happiness as she brought into Merrick's room when she sat by his chair and talked to him as to a person she was glad to see.

Unable to Smile or Sing

Merrick, I may say, was now one of the most contented creatures I have chanced to meet. More than once he said to me: "I am happy every hour of the day." This was good to think upon when I recalled the half-dead heap of miserable humanity I had seen in the corner of the waiting-room at Liverpool Street. Most men of Merrick's age would have expressed their joy and sense of contentment by singing or whistling when they were alone. Unfortunately poor Merrick's mouth was so deformed that he could neither whistle nor sing. He was satisfied to express himself by beating time upon the pillow to some tune that was ringing in his head. I have many times found him so occupied when I have entered his room unexpectedly. One thing that always struck me as sad about Merrick was the fact that he could not smile. Whatever his delight might be, his face remained expressionless. He could weep but he could not smile.

The Queen paid Merrick many visits and sent him every year a Christmas card with a message in her own handwriting. On one occasion she sent him a signed photograph of herself. Merrick, quite overcome, regarded it as a sacred object and would hardly allow me to touch it. He cried over it, and after it was framed had it put up in his room as a kind of ikon. I told him that he must write to Her Royal Highness to thank her for her goodness. This he was pleased to do, as he was very fond of writing letters, never before in his life having had anyone to write to. I allowed the letter to be dispatched unedited. It began "My dear Princess" and ended "Yours very sincerely." Unorthodox as it was it was expressed in terms any courtier would have envied.

Other ladies followed the Queen's gracious example and sent their photographs to this delighted creature who had been all his life despised and rejected of men. His mantelpiece and table become so covered with photographs of handsome ladies, with dainty knickknacks and pretty trifles that they may almost have befitted the apartment of an Adonis-like actor or of a famous tenor.

A Christmas Present for the Elephant Man

Through all these bewildering incidents and through the glamour of this great change Merrick still remained in many ways a mere child. He had all the invention of an imaginative boy or girl, the same love of "make-believe," the same instinct of "dressing up" and of personating heroic and impressive characters. This attitude of mind was illustrated by the following incident. Benevolent visitors had given me, from time to time, sums of money to be expended for the comfort of the *ci-devant Elephant Man*. When one Christmas was approaching I asked Merrick what he would like me to purchase as a Christmas present. He rather startled me by saying shyly that he would like a dressing-bag with silver fittings. He had seen a picture of such an article in an advertisement which he had furtively preserved.

The association of a silver-fitted dressing-bag with the poor wretch wrapped up in a dirty blanket in an empty shop was hard to comprehend. I fathomed the mystery in time, for Merrick made little secret of the fancies that haunted his boyish brain. Just as a small girl with a tinsel coronet and a window curtain for a train will realize the conception of a countess on her way to court, so Merrick loved to imagine himself a dandy and a young man about town. Mentally, no doubt, he had frequently "dressed up" for the part. He could "make-believe" with great effect, but he wanted something to render his fancied character more realistic. Hence the jaunty bag which was to assume the function of the toy coronet and the window curtain that could transform a mite with a pigtail into a countess.

As a theatrical "property" the dressing-bag was ingenious, since there was little else to give substance to the transformation. Merrick could not wear the silk hat of the dandy nor, indeed, any kind of hat. He could not adapt his body to the trimly cut coat. His deformity was such that he could wear neither collar nor tie, while in association with his bulbous feet the young blood's patent leather shoe was unthinkable. What was there left to make up the character? A lady had given him a ring to wear on his undeformed hand and a noble lord had presented him with a very stylish walking-stick. But these things, helpful as they were, were hardly sufficing.

The dressing-bag, however, was distinctive, was explanatory and entirely characteristic. So the bag was obtained and Merrick the Elephant Man became, in the seclusion of his chamber, the Piccadilly exquisite, the young spark, the gallant, the "nut." When I purchased the article I realized that as Merrick could never travel he could hardly want a dressing-bag. He could not use the silver-backed brushes and the comb because he had no hair to brush. The ivory-handled razors were useless because he could not shave. The deformity of his mouth rendered an ordinary toothbrush of no avail, and as his monstrous lips could not hold a cigarette the cigarette-case was a mockery. The silver shoe-horn would be of no service in the putting on of his ungainly slippers, while the hat-brush was quite unsuited to the peaked cap with its visor.

Still the bag was an emblem of the real swell and of the knockabout Don Juan of whom he had read. So every day Merrick laid out upon his table, with proud precision, the silver brushes, the razors, the shoe-horn and the silver cigarette-case, which I had taken care to fill with cigarettes. The contemplation of these gave him great pleasure, and such is the power of self-deception that they convinced him he was the "real thing."

The Elephant Man in Love

I think there was just one shadow in Merrick's life. As I have already said, he had a lively imagination; he was romantic; he cherished an emotional regard for women and his favorite pursuit was the reading of love stories. He fell in love—in a humble and devotional way—with, I think, every attractive lady he saw. He, no doubt, pictured himself the hero of many a passionate incident. His bodily deformity had left unmarred the instincts and feelings of his years. He was amorous. He would like to have been a lover, to have walked with the beloved object in the languorous shades of some beautiful garden and to have poured into her ear all the glowing utterances that he had rehearsed in his heart. And yet—the pity of it!—imagine the feelings of such a youth when he saw nothing but a look of horror creep over the face of every girl whose eyes met his. I fancy when he talked of life among the blind there was a half-formed idea in his mind that he might be able to win the affection of a woman if only she were without eyes to see.

As Merrick developed he began to display certain modest ambitions in the direction of improving his mind and enlarging his knowledge of the world. He was as curious as a child and as eager to learn. There were so many things he wanted to know and to see. In the first place he was anxious to view the interior of what he called "a real house," such a house as figured in many of the tales he knew, a house with a hall, a drawing-room where guests were received and a dining-room with plates on the sideboard and with easy chairs into which the hero could "fling himself." The workhouse, the common lodging-house and a variety of mean garrets were all the residences he knew. To satisfy this wish I drove him up to my small house in Wimpole Street. He was absurdly interested, and examined everything in detail and with untiring curiosity. I could not show him the pampered menials and the powdered footmen of whom he had read, nor could I produce the white marble staircase of the mansion of romance nor the gilded mirrors and the brocaded divans which belong to that style of residence. I explained that the house was a modest dwelling of the Jane Austen type, and as he had read *Emma* he was content.

A Visit to the Theater

A more burning ambition of his was to go to the theatre. It was a project very difficult to satisfy. A popular pantomime was then in progress at Drury Lane Theatre, but the problem was how so conspicuous a being as the Elephant Man could be got there, and how he was to see the performance without attracting the notice of the audience and causing a panic or, at least, an unpleasant diversion. The whole matter was most ingeniously carried through by that kindest of women and most able of actresses—Mrs. Kendal. She made the necessary arrangements with the lessee of the theater. A box was obtained. Merrick was brought up in a carriage with drawn blinds and was allowed to make use of the royal entrance so as to reach the box by a private stair. I had begged three of the hospital sisters to don evening dress and to sit in the front row in order to "dress" the box, on the one hand, and to form a screen for Merrick on the other. Merrick and I occupied the back of the box which was kept in shadow. All went well, and no one saw a figure, more monstrous than any on the stage, mount the staircase or cross the corridor.

One has often witnessed the unconstrained delight of a child at its first pantomime, but Merrick's rapture was much more intense as well as much more solemn. Here was a being with the brain of a man, the fancies of a youth and the imagination of a child. His attitude was not so much that of delight as of wonder and amazement. He was awed. He was enthralled. The spectacle left him speechless, so that if he were spoken to he took no heed. He often seemed to be panting for breath. I could not help comparing him with a man of his own age in the stalls. This satiated individual was bored to distraction, would look wearily at the stage from time to time and then yawn as if he had not slept for nights; while at the same time Merrick was thrilled by a vision that was almost beyond his comprehension. Merrick talked of this pantomime for weeks and weeks. To him, as to a child with the faculty of make-believe, everything was real; the palace was the home of kings, the princess was of royal blood, the fairies were as undoubted as the children in the street, while the dishes at the banquet were of unquestionable gold. He did not like to discuss it as a play but rather as a vision of some actual world. When this mood possessed him he would say: "I wonder what the prince did after we left?" or "Do you think that poor man is still in the dungeon?" and so on and so on.

The splendor and display impressed him, but, I think, the ladies of the ballet took a still greater hold upon his fancy. He did not like the ogres and the giants, while the funny men impressed him as irreverent. Having no experience as a boy of romping and ragging, of practical jokes or of "larks," he had little sympathy with the doings of the clown, but, I think (moved by some mischievous instinct in his subconscious mind), he was pleased when the policeman was smacked in the face, knocked down and generally rendered undignified.

His Happiest Time

Later on another longing stirred the depths of Merrick's mind. It was a desire to see the country, a desire to live in some green secluded spot and there learn something about flowers and the ways of animals and birds. The country as viewed from a wagon on a dusty high road was all the country he knew. He had never wandered among the fields nor followed the windings of a wood. He had never climbed to the brow of a breezy down. He had never gathered flowers in a meadow. Since so much of his reading dealt with country life he was possessed by the wish to see the wonders of that life himself.

This involved a difficulty greater than that presented by a visit to the theater. The project was, however, made possible on this occasion also by the kindness and generosity of a lady—Lady Knightley—who offered Merrick a holiday home in a cottage on her estate. Merrick was conveyed to the railway station in the usual way, but as he could hardly venture to appear on the platform the railway authorities were good enough to run a second-class carriage into a distant siding. To this point Merrick was driven and was placed in the carriage unobserved. The carriage, with the curtains drawn, was then attached to the mainline train.

He duly arrived at the cottage, but the housewife (like the nurse at the hospital) had not been made clearly aware of the unfortunate man's appearance. Thus it happened that when Merrick presented himself, his hostess, throwing her apron over her head, fled, gasping, to the fields. She affirmed that such a guest was beyond her powers of endurance for, when she saw him, she was "that took" as to be in danger of being permanently "all of a tremble."

Merrick was then conveyed to a gamekeeper's cottage which was hidden from view and was close to the margin of a wood. The man and his wife were able to tolerate his presence. They treated him with the greatest kindness, and with them he spent the one supreme holiday of his life. He could roam where he pleased. He met no one on his wanderings, for the wood was preserved and denied to all but the game-keeper and the forester.

There is no doubt that Merrick passed in this re-treat the happiest time he had as yet experienced. He was alone in a land of wonders. The breath of the coun-try passed over him like a healing wind. Into the silence of the wood the fearsome voice of the showman could never penetrate. No cruel eyes could peep at him through the friendly undergrowth. It seemed as if in this place of peace all stain had been wiped away from his sullied past. The Merrick who had once crouched terri-fied in the filthy shadows of a Mile End shop was now sitting in the sun, in a clearing among the trees, arrang-ing a bunch of violets he had gathered.

His letters to me were the letters of a delighted and enthusiastic child. He gave an account of his trivial adventures, of the amazing things he had seen, and of the beautiful sounds he had heard. He had met with strange birds, had startled a hare from her form, had made friends with a fierce dog, and had watched the trout darting in a stream. He sent me some of the wild flowers he had picked. They were of the commonest and most familiar kind, but they were evidently re-garded by him as rare and precious specimens.

He came back to London, to his quarters in Bed-stead Square, much improved in health, pleased to be "home" again and to be once more among his books, his treasures and his many friends.

To Sleep like Other People

Some six months after Merrick's return from the country he was found dead in bed. This was in April 1890. He was lying on his back as if asleep, and had evidently died suddenly and without a struggle, since not even the coverlet of the bed was disturbed. The method of his death was peculiar. So large and so heavy was his head that he could not sleep lying down. When he assumed the recumbent position the massive skull was inclined to drop backwards, with the result that he experienced no little distress. The attitude he was compelled to assume when he slept was very strange. He sat up in bed with his back supported by pillows; his knees were drawn up, and his arms clasped round his legs, while his head rested on the points of his bent knees.

He often said to me that he wished he could lie down to sleep "like other people." I think on this last night he must, with some determination, have made the experiment. The pillow was soft, and the head, when placed on it, must have fallen backwards and caused a dislocation of the neck. Thus it came about that his death was due to the desire that had dominated his life—the pathetic but hopeless desire to be "like other people."

As a specimen of humanity, Merrick was ignoble and repulsive; but the spirit of Merrick, if it could be seen in the form of the living, would assume the figure of an upstanding and heroic man, smooth browed and clean of limb, and with eyes that flashed undaunted courage.

His tortured journey had come to an end. All the way he, like another, had borne on his back a burden almost too grievous to bear. He had been plunged into the Slough of Despond, but with manly steps had gained the farther shore. He had been made "a spectacle to all men" in the heartless streets of Vanity Fair. He had been ill-treated and reviled and bespattered with the mud of Disdain. He had escaped the clutches of the Giant Despair, and at last had reached the "Place of Deliverance," where "his burden loosed from off his shoulders and fell from off his back, so that he saw it no more."

Epilog

This book breaks new ground. I have tried to make it the most thoroughgoing and definitive work about the Very Special People yet published. Many of them have not been discussed at length in books before. I have done my best to tell the stories of all with honesty and accuracy.

With some of the Very Special People, like Tom Thumb, the task is not a difficult one, for the record is clear. With others, however, much is obscure. Human oddities come into the public eye, remain there for a while, and then suddenly plummet out of sight forever. You can't find out whether they married, had children, or where and when they died. In some instances, you're dependent on faded newspaper clippings or old pamphlets that differ astonishingly about the basic facts of their lives or the spelling of their names. Even the great *New York Times,* which we are accustomed to think of as a Gibraltar of information, in its accounts of the Siamese twins Chang and Eng in 1874, the year of their death, interwove fiction with fact.

I probably have done the same, occasionally. However, in researching this book I have diligently tried to sort reality from hearsay and to indicate my doubts with a "reportedly" or "reputedly." I have been aware of contradictions in my sources, and sometimes I've been obliged to choose between them. I hope my choices were the right ones. If you, kind reader, have special knowledge and can supply any dates I've omitted or correct any information I've misconstrued, I should be most grateful if you would write to me in the care of the publishers of this book so I can set the record straight in future editions.

In Appreciation

Writing a book as wide in scope as this one is a weighty task, but the aid of capable, informed people helps to make it lighter. I owe a special debt of gratitude to my publishers, Sidney and Russell Mehlman, who created the idea of this book, gave it its title, and supplied unflagging enthusiasm and advice along the way. Russell also helped greatly in locating illustrations.

My wife, Evelyn, who is reference librarian at the Norwalk Public Library, in Norwalk, Connecticut, provided encouragement, guidance, and an endless stream of reference material, which she obtained from libraries throughout the state of Connecticut. My daughter, Jean, made a trip to the Circus World Museum and brought back research materials and a dream that opened up the whole world of human oddities to me.

No one helped more in providing background information than Robert Parkinson, chief librarian and historian of the Circus World Museum of Baraboo, Wisconsin, and his assistant librarian, William Metzger. "That's what we're here for," said Mr. Parkinson, and proceeded to throw open his files to me. For the hours of personal attention given to me and my daughter I am greatly indebted to these two gentlemen. The museum also furnished a considerable number of the pictures in this book. So did the Harry Hertzberg Circus Collection of the San Antonio Public Library and the Museum of the City of New York.

When the project was in its initial stages, I was given wise and generous advice by John H. Hurdle, curator of the Ringling Museum of the Circus in Sarasota, Florida. Mr. Kenneth Holmes of the Barnum Museum in Bridgeport, Connecticut, also provided useful guidance.

This book owes much to the help of many others. I am especially indebted to:

David L. Rimoin, M. D., of the School of Medicine of the University of California; Jon Friday, carnival authority of *Amusement Business;* Jorn Wounlund of Gothenburg, Sweden; officials of the Library of the British Museum, London; Paul P. Hoffman, head, Archives Branch, Division of Archives and History, State of North Carolina; Mary L. Phillips, local history librarian, Public Library of Charlotte and Mecklenburg County, Charlotte, North Carolina; Mrs. J. J. Cochran, curator of the Medina County Historical Society, Medina, Ohio; Mrs. Susan Knight, reference librarian of the Maryland Historical Society, Baltimore, Maryland; Mrs. Robert D. Nicoll of the Mark Twain Memorial in Hartford, Connecticut; the Reverend C. J. Wayte of Biddenden, Ashford, Kent, England; the Circus Hall of Fame, Sarasota, Florida; the Italian Consul General, New York City; Ruth Adams and Mrs. Walter Pitkin of the Westport Public Library, Westport, Connecticut; the New York Historical Society; the New York Academy of Medicine; the New York Public Library; the Theater Collection of the Library of Performing Arts of New York City; the Cleveland Health Museum, Cleveland, Ohio; the library of the Norwalk Hospital, Norwalk, Connecticut; the local history librarian of the Bridgeport Public Library, Bridgeport, Connecticut; and Martin Laderman of Fair Lawn, New

Jersey, for his infectious enthusiasm and Charlotte Gross for her advice.

The quotation by William Lindsay Gresham on the dedication page is from his book *Monster Midway*. The quotation by Sainte-Beuve is from his poem *"le Joueur d'Orgue."*

Bibliography

This bibliography is suggestive rather than complete. The author has consulted other books and pamphlets, as well as magazines, newspapers, unpublished letters, and other writings too numerous to list.

Autobiography of Chang. London: Arless and Company, 1866.

Barnum, P. T. *Struggles and Triumphs.* New York: Macmillan Company, 1930.

Beal, George Brinton. *Through the Back Door of the Circus.* Springfield, Mass.: McLoughlin Bros., 1938.

Biography of Madame Fortune Clofullia, the Bearded Lady. New York: Baker, Godwin and Company, 1854.

Bodin, Walter, and Hershey, Burnet. *It's a Small World.* New York: Coward-McCann, 1934.

Bradna, Fred, and Spence, Hartzell. *The Big Top.* New York: Simon and Schuster, 1952.

Buckland, F. T. *Curiosities of Natural History.* London: Macmillan Company, 1900.

Calvin, Lee. *There Were Giants on the Earth.* Seville, Ohio: Seville Chronicle, 1959.

Carmichael, Bill. *Incredible Collectors, Weird Antiques, and Odd Hobbies.* Englewood Cliffs, N.J.: Prentice-Hall, 1971.

Clair, Colin. *Human Curiosities.* New York: Abelard-Schuman, 1968.

Clemens, Samuel L. (Twain, Mark). *Pudd'nhead Wilson and Those Extraordinary Twins.* Author's National Edition: The Writings of Mark Twain. Volume XIV. New York: Harper & Brothers, copyright 1894, 1899.

Collins, Pete. *No People Like Show People.* London: Frederick Muller, Ltd., 1957.

Cooper, Wendy. *Hair: Sex, Society, Symbolism.* New York: Stein and Day, 1971.

Dean, Clarence L. *Official Guide: Book of Marvels in the Barnum and Bailey Greatest Show on Earth.* London. 1899.

Desmond, Alice C. *Barnum Presents General Tom Thumb.* New York: Macmillan Company, 1954.

Dingwell, Eric John. *Some Human Oddities.* London: Home & Van Thal, Ltd., 1947.

Durant, John, and Alice. *Pictorial History of the American Circus.* New York: A. S. Barnes and Company, 1957.

Edwards, Frank. *Strange People.* New York: Lyle Stuart, 1961.

Fadner, Frederic. *The Gentleman Giant: Biography of Robert Pershing Wadlow.* Bruce Humphries, 1944.

Fellows, Dexter W., and Freeman, A. A. *This Way to the Big Show.* New York: Viking, 1936.

Fenner, Mildred S. *The Circus, Lure and Legend.* Englewood Cliffs, N.J.: Prentice-Hall, 1970.

Fowler, Gene. *The Great Mouthpiece.* New York: Covici, 1931.

Fox, Charles P. *Circus Parades.* Watkins Glen, N.Y.: Century House, 1953.

Futcher, Palmer Howard. *Giants and Dwarfs.* Cambridge, Mass.: Harvard University Press, 1933.

Geyer, Celesta "Dolly Dimples," and Roen, Samuel. *Diet or Die.* New York: Frederick Fell, Inc. 1968.

Gould, George M., and Pyle, Walter L. *Anomalies and Curiosities of Medicine.* New York: Bell Publishing Company, 1896.

Graham, Harvey. *A Doctor's London.* London: Wingate, 1952.

Gresham, William L. *Monster Midway.* New York: Rinehart and Company, 1953.

Hamid, George A. *Circus.* New York: Sterling Publishing Co., Inc. 1950.

Historical Account of the Siamese Twin Brothers, New York: Elliott & Palmer, 1831.

History of the Two-Headed Girl.

Hollaender, Eugen. *Wunder, Wundergeburt, und Wundergestalt.* Stuttgart: Ferdinand Enke, 1921.

Holtman, Jerry. *Freak Show Man: the Autobiography of Harry Lewiston.* Los Angeles: Holloway Publishing Co., 1968.

Hoskins, R. G. *Endocrinology: the Glands and Their Functions.* New York: W. W. Norton & Company, Inc., 1941.

Hunter, Kay. *Duet for a Lifetime.* New York: Coward-McCann, 1964.

Lee, Polly Jae. *Giant: Pictorial History of the Human Colossus.* New York: A. S. Barnes, 1970.

Lehmann, Alfred. *Zwischen Schaubuden und Karussells.* Frankfurt: Verlag Dr. Paul Schöp, 1952.

Lewis, Arthur H. *Carnival.* New York: Trident Press, 1970.

Lewis, Harry V. *History of Harry V. Lewis.*

Life of the Celebrated Bearded Lady, Madame Clofullia. New York, 1854.

Life of the Siamese Twins. New York: T. W. Strong, 1853.

McCullough, Edo. *Good Old Coney Island.* New York: Scribner, 1957.

McKennon, Joe. *A Pictorial History of the American*

Carnival. Sarasota, Fla.: Carnival Publishers, 1971.

McWhirter, Norris, and Ross. *Guinness Book of World Records*. New York: Sterling Publishing Co., Inc., 1972.

Mannix, Dan. *Step Right Up!* New York: Harper & Brothers, 1951.

May, Earl Chapin. *The Circus from Rome to Ringling*. New York: Duffield and Green, 1932.

Mitchell, Joseph. *McSorley's Wonderful Saloon*. New York: Grosset, 1959.

Montagu, Ashley, and Treves, Frederick. *Elephant Man*. Outerbridge and Dienstfrey, 1970.

Otto, Hermann W. ["Signor Saltarino"]. *Abnormitäten*. Düsseldorf: E. Lintz, 1900.

————. *Artisten-Lexikon*. Düsseldorf: E. Lintz, 1895.

————. *Das Artistentum und Seine Geschichte*. Leipzig: W. Backhaus, 1910.

————. *Fahrend Volk*. Leipzig: J. J. Weber, 1895.

Pilat, Oliver Ramsay, and Ranson, Jo. *Sodom by the Sea*. Garden City, N.Y.: Garden City Publishing Company, Inc., 1943.

Root, Harvey W. *Unknown Barnum*. New York: Harper, 1927.

Rubin, Alan, M.D., editor. *Handbook of Congenital Malformations*. Philadelphia: W. B. Saunders, 1967.

Sanger, "Lord" George. *Seventy Years a Showman*. London: C. Arthur Pearson, Ltd., 1908.

Smith, Anthony. *The Body*. New York: Walker and Company, 1968.

Sprague, Isaac W. *Life of Isaac W. Sprague*. New York: N.Y. Popular Publishing Co.

Stratton, Lavinia Warren. *Memoirs*. Unpublished (Library of the New York Historical Society).

Teel, J. *True Facts and Pictures of Sideshow Freaks and Features*. Petland Press.

Thétard, Henri. *La merveilleuse histoire du cirque*. Paris: Prisma, 1947.

Thompson, C. J. S. *The Mystery and Lore of Monsters*. New Hyde Park, N.Y.: University Books, 1968.

Tietze-Conrat, Erika. *Dwarfs and Jesters in Art*. New York: Phaidon Publishers, 1957.

Tocquet, Robert. *Les hommes-phénomènes*. Paris: Productions de Paris, 1961.

Toole-Stott, R. *Circus and Allied Arts World Bibliography*. Derby, England: Harpur & Sons, 1967.

Unthan, Carl H. *The Armless Fiddler*. London: Allen and Unwin, 1935.

Vail, R. W. G. *Random Notes of the Early American Circus*. Barre, Mass.: Barre Gazette, 1956.

Wallace, Irving. *The Fabulous Showman: the Life and Times of P. T. Barnum*. New York: Alfred A. Knopf, 1959.

Werner, M. R. *Barnum*. Garden City, N.Y.: Garden City Publishing Company, Inc., 1926.

Wood, E. J. *Giants and Dwarfs*. London: Richard Bentley, 1868.

ABOUT THE AUTHOR

FREDERICK DRIMMER has been interested in the Very Special People since childhood, when he first saw them in the circus. In researching this book he has traveled thousands of miles and combed through many unpublished letters and manuscripts penned by such colorful personalities as Chang and Eng (the original Siamese twins), Mrs. Tom Thumb, and P. T. Barnum, as well as old circus brochures, photographs, programs, and other publications in several languages. He has a wide background in scientific and historical subjects, having written a history of medicine for Chanticleer Press and over 100,000 words for the *Reader's Digest Family Health Guide and Medical Encyclopedia,* and contributed to other publications. He is perhaps best known for his work as editor of the monumental three-volume *The Animal Kingdom,* an authoritative book of natural history, and *Scalps and Tomahawks: True Eye-Witness Adventures of Indian Captives.* Mr. Drimmer holds a Master of Arts degree from Columbia University, is a member of Phi Beta Kappa, and has taught at the City College of New York and Norwalk (Connecticut) Community College. He was for many years editorial head of Famous Artists School and the Greystone Press, and is a contributing editor of *The Funk and Wagnalls Encyclopedia.*

MORE!
VERY SPECIAL PEOPLE

THE GREATEST PHOTOGRAPHIC COLLECTION OF HUMAN ODDITIES EVER PUBLISHED!

HUNDREDS OF PHOTOS!

SALE—$3.95
HARD COVER

This is the Big One! SIDESHOW—A Photo Album of Human Oddities. Hundreds of rare and authentic photographs! *Many never seen before!*

Every type of human oddity imaginable (some you never imagined) is pictured in this *large* (8½ x 11") and *fascinating* volume (two-headed people, human "trunks", Siamese twins, giants, dwarfs, plus many, many more).

Currently selling for $4.98. **Save Now!** ☞
Special Offer—$3.95.

YOU WON'T BELIEVE YOUR EYES!

Violetta was born without arms and legs.

Margarite Clark and the Siamese twin
that grew from her chest!

Jolly Bonita the world's smallest fat lady.
Toney the alligator-skinned boy.

Pop-Eyed Perry the man who could pop
his eyes out of his head.

Beautiful Etta Lake could stretch her skin
6 inches from her cheek.

The Human Pin Cushion knew no pain.

Serpentina the serpent girl claimed she
was born with no bones in her body!

Pasqual Pinon the two-headed Mexican.

Roberta-Robert—half-man, half-woman.

Tom Ton—645 pounds!

Joe Pearl born with three legs and
double sexed.

Frances O'Conner, armless, was able to
use her toes as well as most people
use their hands.

Alzora Green was only 2 ft. tall, had six
fingers on each hand and was
married twice.

"Priscilla", the monkey girl, was covered
with hair from head to toe and married
the "Alligator-Skinned Man".

PLUS MANY, MANY MORE!

Bantam Book Catalog

It lists over a thousand money-saving best-sellers originally priced from $3.75 to $15.00 —bestsellers that are yours now for as little as 50¢ to $2.95!

The catalog gives you a great opportunity to build your own private library at huge savings!

So don't delay any longer—send us your name and address and 25¢ (to help defray postage and handling costs).